10-22-74

DEATH AND EASTERN THOUGHT

DEATH AND EASTERN THOUGHT

Understanding Death in Eastern Religions and Philosophies

Edited by Frederick H. Holck

Abingdon Press • Nashville and New York

Death and Eastern Thought

Library of Congress Cataloging in Publication Data

HOLCK, FREDERICK H. 1927– Death and Eastern Thought. Includes bibliographical references. 1. Death—Comparative studies. I. Title.
BL504.H6 128'.5 74-10650

ISBN 0-687-10341-X
ISBN 0-687-10340-1 (pbk.)

MANUFACTURED BY THE PARTHENON PRESS AT NASHVILLE, TENNESSEE, UNITED STATES OF AMERICA

Contents

Foreword

I

I am pleased to respond to Professor F. H. Holck's invitation to furnish an introduction to his book, *Death and Eastern Thought*. It is a healthy spiritual sign of our times that contemporary thinkers of the West have begun to reflect increasingly upon the problem of death and to draw the attention of others to it. Psychoanalysis drew people's attention to this problem a few decades ago, but the mainstream of psychology and philosophy continued to ignore it. Yet the present age, despite its scientific and technological achievements with all the hopes and promises of an eternal life without disease, old age, and death, has not prevented man from looking into the basic features of human existence, however overgrown with the glamor of cultural superstructures. Death is one such basic feature. There is a saying in India to the effect that although every man is sure to die somewhere and sometime, he should work for his life, prosperity, and family as though he were eternal. On the other hand, recall the question posed by the angel (*yakṣa,* "a spiritual being") to Yudhiṣṭhira to which he had to answer on pain of losing his brothers: "What is the greatest wonder in the world?" The answer was: "Although every man knows that he is sure to die sometime, he rarely cares about it."

This ambivalent attitude toward death is found in both East and West. This holds true in a pervasive way both for thinkers and for the general run of men. One often hears that Western man knows how to live and Eastern man how to die—which means that the former knows how to plan for a decent and comfortable life in terms of worldly values, while the latter knows how to plan for death under the guidance of spiritual values without anxiety, fear, and grief. Yet, frequently, one comes across Western wives and daughters shedding few tears at the loss of loved as well as earning members of their households, as though they were prepared for all events; and Eastern wives and daughters bemoaning such losses and wailing aloud for entire days, as though they were visited by the unexpected. If we take only the thinkers of the East and West into consideration, we find important differences of emphasis, although for any view in the West we can find a more or less corresponding view in the East, and vice versa. I cannot forget Lord Macaulay's branding of Socrates as an oriental: who else could speak enthusiastically of death creeping into his body and conquering it bit by bit, from toe to ankle, thus removing restrictions upon his conversing with gods? The majority of Western thinkers are more concerned with the world and the personality of waking consciousness: with the social, ethical, and political organization of man rather than with man and his personality traversing the states and worlds of wakefulness, dream, and deep sleep (see Rao's and Sundararajan's chapters), and even transcending them. Eastern thinkers who are more concerned with the world and personality of man in his wakefulness, that is, in his social, ethical, and political relationships—like Manu, the lawgiver in Hinduism—do not enjoy the prestige of those philosophers who consider the world and personality of man in his wakefulness as only a part of an illimitably comprehensive whole.

When a philosophy regards personality as extending beyond life and death, it treats the subject of death more earnestly and positively. When the contrary view is taken, namely that death puts an end to life and personality since these belong only to waking consciousness, then death becomes an issue to be generally evaded, however inevitable an evil it is. Nevertheless, and particularly in the East, the idea of one's self as traversing and transcending the three states of wakefulness, dream, and deep sleep has taken shape through various forms and stages in the history of man's self-reflection. Accordingly, what we call death took on the significance and appeal of changing old clothes for new and better ones (see the *Bhagavadgītā*), and the meaning of physical death became that of a moment in the unending process of life. Thus the word "life" is not restricted in its meaning to the span of the life of man between birth and death. Life is a process; there is no process without change, no change without becoming, and no becoming without the intervening moments of discarding dispensable elements of the life-process. Death is one such moment.

This typically Indian view is shared by Hindus, Buddhists, and Jains alike. Life is an unending drive from birth to birth. Yet it is not the same as immortality. It is within the realm of mortality, change, and becoming.

II

According to the orthodox schools of Indian thought as well as of Buddhism and Jainism, it is the realization of what one's essential self is that takes man beyond the cycle of births and deaths. This shows that man in India desired not only the conquest of the particular, impending death in this life, but also of all future deaths in all future lives. When one realizes what one essentially is, there is no room in his mind for the fear of death, and he is freed from the cycle of births and deaths. Since this realization is possible in the present body, both Buddhism (see Amore's chapter) and the

Vedānta accept two stages of salvation: first, in the body; second, at physical death. Physical death is no death for the man of enlightenment or knowledge (*buddha* or *jñāni*). What dies is his physical body, not his *I-am*. For most schools of Buddhism, the I-am has no being; for the Vedānta, the I-am of the enlightened is disentangled at death both from the physical body—which is composed of three attributes (or *guṇas: sattva, rajas,* and *tamas*)—and from the subtle body (*sūkṣma-śarīra,* including the causal body or *kāraṇa-śarīra,* which corresponds to the lower *vijñāna* of the vijñāna-vādin Buddhists, which contains the individual's *kārmic saṃskāras* or ethical potencies).

In Buddhism (particularly in the Hīnāyana form) the I-am has no ontological status. Realizing this renders one immune to the fear of death since there is really nothing which death can attack. We may say, therefore, that whether or not a school accepts the two-stage emancipation view, the conquest of death is obtained by the realization of the true nature of one's I-am; namely, that it is not the body, that it is not what it appears to be in any or all the states of wakefulness, dream, or deep sleep, and that it transcends the worlds of all three. (From a higher point of view, of course, we should bear in mind that death is but a moment in the process of life itself.)

Thus we have the question: Can the I-am think or imagine its own destruction or death? It is true that every living being is instinctively afraid of death and that, so far as its present mundane life goes, its life is a life unto death. It may also be admitted that I become intensely aware of my being or existence and that I evoke my ontological sense (particularly when confronted by the dread of nonbeing) when my being, projected on diverse objects which are in several ways only "mine" but not "I" myself, is turned back into itself; as though chased by nonbeing (death), it retreats into its cell, its castle, or real home. The fear of death implies also that my being (*sattā*) is not in any object, including my own body and mind, but that it transcends all of them inwardly. It shows, furthermore, that true transcendence lies inwards through my I-am, but not in the endless directions of space and time.

A dialogue between a child and her father perhaps helps reveal the truth about this fear. While being led into an absolutley dark room, she said she was afraid. "What are you afraid of?" asked the father. "Nothing," replied the child. "How can you be afraid of nothing?" he asked. She could not answer, but only cried. The truth is that she did not see anything. Not knowing anything produced fear. This is the fear of "nothing." But was she not aware that she herself was there, and so there was really no "nothing"? Or was she afraid that she would be swallowed up by "nothing"? The idea of being swallowed by a tiger and forced to live in its stomach, for example, does produce fear in children. But if we analyze their minds and attitudes, we cannot find the idea of total annihilation: the idea is impossible for them.

How can I have the idea of the total annihilation of myself without my "I" being there to entertain the idea? I can think of my annihilation only as consistently as I can think of the circular square. If my I-am is there to think, then the Cartesian *cogito* will affirm what it thinks and takes to be negated. So the annihilation of the I-am cannot be really envisaged by the same I-am. The fear of death of which the existential philosophers of the West speak continually is really the fear of the possibility of not knowing *any* objects, human or nonhuman; of losing what appears to be familiar, to be "my world"; and so, of being lonely. (Compare this, for example, with Sartre's idea of the world being alien and ask, Can it be completely alien when it is "my world"?) The *Bṛhadāraṇyaka Upaniṣad* says that when the Supreme Ātman (Brahman) desired to create the worlds, he first said, "I am." He thus acquired the name of "I" (*aham*). This narrative reminds us of the God of Israel telling Moses that he had no name. He is only I AM. Afterwards, the Brahman, feeling lonely and unhappy, created the different species of animate and inanimate creatures.

Note that this lonely I-am is not the original supreme I-AM, but a derivative. It is the supreme Ego, called by various names like Iśvara, which cannot exist or be happy without the other Ātmans (spirits) or the physical world. The supreme I-AM is pure self-consciousness of being (*sattā*), and has no fear of facing "nothing" or nonbeing. All the lower I-am's from Iśvara (personal God) downwards, are its reflections, images increasingly imperfect. (Compare this with the Christian concept of man as the image of God, and then ask what kind of image it is). Their destiny or salvation lies in realizing their oneness with the supreme I-AM; it is of the very nature of the I-am not to be able to confront its own nonbeing.

The only alternative to this position, so far as I can see, is that the I-am is a categorical mistake, a grammatical error, an illusion, a mere nothing. There ought to be, then, no fear of the destruction of mistakes and illusions. Nonbeing cannot affect and destroy nonbeing. This may also be one of the Buddhist answers; but considered from the strictly human point of view, I am infinitely concerned with my I-am, whatever other people say it is. It may be said that the illusory fear of a positive I-am confronting nonbeing is similar to the illusory fear of an illusory I-am confronting nonbeing. But if the I-am is an illusion, then the whole objective world becomes an illusion, since it is absolutely illogical to accept the reality of the objective world which my I-am confirms without accepting the reality of the confirming I-am. (This I see to be the defect in Sartre's thought. If the I-am or being-for-itself is nonbeing, then how can the being of the objective world, being-in-itself, be confirmed and by whom can it be confirmed? By non-being?) How can I be at all certain that that which an unreality, a phantom, asserts is true? If the I-am is not real, then nothing can be certain—a literary expression which is not strictly correct, for even "nothing" cannot be certain. However, this matter would lead us deep into epistemology and metaphysics, quite beyond the scope of a foreword.

III

If death cannot destroy the I-am, then what can death destroy or change? The I-am transcends both space and time and is not within the reach of death. The fear of death, then, is due to the identification of the I-am with the objects in space and time which are subject to change and destruction. This is what Hinduism (Vedānta) and Buddhism assert, although for many schools of Buddhism the ultimate nature of the I-am is the inexplicable nothing (*śūnya*). The physical body is in both space and time, but life (*prāṇa*) and what in Western philosophy and psychology is called mind are not in space (i.e., they are not spatial or extended), but are in time.

Here the words "life" (*prāṇa*) and "mind" (*antaḥkaraṇa,* "inner instrument," or, roughly, the "common sense" of Aristotle's philosophy) need some explanation. In the above sections the word "life" was used in a very general sense as the continuation of a person's existence or being, as an endless *durée,* an élan vital, of which death and birth alike are but incidental moments. But the word is used also to mean the existence of the individual between birth and death, as in the statement: "The life of no man has lasted more than two hundred years." In this sense, what we mean by life is affected by death. In the present context of Indian thought, life (*prāṇa*) is not affected by death except as its detachment from a physical body. Yet it has additional significance as the principle of coordination or integration of both the voluntary and involuntary processes of the physical body. It belongs to both the macrocosm and the microcosm. The corresponding macrocosmic principle in the cosmos is personified as *Hiraṇyagarbha* ("the golden womb") and also as *Sūtrātman* ("the connecting thread of multiplicity"). When life as the microcosmic connecting thread leaves the body, the latter decomposes into the separate elements that compose it and dies.

In Western thought, the meaning of the word "mind" is rather ambiguous. What corresponds to it in Sanskrit philosophy is the comprehensive term *antahkaraṇa* ("inner instrument," generally of cognitions and for differentiating pains and pleasures). It excludes the outer instruments, the senses and the organs of action. This inner instrument, also translated as "inner sense," includes reason (*buddhi*), ego (*ahāṃkāra*), and mind (*manas*). The function of mind (*manas*) is to join or separate sensations derived from objects and to perceive pains and pleasures. The ego (*ahāṃkāra*) does not correspond exactly to Descartes' and Kant's meaning, but rather to the appropriating function, in the sense of "mine" as opposed to "thine." It is related to egoity and egoism, but not to the meaning of I-am. *Buddhi* is the decision-making function as employed in the statement, That *is* a horse. These meanings hold more or less true for all Indian schools of philosophy.

According to the Vedānta and Hinduism in general, what leaves the physical body at death is called the *jīva,* ("that which lives"). But it is not merely the life principle. The word may rightly be translated as "the soul." It includes the inner sense, the vital principle, and the outgoing psychological senses (not the visible, physical ones), all lying inward. We should note that the vital principle is not destroyed at death, but transmigrates as part of the *jīva* and coordinates the voluntary and involuntary processes of the future body. This *jīva,* called the subtle body (*sūkṣmaśarīra*), according to the nondualistic Vedānta, includes the causal body, which is something like the id or libido, and contains latently, in a soteriological and eschatological sense, all the causal potencies for future births.

But it should not be thought that the Ātman transmigrates. It is the *jīva* (soul) that transmigrates. Although the word Ātman is used occasionally in the sense of the *jīva,* it must be interpreted according to context. However, the soul cannot exist apart from the Ātman (spirit), which is the support of everything and not really subject to the vicissitudes of transmigration, always remaining an onlooker despite its ever conferring being on everything. It is the same as the Brahman (Absolute); therefore, the I-am is essentially the Brahman. This realization enables me and everyone else to rise above the realm of becoming and so of death.

There are two views in the Upsaniṣads about the state of the transmigrating soul (see Chan et al., *The Great Asian Religions: An Anthology* [New York: Macmillan, 1969], pp. 43 and 45). According to one view, the state is like that of a dream, a twilight in which the soul (*jīva*) stays for a time involuntarily searching for the right parents and incarnation. On the other account, the soul leaving the physical body is like a caterpillar with its tail end on the leaf it is leaving behind while its front end is on another leaf to which it is leaping. Thus, there is no ghostly existence, no merely incorporeal, dreamy existence.

The Buddhists, unlike the Vedāntists, do not seem to have elaborated the idea of a subtle body, apparently because the idea of a durable subtle body conflicts with their doctrine of momentariness.

But for logical reasons, the idea of a subtle body must be posited. Otherwise, we cannot understand what transmigrates. If it is only some *karmic* ("ethical") potencies which transmigrate, then the being from which they are transmitted will have to be different from that to which they are transmitted. Thus, the former being need not worry about transmigration at all because it perishes absolutely after only a moment. Its perishing must be as good as emancipation, and salvation, consequently, ought to be spontaneous and instantaneous. But such could not have been the view of the Buddhist teachers. There is, therefore, a lacuna in their argument.

However, according to Buddhism (and in a sense Hinduism also) death pertains to aggregates or compounds. For Hinduism, death occurs to the physical body when it decomposes. The Buddhists regard man's psychophysical personality (*pudgala*) as consisting of five aggregations of physical and psychological elements (*dhātus*). When these are separated, there will be no remainder that calls itself Ātman, and there can be no death of that which never existed. (See Amore's chapter.) Death can be said to attack the aggregates by separating and decomposing them. The view that there is no remainder after decomposition belongs in a general way to all schools of Buddhism. A small number of Hīnayānists and many Mahāyānists, particularly the Vijñāna-vādins, would say that there is a remainder, but they do not agree on how that consciousness can be described. Some, like Asaṇga and Śāntarkṣita, do not even mind calling it the Ātman, which has no death and is an eternal moment.

IV

It is generally held that love and death affect human emotions most intensely by gripping man's very being. But we find stated in the Upaniṣads that birth affects the embryo and foetus with intense grief, regret, remorse, and depression. In the case of some abnormal (infranormal) individuals, a faint memory of life in the womb results in painful pathological conditions. If such memory occurs in the minds of supranormal individuals—the religious literature of India declares—the desire is strengthened to avoid all future births. The *Garbhopaniṣad* (the Upaniṣad of the Womb or Foetus) says that the foetus becomes aware in the ninth month of all its past lives and miseries and longs for escape (delivery) from the womb (full of filth and inserted between the bladder and the colon), vowing that it will spend its life in devotion to God and working for salvation. As soon as the baby is delivered, one of the vital principles (*vaiṣṇavi vāyu*) makes it forget its past, including its life in the womb. The birth of a baby may be a happy event for the parents, their friends, and relatives; but for the baby itself, until the above forgetfulness overtakes it, birth is said to be a misery. The Buddhist twelve-linked chain of causation (*pratītya-samutpāda*) mentions that suffering consists of birth (rebirth), old age, and death. Birth is a misery not only because it leads to death, but also in itself, since life in the womb is inevitable. Both birth and death can be avoided only by liberation. Life in the general sense—including death—makes not only death but also birth a moment of itself.

V

The general Hindu and Buddhist attitude toward death views it (1) as happening mainly to the physical body by destroying the organization of the elements which constitute it, (2) as a necessary step in the continuity of personal life from birth to birth, and (3) as escapable only by transcending birth itself through the disentanglement of one's ontological self—generally negative and illusory in the case of Buddhism—from the world of becoming. The dread of death and the suffering that precedes it are due to a false identification of one's self with the constituents of becoming, such as mind and body, which belong to Prakṛti "primeval physical nature" according to the Sāṃkhya and the Yoga, and to Māyā according to the nondualistic Vedānta and Mahāyāna Buddhism. For the Hīnayāna, this dread and suffering is the result of the belief in a substantial self, which is only an illusion, an idea which is accepted with some modifications by the Mahāyāna schools as well.

It should be noted that in both Hinduism and Buddhism there is recognition of an instinct called the Nirvāṇa instinct, which in one sense corresponds to the death instinct of Freud, but in another sense does not. Both the Nirvāṇa and death instincts are drives, either normal or abnormal, to escape or rise above the world of suffering. The death instinct is an earth instinct, a matter instinct —the desire to turn into matter, which is immune to the pains and pleasures of living beings. The Nirvāṇa instinct, on the other hand, is the drive to be one's true self without false self-identification and involvements. Freud seems to identify the two (see P. T. Raju, "I-consciousness: Its Depths, Normal and Abnormal" in the *Problem of the Self* [The Hague: Martinus Nijhoff, 1968]). It is, as Schopenhauer says, the will to liquidate one's particularized finite will and identify it with the Supreme Will. In Buddhism, this liquidation of the finite will and ego finally ends as unity with the Śūnya; in the Hindu Vedānta it amounts to becoming one with Being. In either case, it is not exactly the death instinct of Freud. For him, the opposite of the death instinct is the life instinct or love instinct. For Hinduism and Buddhism, the opposite of the Nirvāṇa instinct is the birth instinct, the tendency to be born again and again to enjoy the values of the world. As a drive for living and love in the ordinary sense (*kāma*), it does have some similarity to the life instinct of Freud. However, it also contains the drive toward outward activity (*pravṛtti*) which may remind us of Jung's extroversion. Though Jung's extroversion has a psychopathic sense, this is not the case with *pravṛtti*. Therefore, the opposite of the Nirvāṇa instinct, which is the instinct of disinvolvement or disentanglement from the deterministic world of change and becoming, will be the instinct to get involved or entangled in it. These two opposite instincts are called respectively *nivṛtti* and *pravṛtti* in Sanskrit. They are natural drives in man to withdraw from, or get involved in, external activity. The withdrawal is inward, but is not to be confused with Jung's introversion, which is obsessively concerned with man's finite ego. For Nirvāna is the liquidation of the finite ego itself.

In Hinduism, Buddhism, and Jainism, death through starvation was permitted for various reasons, although suicide itself was condemned. Fasting and starvation were forms of self-purification. Where the sin was the greater, the self-punishment was the more severe. In Jainism and some forms of Buddhism, absolute starvation to death was practiced with the permission of the elders of the monastery when the monks felt so completely enlightened that no purpose would be served by further worldly existence. We even read in the Purāṇas (the ancient Hindu legends) of instances in which the fast unto death (*prāyopavesa*) was practiced for purification from great sins. Now and then such resolves were broken when sages and saints would intervene. However, on the whole, fasting unto death was not characteristic of orthodox Hinduism. Yet the very existence of the practice indicates that the span of time between birth and death was not considered the totality of life. Rather, there could be as many lives as one wanted for purification from sin and for development of spiritual consciousness.

VI

The indigenous Chinese and Japanese attitudes toward death are pre-Buddhist and, despite many similarities to Indian views, have a number of peculiarities of their own. The Confucian attitude is certainly more socially oriented, more human and worldly, than the Taoist and Mohist. The Taoist is akin to the Vedāntic and the Buddhist. One can almost trace idea for idea in the two traditions: most noteworthy in what is called the Indian epic literature which mixes popular narratives, sentiments, and opinions with highly philosophical views, one can find almost all the Confucian views as well. Very often an Indian scholar may find what is called a peculiarly Chinese view—for example, the Confucian with its advice on familial, political, and social relationships—in the voluminous epic literature of India, which for some reason is not treated by the Indians themselves as particularly philosophical. However, I have not come across any sect in India similar to the Mohists, who would fight and die on behalf of a victim of aggression, whether an individual or the state. Though history contains episodes of Hindu monks who organized themselves to fight the oppressors of their religion, the "altruistic" deaths of the Mohists were foreign to them. It would be interesting for a scholar of Indian history and philosophy to collect accounts of such organizations, their philosophies and practices. All of them, fighting more or less against superior opponents, must have had a practical philosophy of death. It is said that the Nayak (Telaga) regiments of the dismembered Vizianagar Empire in the south of India, even after joining the British army, spent their evenings in peacetime singing about the transience of life, the illusoriness of the world, the glory of death on the battlefield, the greatness of God and the bliss of salvation, rather than indulging in loot, arson, and rape. It was the dismembered Marata armies, particularly the Pindaris and the Thugs, who indulged in such activities until the British destroyed them.

Of the two attitudes toward death, the Chinese and the Japanese, the latter contains one of the most interesting transformations of the Buddhist attitude. The Japanese Samurai ideal, that death is to be one with the cosmic process—apart from its connection with the idea of dying for identity with or out of loyalty to one's overlord or superior (an idea which is found in a different form in Mohism)—is at once spiritual, ethical, and aesthetic. It is spiritual or religious in the sense that death is undergone as the final extinction of an ethically pure soul, which every great Samurai as well as every Japanese Buddhist saint understood himself to be. It is the same as Nirvāṇa entered into either on the battlefield or in a quiet corner of the monastery. An ideal akin to the Samurai's is found in Hinduism also, and is called the heroic ideal or the heroic practice for salvation. The Samurai ideal is again ethical in that it demands that man should obey the laws of the cosmic process, one of which is that he is to be born and die. This demand does not mean in Hinduism and Buddhism that man ought to seek death in any way, but that he should face it boldly and dispassionately when it comes. The third aspect of the Samurai ideal, that to try to flee from death is unaesthetic, does not seem to be enunciated in so many words in the ancient Sanskrit and Buddhist literatures of India as it is in the Japanese, but it is possible to read this view into them. If Nirvāṇa is blissfulness and the basis of all aesthetic pleasure, as the Indian aestheticians say, and if death (overlooking the bodily pains that precede it) is blissful in a way, then death can be a pointer to the source of aesthetic pleasure. But the Japanese Buddhists seem to intend much more than this: without death, not only the picture of the cosmos, but the life of man as well will lose its aesthetic appeal and value; both will be ugly. The Japanese seem to think that human life is ugly without death, not merely because of the misery and tastelessness of an eternal old age with its disillusionment about worldly values, but also because the soul realizes its natural inherent beauty in going through the process of death. A dead body may have no aesthetic appeal to the onlookers. But to the soul within, if it is self-conscious and conscious of passing out of the body and without longing for or attachment to friends, relatives, and property, the event can have tremendous aesthetic value, provided aesthesis is understood not only as the pleasant state of mind produced by the sense perception of the beautiful object, but also as the sense of intensity, fullness, and integrity of one's being. The Japanese seem to mean both, as their culture is essentially an aesthetic one.

VII

Whitehead said that the history of Western philosophy might be regarded as a series of footnotes to Plato. Yet, Plato was a disciple of Socrates. If, as Macaulay opined, Socrates is oriental in his attitude toward life and death, and the Socratic dialogues are indeed the foundation of Western philosophy, then we will expect much in common between the attitudes of Eastern and Western thought toward death. It is said further that the history of Western thought, from about the time of the Church Fathers, is a series of permutations and combinations of Judeo-Christian dogmas and Greek thought, with omissions and additions. Then again, even if we refrain from giving rational and psycho-spiritual explanations of the dogmas, the factor of Greek thought has many elements in common with Eastern thought, particularly the Indian, so that we cannot but find much that is similar in both East and West. Apart from Indian thought which, like Greek thought, has its origins in the mind of the Aryan peoples, even Mishima's idea of death as found in Japan echoes Greek classical thought. But what may prove of interest to a serious thinker is the application of highly metaphysical and spiritual ideals to situations of a mundane nature. For instance, the ethical ideal of identity with cosmic law may be, and indeed has been, used to justify loyalty or identity with the overlord or even immediate superiors. Lack of such identity may be equated with treachery. The cosmic law is the mode of behavior of the Cosmic Person or Logos, which is infinite and incapable of mistakes. The overlord, on the other hand, is a finite human being capable of error. Apart from such applications of basic truths, the fundamental attitudes toward death in Eastern and Western philosophies do not seem to be so very different as is commonly supposed. Furthermore, it is as mistaken to think that the Western attitude is consistently and continuously the same throughout history as it is to dub some particular attitude in the East as *the* Eastern attitude. For despite the many common features, there are notable differences in emphasis and in the application of principles in the different lands of the East, as can be seen in the chapters of this book. This plurality serves, however, to make this study interesting to the reflective reader. Professor Holck is to be congratulated for hitting upon the idea of this book and working strenuously to develop it. It is certain to be a valuable companion volume to Choron's *Death and Western Thought.* The two together offer material for a profitable study in comparative philosophy, especially in a comparative philosophy of religion. I wish the book success and commend it to every serious student of human existence.

P. T. Raju

I

The Vedic Period

F. H. HOLCK

Some three thousand five hundred years ago numerous seminomadic tribes calling themselves Āryas[1] left their East European and Northwest Asian homelands in search of new territories. Some moved westward, others southward. Many migrated southeastward towards the Indian subcontinent and were later known as the Indo-Aryans. A courageous people, full of energy and determination, they overcame great obstacles; the rough snow-covered mountains of the Hindu Kush (Hindu-killer) took many lives. Entering the plains of northwest India, they had to fight the indigenous population and cope with the new climate.

First they settled as tribes in villages in the upper Indus Valley and the Punjab region. From there they expanded gradually southeastward, while other Aryan newcomers from the northwest filled the vacuum. For many years the invaders were constantly battling the black-skinned indigenous inhabitants, the Dāsas, whom they described as the black, noseless devils.[2] Yet some of the settlers took Dāsa wives, which may account for the Dravidian influence. Ancient hymns telling of intertribal struggles for predominance and later the great epics, Mahābhārata and Rāmāyaṇa, prove that the Aryans were warlike people.[3]

When the Aryans entered India, they brought with them a pastoral culture living on a diet of milk and meat. Cattle breeding was their basic occupation. Gradually, however, as they became more settled, they also developed an agriculture. The combination of both gave them an affluence which is clearly reflected in the sacrificial character of their religion. Already in their early age, known as the Vedic Age, both the economic and the religious significance of the cow was recognized.

Economic and social conditions were the factors that led to the development of a system of social classes. Traces of a classified society among the Aryans can be found even before their entry into India. After numerous cases of intermarriage between Aryans and Dāsas, class divisions were increasingly emphasized which resulted finally in the establishment of a caste system where each caste had its special responsibilities and duties. The highest caste were the priests (*brāhmaṇa*), the intellectual and spiritual elite of the Vedic society and the authors of a vast body of religious and philosophical literature called the Veda[4] which they orally transmitted. One of their main functions was to supply the other castes with sacrificial services for which they received cattle, the official currency, as payment. Next were the warriors (*kṣatriya*) whose responsibility was to govern and protect the tribe in time of war. The mercantile class (*vaiśya*) constituted the third caste, whereas the servant class (*śūdra*), no longer considered pure Aryan, was the lowest in the caste system. Later, below the fourth caste, were the large number of untouchables who were entirely outside the Aryan society.

From their extensive literature we get the vivid impression they were an uninhibited, merrymaking people who enjoyed life to the fullest. There was no trace yet of the later pessimistic outlook on life and the world. They liked dancing, singing, instrumental music, drinking intoxicating beverages and gambling which was frequently reprobated by the priests. A distressed gambler in a Ṛg-Vedic hymn is quoting the god Savitṛ's advice:

'Don't play with dice, but plough your furrow!
Delight in your property, prize it highly!
Look to your cattle and look to your wife,
you gambler!' Thus noble Savitṛ tells me.[5]

That the early Indo-Aryans also had their serious concerns is clearly manifested in a large number of Vedic passages where their sages and poets deal with profound questions and offer various solutions. Their close relationship to nature sharpened their awareness of the predictable and unpredictable natural phenomena of order and chaos in the universe. Although they experienced the fury of natural forces in their new environment, they believed in the predominance of an independent all-pervading cosmic principle (*ṛta*) to which they attributed regularity in nature and order in the moral and social spheres of life. Thus, the regular changes in the seasons, the peaceful flourishing of a community, or the faithful adherence to a given promise were due to the influence of Ṛta. This cosmic law had its divine protectors, Varuṇa and Mitra, who were the ethical deities of the Ṛg-Vedic pantheon. The numerous other gods and goddesses were primarily nature deities with individual areas of competence. The mighty Indra, whose weapon was the powerful thunderbolt, was the god of storms and patron of the Aryan armies. Agni, the beloved god of fire and protector of altar and hearth, mediated between gods and men. The god Soma represented the intoxicating power of the lifegiving soma liquor. The majority of these gods, however, lacked distinctive individual traits. They were addressed either individually or collectively in hymns and prayers or through sacrifices. The worshiper asked for material blessings and long life or deliverance from specific evils.

Questions concerning the origin of the universe were of great interest to the Vedic Aryans. Their literature contains a variety of cosmogonic myths and speculations, some of which reveal the remarkable intellectual and philosophical potentiality of the Indian mind. In the course of several hundred years, when they were still pushing eastward and southward, their thinkers developed ideas of this great mystery independently of one another which explains major differences and apparent inconsistencies. From the mythological point of view, some saw the universe as the work of gods who used existing material in their creative efforts. In a hymn a poet wonders from what kind of wood they built heaven and earth, since this material was lasting without decay (*RV*, X. 31. 7). Others tried to explain the origin of the world as the result of a primeval sacrifice where the gods immolated the cosmic giant (*puruṣa*), out of whose parts came forth the entire creation (*RV*, X. 90). We also find the idea that the universe emerged from a "Golden Embryo" *hiraṇyagarbha*) (*RV*, X. 121. 1, 7). This is an anticipation of the later cosmogonic theory of the "Golden Egg" which developed in the cosmic waters (Śatapatha-Brāhmaṇa, XI. 1. 6. 1). Another attempt to account for this world is found in the Atharva Veda (XIX. 53) where Time (*kāla*), an abstract principle, was believed to be its cause. Perhaps the profoundest of all Vedic cosmogonies is the following monistic speculation where an anonymous thinker suggests:

> Then was not non-existent nor existent: there was
> no realm of air, no sky beyond it.
> What covered in, and where? and what gave shelter?
> Was water there, unfathomed depth of water?
> Death was not then, nor was there aught immortal:
> no sign was there, the day's and night's
> divider.
> That One Thing, breathless, breathed by its own
> nature: apart from it was nothing whatsoever.
> Darkness there was: at first concealed in darkness
> this All was undifferentiated chaos.

All that existed then was void and formless: by the
great power of Warmth [Tapas] was born that One.
Thereafter rose Desire in the beginning, Desire [Kāma],
the primal seed and germ of Spirit.
Sages who searched with their heart's thought
discovered the existent's kinship in the non-existent.[6]

According to this view the world has its origin in the absolute, yet nondistinct, ground of Being, containing in itself the cosmic principle Tapas, by whose impulse Being evolved into existence. The next step in this evolution was the powerful action of Kāma which effected a spontaneous, distinct self-manifestation of reality. But who knows if this is true, wonders the skeptical author of this hymn, adding that even the gods may be ignorant, since they "are later than this world's creation."

Closely related to their cosmogonic theories is their anthropology. Vedic man sees himself living in a world in which he belongs, and which is the arena of his actions. He is one with the universe and one with the divine in whatever form it is encountered.[7] This divine-human relationship finds its expression in numerous Vedic passages.[8] One of the most pointed references to man's divine nature can be found in the famous Puruṣa Sūkta (*RV*, X. 90), the above hymn of the primeval man[9] whose self-sacrifice was an act of creation. According to this hymn all living beings, gods, men, animals, as well as the rest of creation (including the four Vedas), originated from the divine Puruṣa. It is of particular interest to see that man does not occupy a privileged position among the living beings.[10] The hymn, however, makes reference to the four castes, identifying the Brāhmin with the Puruṣa's mouth, the warrior with his two arms, the Vaiśya with his thighs, and the Śūdra with his feet.

That man has not only a body, but also a more permanent part, is hinted at early in a Ṛg-Vedic cremation prayer addressed to the god Agni, requesting him not to consume the dead person entirely, but to dismiss him to the Fathers. His eye is to go to the sun, his Ātman ("breath") to the wind, etc. (*RV*, X. 16. 1-3). Ātman, especially, developed later into an all-important concept, denoting not only the individual self, but also the world soul. In the Ṛg-Veda Ātman has several meanings besides breath: sometimes it stands for body, but it may stand for life and the life principle; at other times it signifies the soul of man or man's self. It was the general understanding of the Vedic Aryans that every human being is an individual, personal self which is to be distinguished from his physical aspect. His death and subsequent physical destruction are not accompanied by the annihilation of the self.[11]

The divine-human relationship is also revealed by another concept of great future significance, equally important as Ātman, which appears in the Atharva Veda: Brahman. Originally meaning "sacred word," next the power behind the sacred word, it was finally applied to the one who possessed this power, either the creator god Brahmā or the members of the priestly caste who had knowledge of the sacred word. Thus, Brahman, the sacred power present in man, is identical with the same power in the god Brahmā. Furthermore, it sustains the earth; it is even identified with the sky above and the atmosphere (*AV*, X. 2. 21-25). Its presence in the universe is unlimited. R. C. Zaehner sees in this hymn an implication "that man, through his participation in Brahman, is co-extensive with the universe." [12] This applies especially to the Brahmacārin, the Vedic student, who because of the inherent power of Brahman, is extolled as Prajāpati, god of creation (*AV*, XI. 5. 16).

Another significant point of this early period which must not be overlooked in our context is contained in Atharva Veda (X. 8. 2). Here, the identity between Brahman, the sacred power and by now also the objectified impersonal essence of the universe, and the individual personal self, Ātman, can be inferred. At the end of this remarkable hymn (*AV*, X. 8. 44) the ancient thinker proclaims emphatically that the knowledge of this great reality, which he chooses here to call Ātman, though he could name it Brāhman, or Puruṣa as well, will eliminate man's fear of death. We have here in a nutshell "the whole teaching of the Upanisads: it is the recognition within the human soul of an immortal something that participates in, is of the same nature as, or is actually identical with the immortal Brahman which sustains and ensouls the entire objective cosmos." [13]

These introductory remarks will give us the necessary background for better understanding Eastern thought about the finiteness of one's earthly life and Eastern attitudes toward death.

Death and the Saṃhitās

A dogmatic treatment of eschatological questions has not been developed in the Ṛg-Veda, which probably is due to the vivacity and lightheartedness of the Vedic Aryans. Yet despite the prevailing cheerful and optimistic atmosphere among them, there was an awareness of man's limitations. Man is subject to evil, to suffering, and finally to death. Death was inevitable. Nobody, rich or poor, could evade it because man is by nature mortal. "Hunger was certainly not meant as a means of death by the gods. For also him who has eaten his fill, death befalls in various forms." [14] At this early period we do not clearly find the belief in reincarnation; there seems to be only one life and one death on earth, and since life was basically good and satisfying, the ideal in the earlier parts of the

Ṛg-Veda was to prolong life and postpone death. A limited interest in a future life beyond with the Fathers and the god Yama developed later and found its expression especially in the ninth and tenth books of the Ṛg-Veda. There are various views concerning the fate of the deceased. However, in spite of those differences, there is a common concern for the body, which is not to be injured by birds, ants, snakes, or wild beasts (*RV*, X. 16. 6) when buried or cremated since the whole person in all his aspects—body, life, mind, limbs, sap, and bones—is to be restored in the next world. Arthur B. Keith[15] holds this idea to be the regular view in the Veda. The belief according to which the eye of the deceased is to go to the sun, the breath into the wind, and the other bodily elements in conformity with their nature to heaven, earth, water, or plants (*RV*, X. 16. 3) is merely a deviation from the generally accepted position.

In a rather undogmatic way the Vedic thinkers deal with the life beyond. There are "two paths for mortals, that of the Fathers[16] and that of the gods" [17] by which the deceased depart from this world. In a funeral hymn the survivors address the dead, advising him to proceed on the old ancestral paths (*pitṛyāna*) to Yama's realm (*RV*, X. 14. 7) where, if he was a liberal giver and had acted in compliance with Ṛta, he may now join forever the blessed company of Yama, the Fathers, and the gods.[18] This heaven had rather mundane and materialistic features (*RV*, IX. 113. 7-11). Although such pleasures of this world as the drinking of soma, milk, and honey and experiencing love[19] could be enjoyed in Yama's kingdom, the Vedic Aryan was not particularly eager to enter heaven; he was too much this-worldly oriented.

Yama, the king of this heavenly realm, "was the first of men that died, and the first that departed to this (celestial) world (Muir, 292; *AV*, XVIII. 3. 13). Therefore, reverence was due "to that Yama, to Death, who first reached the river, spying out a path for many, who is lord of these two-footed and four-footed creatures."[20] With his twin sister Yami he was also believed to be the parent of the human race (*RV*, X. 10. 1-14) and thus the Father of the Fathers. In the later Saṃhitās he became identified with death, or at least was closely "connected with Antaka, 'the ender', Mṛtyu, 'death', and Nirṛti, 'dissolution'."[21] Occasionally, the character of Yama is ambiguous. Although in most passages he may be visualized as a glorious king who dwells in the perpetual light of heaven, receiving the pious into eternal joy (*RV*, IX. 113. 7-11; X. 14. 9), he may also be represented as a frightening ruler from whose bonds deliverance is sought.[22]

In the Ṛg-Veda we do not find the idea of a judgment in the world of the dead. Rather, admission to Yama's paradise and the everlasting enjoyment of all the heavenly pleasures, including the restoration of a sick body, the maintaining of family relations and the highly desired apotheosis, is considered to be reward for sacrifice to the gods and good works.[23] The absence of a judgment, however, does not exclude the belief in well-deserved punishment of the wicked, particularly when the admission to paradise was dependent on a virtuous life (*RV*, X. 154. 1-5). It is not beyond dispute whether or not there is in the Ṛg-Veda a hell or a place of punishment after this life. We read of a deep abyss which "has been produced [for those who], being sinners, false, untrue, go about like women without brothers, like wicked females hostile to their husbands (Muir, 312; *RV*, IV. 5. 5). In a hymn to Varuṇa a sick man implores the god not to send him into the "House of Clay" which is, unlike the cheerful realm of the Fathers, apparently a kind of gloomy underworld, reserved for the wicked whom Varuṇa had afflicted with diseases, especially dropsy and consumption.[24] We also learn that the gods Indra and Soma throw the evildoers into the deepest darkness from which they can never get out (*RV*, VII. 104. 3).

The Atharva-Veda is more explicit on the subject of hell; there appears "the word Naraka Loka in contrast to Svarga, heaven, as the place for female goblins and sorceresses." [25] For those who spit upon a Brahmin or who demand tribute from him, the place of punishment is described as a pool of blood, where they sit chewing hair (*AV*, V. 19. 3). A form of increased punishment is mentioned in the Kauṣītaki Brāhmaṇa where man is threatened "with being eaten in the next world by the animals which he devoured in this, unless he adopts a certain ritual practice of special potency." [26] As time went on, these ideas were further developed until finally, in the time of Buddhism, elaborate descriptions of all the tortures of hell found entrance into the religious literature, greatly disquieting the minds of the people.

The phenomenon of death was for the Vedic poet as much a shocking and mysterious experience as it was for any other man of this period. He knew very well that as his elders, parents, friends, and neighbors passed away from this earth, so he, too, someday had to die. (*RV*, X. 117. 1). Nevertheless, the inevitability of death did not prevent him from wondering why there was death. His monistic speculation that in the very beginning there was neither death nor immortality (*RV*, X. 129. 2) leaves room for the assumption that in the evolutionary process of the One, the appearance of death and the negation of it (immortality) were necessary features of that cosmogony. If this was true, death could not be considered a punishment. Could it be, therefore, that the experience of death was simply a given fact in everybody's life which had to be met? The unsophisticated majority of the Vedic people would probably not choose such an interpretation. Although the Ṛg-Veda does not offer an explanation for the origin of death, various passages establish a causal relationship between sin and death, or more accurately, between sin and the time of death. "Slay us not for one sin, nor for two, nor for three, nor for many, O hero," the god Indra is implored (Muir, 112; *RV*, VIII. 45. 34). The sin here referred to is not so much a transgression as a failure to worship him or to bring him sacrifice. A similar request is addressed to the god Varuṇa to forgive daily transgressions against his laws and not to deliver the sinner unto death (*RV*, I. 25. 1-2), but to spare his life.[27] Professor Organ's view that "death was not regarded as a punishment . . . [and] not to be dreaded," [28] would have hardly convinced the frightened worshiper who asked Varuṇa's forgiveness in fear of being slain by him.[29] The comforting outlook that Yama has prepared an eternal pasture with the departed forefathers, perhaps a reunion with wife and children (*RV*, X. 14. 2; *AV*, XII. 3. 17), or a long life among the gods (*RV*, X. 14. 14) may have made it easier to face death. However, the numerous Vedic passages dealing with human emotions and fears make it hard to accept Professor Ghosh's generalized statement that the Ṛg-Vedic Indians "were not afraid of death." [30] Rather, the Vedic sources support Maurice Phillips' position in which he relates man's instinctive fear of death to fear of punishment for trespassing the laws established by the gods.[31] This fear also finds its expression in the idea of Yama's two four-eyed underworld dogs with big nostrils who roam among men threatening them or in the dove as the ill-omened messenger of Death (*mṛtyu*) (cf. *RV*, X. 165; X. 14. 10, 12).

To be sure, as there are in any civilization individuals with higher, loftier ideas, so we may find them among the Vedic poets who reveal in some of their hymns a more spiritual orientation. They visualize the immortal life as one aspect of man's total existence, where he enters into a perfect state of being: "Boneless, cleansed, purified by him who cleanseth, they go resplendent to the world of splendour." [32] Yet, it must not be overlooked that the second part of this verse alludes to a very worldly pleasure, when the faithful are assured that "fire burneth not their organ of enjoyment." Certainly, these ideas had some influence upon their attitude toward death; nevertheless, there is no statement during this period that would indicate a desire to die in order to enter the perfect realm of heaven. Despite hope for immortality, a joyful life on earth was preferred over any questionable existence beyond. The Vedic people, therefore, tried to prolong life as much as possible with all means available. The ideal during the period of the Saṃhitās and Brāhmaṇas was to live a hundred years.[33] To this end liberality[34] was recommended, and many incantations, spells, prayers, and rituals as well as primitive medical and surgical arts were applied. What, then, could reflect better the deep concern of the worshiper than his request, addressed in general to various gods and specifically to Mṛtyu ("Death"):

Go hence, O Death, pursue thy special pathway
apart from that which Gods are wont to travel.
To thee I say it who hast eyes and hearest: Touch
not our offspring,[35] injure not our heroes. (1)

Divided from the dead are these, the living: now
be our calling on the Gods successful.
We have gone forth for dancing and for laughter,
to further times prolonging our existence. (3)

Here I erect this rampart for the living; let none
of these, none other, reach this limit.
May they survive a hundred lengthened autumns,
and may they bury Death beneath this mountain. (4)

As the days follow days in close succession, as
with the seasons duly come the seasons,
As each successor fails not his foregoer, so
form the lives of these, O great Ordainer. (5)

Live your full lives and find old age delightful,
all of you striving one behind the other.
May Tvashṭar, maker of fair things, be gracious
and lengthen out the days of your existence. (6)

(Griffith, II, 406; *RV*, X. 18)

Though the desire for a long and happy life is the main theme in this hymn, there is no resentment against the inevitable fact of death. The Vedic Aryan knows that as human beings we "are akin to death," i.e., mortal.[36] Accepting this fact, the poet implores the fate-ordaining deity to terminate individual lives "in due order of seniority" (Griffith, II, 406; *RV*). Among the hundred and one modes of death, only death as a result of old age is accepted as a natural event. Thus, on the occasion of the birth of a boy a ceremonial benediction for a happy life is recited, containing the following verses:

This Child, Old Age! shall grow to meet thee
only: none of the hundred other deaths shall
harm him. (1)

Let not breath drawn or breath emitted fail
him. Let not his friends, let not his foemen
slay him. (3)

Let Heaven thy father and let Earth thy mother,
accordant, give thee death in course of nature,
That thou mayst live on Aditi's bosom, guarded,
a hundred winters, through thy respirations. (4)[37]

We have seen so far that the Vedic Aryan considered death an inevitable evil to be postponed as long as possible and at all costs. To die meant "to pass into the order of nonexistence,"[38] a state of being outside the familiar laws of nature (*ṛta*). Affirmation of life and fear of losing prematurely one's life, the most precious possession of each individual, characterize the general attitude toward death. Despite hardships and problems, everyone knew how life in this world could be enjoyed, whereas no one knew for sure what was to follow. This applies especially to the lower classes who did not have the same confident expectation regarding immortality as did the members of the upper castes. Hermann Oldenburg, pointing to this fact, states:[39]

> So zeigt sich der Unsterblichkeitsglaube in den Totenliedern des letzten, jüngsten Ṛgvedabuchs durchaus in der Färbung der Aristokratie, deren Angehörige gewiss sind, in der lichten Himmelswelt von ihren göttlichen Freunden mit hohen Ehren empfangen zu werden. Die Vorstellungen aber von den in der Erdtiefe hausenden Seelen, . . . von Gespenstern: all das liegt so gut wie ganz ausserhalb des Horizontes jener Totenlieder.

In the later part of the Atharva-Veda a change of attitude gradually took place, heralding the advent of a new age of thought. A grandiose, perennial idea began to evolve which was to take the sting out of death.[40] When we read that knowledge of the highest reality eliminates the fear of death, we have a foretaste of the Ātman-Brahman theory that was to find its classical expression in the great Upaniṣads.

Death and the Brāhmaṇas

Parallel with the development of this new philosophy which has to be seen, at least in part, as a reaction to the increasing predominance of the Brahmin caste over the rest of the Vedic society, the old sacrificial system expanded rapidly. Ritual commentaries and manuals in prose, known as the Brāhmaṇas,[41] were composed by the various priestly orders and their schools. Their high social position was due largely to the general belief in their magical powers. In order to obtain a desired good or to prevent the occurrence of a certain evil, highly specialized priests with extreme care and in accordance with their sacrificial manuals performed ritual acts for their paying clients. Any deviation from the established ceremonial order could invalidate a rite or even produce dangerous consequences.

In this period of the Brāhmaṇas, beginning approximately in the tenth century B.C., the gods of the Saṃhitās have lost their former significance. Instead, the sacrifice now takes the place of the ruling powers in the universe. "The sacrifice is here no longer the means to an end, but it is an aim in itself, indeed, the highest aim of existence." [42] The gods depend as much on sacrifice for survival and strength as do human beings.[43] In fact, there is hardly any distinction between gods and Brahmins. The priestly author of the following Śatapatha-Brāhmaṇa passage makes his position quite clear when he states that "there are two kinds of gods; for the gods, forsooth, are the gods; and the learned Brāhmans versed in sacred lore are the human gods. And the sacrifice to them is twofold, oblations (being the sacrifice) to the gods, and gifts to the priests being that to the human gods, to the learned Brāhmans versed in sacred lore." [44] The same passage then goes on to show divine and priestly appreciation for gifts received, and promises to the giver the inheritance of heaven. In the hands of the learned priest-magicians the sacrifice became the most powerful weapon which raised the Brahmins not only over their fellowmen, but ultimately even over the gods.

About this branch of Vedic literature, saturated with lengthy ceremonial elaborations and often incomprehensible speculations, the judgment has been made "that all that is noble and beautiful in Hinduism was foreshadowed already by the Rigveda, and all that is filthy and repulsive in it, by the Brāhmaṇas." [45] But we may also find parts in these otherwise biased writings that contain important ideas relative to the main theme of our investigation as well as old creation legends and etiological myths. Whereas in the Saṃhitās eschatological concepts were still very vague, the Brāhmaṇas are more definite on this subject. According to a speculation in the Śatapatha Brāhmaṇa (*ŚB*, X. 4. 3) Death was identified with Time, symbolized by the Year, and also identical with the divine principle, Prajāpati, the Lord of creatures, who created the gods and the mortal beings as well as Death, their consumer (*ŚB*, X. 1. 3. 1). The then mortal gods lived in constant fear of Prajāpati, "the Year, Death, the Ender, lest he, by day and night, should reach the end of their life." [46] In their anxiety they attempted, at first unsuccessfully, to attain immortality through sacrificial rites. Only after building a fire altar exactly according to Prajāpati's specifications did they become immortal (*amṛta*).[47] There was in this, however, a potentially dangerous consequence which could upset the natural order. If the human mortals should employ the same method, they could share immortality with the gods and thus cheat Death out of his right. Therefore, the gods decided that no living being should enjoy immortality with a body. First Death (*mṛtyu*) was to receive his portion, whereafter "he who is to become immortal either through knowledge, or through holy work, shall become immortal after separating from the body." [48]

The ritual construction of a fire altar, a symbolic manifestation of Prajāpati, conveys immortality to the nonbodily aspect of the worshiper who in a mystical way partakes of the immortal essence of the god and thus transcends death. The physical body of a god as well as the bodies of men, consisting of "the hair on the mouth, the skin, the flesh, the bone, and the marrow" is subject to decay, whereas "the mind, the voice, the vital air, the eye, and the ear" (*ŚB,* X. 1. 3. 4; *SBE,* XLIII, 290) constitute his immortal part. However, the deep-seated desire of the Aryans of this period was still for total immortality. Their great concern for the survival of the entire being finds its expression in the same Brāhmaṇa. Here the gods are determined to make Prajāpati, manifested as the fire altar, immortal by encompassing his mortal part (layers of earth) with layers of bricks (representing his immortal part), topping the structure with scattered chips of gold and placing fire on it. By this sacrificial act, i.e., the Agnihotra, Prajāpati became entirely immortal. In like manner the mortal human sacrificer "by this sacrificial performance . . . makes his body uniformly undecaying and immortal (*ŚB,* X. 1. 4. 1; *SBE,* XLIII, 292). An all-inclusive personal immortality, the highest good in this universe (*ŚB,* VIII. 7. 4. 18), is available for the faithful sacrificer[49] in the blessed realm of the gods, but the path to this future life leads through the painful experience of death, when Death will take temporary possession of man's physical part.[50]

The basic attitude of the worshiper who has knowledge (*vidyā*) or who does holy work (*karman*) is optimistic because of his confidence in the efficacy of the sacrificial system (*ŚB,* XII. 3. 5. 1-4). His life-affirming spirit counters the fear of death by stressing the victory of life over the necessary transitory destruction. Indeed, there are three births and only one earthly death for him. His first birth is from his parents, his second birth occurs through the performance of the all-important lifegiving sacrifice, and the third and final birth takes place in heaven after his earthly death and cremation (*ŚB,* XI. 2. 1. 1). The Ṛg-Vedic ideal of a prosperous life of a hundred years is still maintained (*ŚB,* XII. 8. 1. 20), but now with less emphasis. On the other hand, life in heaven is more clearly conceived than in any of the Saṃhitās. It is seen in relation to the sacrificial activities of an individual. In proportion to his sacrificial credits is his need for food in the next world which may range from two meals a day to one meal every hundred years or more.[51] The performance of sacrifices during his lifetime determines the length of his earthly life as well as his future condition in heaven and confers to him sustenance and strength. It appears that one can infer from a fulfilled life of a hundred years on earth a blessed immortality in heaven.

Despite optimism and confidence, traces of apprehension and concern are not absent in this period. The dreaded possibility of redeath (*punarmṛtyu*) in the realm beyond occupied his mind. He held that acts performed in this life will find their recompense in the next, where the gods place the good and evil deeds of a person in a balance. "Whichever of the two will rise that he will follow, whether it be the good or the evil." [52] In fact, man is the architect of his own future. "He is born into the world made by him" (*ŚB*, VI. 2. 2. 27; *SBE*, XLI, 181). This idea does not yet constitute the famous Hindu doctrine of transmigration, as rebirth takes place not in this world, only in the next. But the thought of appropriate punishment or reward, together with the possibility of recurring deaths and consequent births, needed only a minor shift of emphasis to develop into the Upaniṣadic theory of Karma-Saṃsāra.

Death and the Upaniṣads

A major development relative to the theme of our investigation takes place in the last branch of Vedic literature or Śruti which has influenced the Indian mind most profoundly; i.e., the Upaniṣads. The generally accepted meaning of this word, viz., "sitting down near" a teacher to be instructed in esoteric doctrine, already indicates the character of this class of literature which is also known as Vedānta or "end as well as goal of the Veda." According to Indian tradition the 108 extant Upaniṣads, of which ten to thirteen are classified as principal Upaniṣads, are basically speculative and to be studied only by people who have achieved a certain spiritual maturity. It is impossible to determine their authorship and their exact age. It is generally assumed, however, that the early prose Upaniṣads were composed before the appearance of the Buddha. Despite the fact that the Upaniṣadic speculations are different in spirit from the magico-sacrificial speculations of the Brāhmaṇas, it would be wrong to deny a continuity between the two. The Āraṇyakas, the contemplative texts of the forest hermits, successfully mitigate any possible reaction and help to maintain a clear connection between the deep concerns of the Brāhmaṇas and the new approaches of the earliest Upaniṣads. In fact, similar speculations with regard to the universe, man, and sacrifice can be found in both the Brāhmaṇas and the Bṛhad-āraṇyaka and Chāndogya Upaniṣads. R. C. Zaehner sees the Upaniṣadic identification of the human soul (*ātman*) with the world soul (*brāhman*) as resulting from "the purely magical identifications [in the Brāhmaṇas] of details of the sacrifice with various objects in the phenomenal world." [53]

The Upaniṣads are not systematic treatises. They are religio-philosophical expositions of various lengths, often using the forms of dialogue and parable to communicate new intuitive insights regarding the nature of reality. Questioning the efficacy of sacrifices, they no longer concentrate on sacrificial rites, but develop new ways and mystical methods that lead to the realization of the highest good, i.e., eternal liberation. Thus, they relate to the speculations already encountered in some of the mantras of the Ṛg-Veda and Atharva-Veda.

In order to understand their thoughts about death, we first have to acquaint ourselves with their major concepts and their ideas about man. We find as early as the period of the Ṛg-Veda a trend towards monism in some hymns (*RV,* X. 129), expressed through various identifications and equivalences. According to early Upaniṣadic thought, there is one single entity underlying the multiplicity of ever-changing phenomena. It is called by different names: Ātman, Brāhman, Puruṣa, meaning either the unchanging ground of the universe or the essence of the immortal human soul.[54] Ātman, in its microcosmic aspect, the principle of one's life, is different from the mortal body, mind, and even intellect. It is unborn, pure existence, and unconditional. Radhakrishnan calls it "the superreality of the *jīva,* the individual ego." [55] In its macrocosmic aspect, it is the same subtle essence that underlies the entire world (cf. Chāndogya Upaniṣad VI. 8. 7). While the term Ātman —originally meaning the breath of life[56]—represents in its development a movement from microcosm to macrocosm, the term Brāhman, as the eternal ground of the universe, represents movement in the opposite direction by way of emanation. The two meet in man and become identical when he, in a mystical experience, not in a reasoning thought process, realizes the great oneness with totality (*sarvam*).[57] Duality is transcended and with it, time and space, moral and social categories, suffering and death.[58] The Upaniṣadic thinkers call this great experience of emancipation from *mṛtyu,* "plurality and relativity," and from *Punarmṛtyu,* "attachment, fear and death," Mokṣa. It is a supraconscious state of the one who "knows," whether alive (*jīvanmukti*) or after his physical death. Since there is no continuation of a personal entity with individual features, immortality has to be understood as an eternal merger of the microcosmic self (*ātman*) into the universal self (*brāhman*).[59]

Unfortunately, not everyone is capable of gaining this liberating knowledge. It cannot be attained by way of instruction or through the performance of magic rituals; rather, it requires a radical change of attitude towards the phenomenal world—elimination of selfish desire, an ascetic life, and the application of Yogic practices (cf. Maitrī Upaniṣad VI. 34). Mokṣa, as seen in most of the Upaniṣads, depends on the disciplined self-effort of the seeker.[60] Man, by his action and attitude, is ultimately responsible for the course of his life. Neither a supreme being, nor magic formulas, nor sacrifice ultimately determines his future, only his own deeds (*karman*). At death, when the various components of a person unite with their corresponding counterparts in nature, the totality of his Karman remains attached to his Ātman. This Karman then is the force which decides his fate in his next existence, where he will receive exactly what he deserves. If his conduct was good, he will be reborn as a member of an upper caste. If it was evil, he will be reincarnated as a dog or lower animal.[61] This is an ongoing, autonomous process based on the principle of cause and effect. The perpetual cycle of births, deaths, and reincarnations (*saṃsāra*) will last as long as its cause, Karman—the result of action itself—is being produced. All are subject to the force of Karman, even the gods. All are afraid of the many deaths lying ahead of them. Life as such came to be viewed as something evil because of its brevity and the fatal consequences of one's actions whether good or bad. Birth was understood as the beginning of suffering (cf. Bṛhad-Āraṇyaka Upaniṣad IV. 3. 8). The apparent pessimistic attitude and the contempt of worldly pleasures of the possibly Buddhist-influenced Maitrī Upaniṣad can hardly be surpassed:

In this foul-smelling, unsubstantial body, a conglomerate of bone, skin, muscle, marrow, flesh, semen, blood, mucus, tears, rheum, faeces, urine, wind, bile, and phlegm, what is the good of the enjoyment of desire? In this body which is afflicted with desire, anger, covetousness, delusion, fear, despondency, envy, separation from what is desired, union with the undesired, hunger, thirst, old age, death, disease, sorrow, and the like, what is the good of the enjoyment of desire? [62]

With great concern the Upaniṣadic thinkers wrestle with the problem of suffering and search for ways out of this vicious cycle of unending painful death experiences. When we ask for the root of the chain of empirical existences (*saṃsāra*), we are told that it is desire: "A person consists of desires. As is his desire so is his will; as is his will, so is the deed he does, whatever deed he does, that he attains. The object to which the mind is attached, the subtle self goes together with the deed, being attached to it alone. Exhausting the results of whatever works he did in this world he comes again . . . to this world for (fresh) work." After having shown the predicament, the author offers his solution: "This (is for) the man who desires. But the man who does not desire, whose desire is the self . . . he goes to Brāhman. When all the desires that dwell in the heart are cast away, then does the mortal become immortal." [63] Thus, actions as such do not necessarily produce Karman; this occurs only when they are motivated by passionate desire, when the deluded doer in his ignorance (*avidyā*) of the true reality is attached to the phenomenal world. In this context Radhakrishnan in his commentary to the Iśa Upaniṣad stresses the importance of action while one is embodied. Works have to be performed, however, "by merging the individual in the cosmic purpose and by dedicating all action to God," [64] if they are not to lead to new Karman and thus prevent immortality.

To the spiritually gifted person who has the capacity for reaching the lofty sphere of the Absolute, the Upaniṣads are sources of hope and strength. In his encounter with the problem of death he can chant with confidence the famous prayer: "From the unreal lead me to the real, from darkness lead me to light, from death lead me to immortality." [65] He is no longer afraid of life or death since he can detach his true self from the evils of his current embodiment, and when he dies, he leaves all suffering behind forever.[66] To the ignorant, on the other hand, the Upaniṣads do not offer much hope. The routine performance of the Vedic ritual produces only inferior Karma. Instead of making spiritual progress, fools sink deeper when their Karma is consumed. Their attachment to ephemeral things only increases their folly and keeps them chained to the fatal cycle of births and deaths. Not even a limited stay in heaven on account of good works has any liberating value (cf. Muṇḍaka Upaniṣad 1. 2. 7-10). Even if some stern statements in the Muṇḍaka Upaniṣad are softened by the exaltation of the wise mendicant (*saṃnyāsin*), they nevertheless reflect the prevalent attitude of the Upaniṣads.

A classical episode that clearly illustrates the Upaniṣadic attitude towards death is found in the Kaṭha Upaniṣad. It is the Upaniṣadic version of the ancient story of Yama, the lord of death, and Naciketas, a boy—a story also found in the Ṛg-Veda (X. 135) and in the Taittirīya Brāhmaṇa (III. 11. 8). In accordance with the ideal in the Brāhmaṇas, salvation in the Brāhmaṇa version is understood as freedom from the much feared final redeath (*punarmṛtyu*) in a life beyond by means of sacrificial acts. A different attitude manifests itself in the following version of the Kaṭha Upaniṣad:[67] Vajarasravasa, a typical representative of Vedic ceremonialism, performs a sacrifice in hope of gain. Impoverished, he remunerates the priests by giving them some worthless cows. His searching son Naciketas, representing the new spirit of the Upaniṣads, is upset by his father's hypocritical formalism and—knowing the dangerous consequences of his father's action—offers himself as payment (*dakṣiṇā*) to the sacrificial priests. His father, angry about his son's persistence, says to him: "Unto Death shall I give thee" (I. 1. 4). The obedient son goes to Yama's abode, first revealing his thoughts about death. He sees his death as a temporary event, comparing it with the natural process in the realm of vegetation: birth, growing, ripening, decaying, and again, new life. Death, for him, is the gate to a new, though limited, existence on earth, whereas to his father, it is hopefully leading to a blessed life in heaven without a second final death. Upon entering Yama's world, Naciketas has to wait for three days and nights, due to the absence of the host, without receiving the usual hospitality. As soon as Yama arrives, he grants him three boons to make up for the suffered inconvenience. The first request of Naciketas is to return alive to his appeased father. In connection with the second boon, Naciketas discusses with Yama the traditional idea of heaven: "In the world of heaven there is no fear whatever; thou [Death] art not there, nor does one fear old age. Crossing over both hunger and thirst, leaving sorrow behind, one rejoices in the world of heaven" (I. 1. 12). According to this essentially pre- or extra-Upaniṣadic concept of heaven, death and all the other human problems belong only to the earthly sphere. All, including death, appear to be equally undesirable.[68] Now, as his second boon, Naciketas wants to know how the heavenly citizens attain immortality; i.e., what he himself can do to enjoy the effects of his good works (in the ritual sense of the Brāhmaṇas) forever. In response, Yama instructs him in the threefold fire sacrifice, henceforth called the Nāciketa rite, as the sure means of gaining access to heavenly immortality.[69]

Naciketas' third wish reveals the spirit of the Upaniṣads best. In leaving behind the lower epistemological level of the first two boons, he now moves towards a higher level of knowledge, i.e., illumination. This becomes apparent in his third request: "There is this doubt in regard to a man who has departed, some (holding) that he is and some that he is not. I would be instructed by thee in this knowledge" (I. 1. 20). Yama reacts most uncomfortably. Since Naciketas' question is so difficult to answer, Yama suggests choosing other favors such as sons, grandsons, wealth, a long life and enjoyment of any imaginable pleasure. But Naciketas refuses, realizing the transitoriness of these questionable goods. Finally, when Yama sees that the youth is interested only in the absolute reality which is not subject to transmigration, he is willing to reveal the secret doctrine of the immortal self to him: "The knowing self is never born; nor does he die at any time. . . . He is unborn, eternal, abiding and primeval. He is not slain when the body is slain" (I. 2. 18). This is the direct answer to his question about the mystery of death. This true, unchanging self "constitutes the inner reality of each individual."[70] It is beyond fear, sorrow, and death. No instruction or intellectual power can grasp it, because it is "without sound, without touch and without form, undecaying, is likewise, without taste, eternal, without smell, without beginning, without end, beyond the great, abiding, by discerning that, one is freed from the face of death" (I. 3. 15). Thus ends the Upaniṣadic version of the story of Yama and Naciketas.

In this Upaniṣad, which is representative of most Upaniṣads, the basic concern is emancipation of the immortal Ātman from Saṃsāra. This deliverance from births and deaths can be achieved only through the cultivation of self-knowledge. To know the self's identity with Brāhman is immortality; to be ignorant of it is death.[71]

Notes

1. Aryans, meaning "noble"; this designation refers more to linguistic similarities than to racial affinity among the tribes.
2. A. L. Basham, *The Wonder That Was India* (New York: Grove Press, 1959), p. 32. Relates the Dāsas to the earlier Harappā culture which definitely has influenced the development of Indian thought and life.
3. One of the leading tribes was the Bharatas, after whom the entire country was named. The Indians still officially refer to their country as Bharat.
4. The Veda, the Indo-Aryan literary harvest of a period of several thousand years, had its beginning in protohistoric times before the Aryan invasion of India. Most hymns, prayers, and charms, however, were composed in India since the middle of the second millennium B.C. The literature has been divided early into four parts. The first part consists of four collections or Saṃhitās: Ṛg, Yajur, Sama, and Atharva. The Ṛg-Veda (*RV*), consisting of hymns and prayers, and for our study the most important part, is the oldest collection. The Atharva-Veda (*AV*), a collection of spells and magical incantations, is the youngest in the group. The Brāhmaṇas, the priestly interpretations of the Saṃhitās, make up the second, and the "Forest Texts," the Āraṇyakas, the third. Finally, the Upaniṣads constitute the philosophical conclusion of the Vedic literature.
5. X. 34. 13, trans. Basham in *The Wonder That Was India,* p. 405.
6. *RV,* X. 129. 1-4, trans. R. Griffith, *The Hymns of the Ṛg Veda,* (Benares: 1896-7), volume 2, p. 575.
7. E.g., Goddess Vāc is represented as the life principle and soul of man. *RV,* X. 125. 4, 6.
8. *RV,* I. 164. 33; X. 183. 3; X. 184. 1; *AV,* XII. 1. 19.
9. Probably identical with god Prajāpati, the Lord of Beings.
10. *AV,* X. 10. 33 f. makes gods and men dependent for life on the cow. What distinguishes man from the other creatures is his ability to reason. As Aristotle defined man a rational animal, so did the Vedic thinkers, by naming the postdiluvial progenitor of humanity Manu. This name, as M. Phillips, *The Teachings of the Veda* (London: 1895), p. 137, points out, is derived from the Sanskrit root *man* which means to think and which is related to (Latin) *mens* and (English) man and mind.
11. See T. W. Organ, *The Self in Indian Philosophy* (The Hague: Mouton & Co., 1964), p. 28.
12. R. C. Zaehner, *Hinduism* (New York: Oxford University Press, 1966), p. 48.
13. *Ibid.,* p. 50.
14. *RV,* X. 117. 1, quoted from R. C. Majumdar, ed., *The Vedic Age* (Bombay: 1965), p. 345.
15. Keith, *The Religion and Philosophy of the Veda and the Upaniṣads* (Cambridge: Harvard University Press, 1925), p. 405.
16. The Fathers (*pitaras*) are the blessed ancestors who reside now in heaven.

They are invoked to intercede for their descendants on earth. See *RV*, X. 15. 1,2,5.

17. *RV*, X. 88. 15; trans. J. Muir, *Original Sanskrit Texts*, vol. 5, 3rd ed. (London: Trubner & Co., 1884), p. 287. Cited in text as Muir, *RV*.
18. *RV*, X. 107. 2; I. 125. 5, 6; X. 14. 8. The drinking of *soma*, the divine ambrosia, was also believed to convey immortality; cf. *RV*, VIII. 48. 3.
19. When cremated, "Agni does not consume their generative organ; in the celestial sphere they have abundance of sexual gratification" (*AV*, IV. 34. 2); trans. J. Muir, *Original Sanskrit Texts*, vol. 5, p. 308. Cited in text as Muir, *AV*.
20. Muir, 291; *AV*, VI. 28. 3. Compare also *RV*, X. 14. 1.
21. Keith, *The Religion and Philosophy of the Veda and the Upaniṣads*, p. 408.
22. *RV*, X. 97. 16. Cf. J. Ehni, *Die ursprüngliche Gottheit des vedischen Yama* (Leipzig: 1896). The author in this elaborate monograph attempts to trace the various features of Yama as a nature and sun god, as a god of fire, as king of the blessed dead, as a terrible deathbringer and judge, as well as a human being.
23. *RV*, X. 14. 8; *AV*, XII. 3. 17; VI. 120. 3; *RV*, IX. 113. 7-11.
24. *RV*, VII. 89. 1; see also Basham, *The Wonder That Was India*, p. 237.
25. Keith, *The Religion and Philosophy of the Veda and the Upaniṣads*, p. 409. See also *AV*, XII. 4. 36.
26. Keith, p. 410.
27. *RV*, I. 24. 11. The relationship between sin and suffering in general is hinted at in numerous passages, e.g., *RV*, I. 23. 21-22; VII. 88. 5-6; VII. 89. 5; X. 37. 12.
28. Cf. Organ, *The Self in Indian Philosophy*, p. 28.
29. *RV*, VII. 86. 3-5; see also Keith, *The Religion and Philosophy of the Veda and the Upaniṣads*, pp. 425, 427.
30. Majumdar, ed., *The Vedic Age*, p. 352.
31. Phillips, *The Teachings of the Vedas*, p. 168. Cf. *RV*, I. 121. 13; *RV*, I. 133. 3; II. 29. 6; IX. 73. 8; X. 97. 16.
32. *AV*, IV. 34. 2. Trans. Ralph T. Griffith, *The Hymns of the Atharvaveda*, 2 vols. (Benares: 1895-6), volume 1, p. 176 (hereafter cited as Griffith, *AV*). See also *AV*, IV. 4. 16; IV. 11. 6. *RV*, X. 15. 1; X. 14. 8.
33. This general attitude was to last until a new philosophy evolved which changed the naive, optimistic, this-worldly mood into an apparent pessimistic outlook toward life.
34. "The givers of rich meeds are made immortal; the givers of rich fees prolong their lifetime," *RV*, I. 125. 6. Trans. Ralph T. Griffith, *Hymns of the Rig-veda*, 4 vols. (Benares: 1889-92), vol. 1, p. 174 (hereafter Griffith, *RV*).
35. Concern for survival of offspring and heroes (i.e., daughters and sons, according to Sayana. See Griffith, II, 406; *RV*.) can also be related to the idea of immortality through children. In *RV*, V. 4. 10, the poet prays to the god Agni: "As I . . . a mortal, call with might on thee Immortal . . .

may I be immortal by my children." (In Griffith, I, p. 471.) Also, *RV*, VI. 70. 3: "He in his seed is born again" (*idem.*, p. 643).

36. *RV*, VIII. 18. 22 (Griffith, II, p. 144); cf. also *RV*, X. 95. 18. See also H. Zimmer, *Altindisches Leben* (Berlin: 1879), p. 400.
37. Griffith, I, 67 f.; *AV*, II. 28. Cf. also *AV*, I. 30. 3; VIII. 2. 27; see also Griffith, I, 217; cf. also *RV*, I. 89. 9.
38. A. T. Embree, *The Hindu Tradition*, Modern Library (New York: Random House, 1966), p. 29.
39. H. Oldenberg, *Die Religion des Veda* (Stuttgart: 1923), p. 11.
40. Griffith, II, 39-42; *AV*, X. 8. 26,27,37,44: "This fair one is untouched by age, immortal in a mortal's house. . . . Thou art a woman, and a man; thou art a damsel and a boy. Grown old thou totterest with a staff, new-born thou lookest every way. The man who knows the drawn out string on which these creatures all are strung, the man who knows the thread's thread, he may know the mighty Brāhmaṇa. Desireless, firm, immortal, self-existent, contented with the essence, lacking nothing, free from the fear of Death is he who knoweth that Soul courageous, youthful, undecaying."
41. To each of the four Saṃhitās belong a number of Brāhmaṇas, some of which have been lost. Cf. M. Winternitz, *A History of Indian Literature* (Calcutta: 1959), vol. 1, pp. 163-96. Also H. Gowen, *A History of Indian Literature* (New York: Greenwood Press, 1968), pp. 93-104.
42. Winternitz, *A History of Indian Literature*, p. 172.
43. Cf. Gowen, *A History of Indian Literature*, pp. 97 f.
44. Śatapatha Brāhmana (*ŚB*), IV. 3. 4. 4. In F. Max Müller, ed., *The Sacred Books of the East Translated by Various Oriental Scholars*, 50 vols. (Oxford: Clarendon Press, 1879-1900), vol. 26, p. 341. Hereafter cited as *SBE*.
45. Majumdar, ed., *The Vedic Age*, p. 422.
46. *SBE*, volume 43, p. 356. Prajāpati himself was half mortal and with that part of him, he was afraid of death. Cf. *ŚB*, X. 1. 3. 2 ff.
47. Another etiological myth explaining the attainment of immortality is found in *ŚB*, III. 6. 1. 28.
48. *ŚB*, X. 4. 3. 9. This new emphasis on knowledge in the pursuit of liberation (*mokṣa*) was soon to become a main feature of Indian thought. Cf. also *ŚB*, X. 5. 4. 16.
49. *ŚB*, IV. 2. 5. 10: "Every sacrifice is a ship bound heavenwards" (*SBE*, vol. 26, p. 311). See also *ŚB*, XI. 1. 8. 6.
50. *ŚB*, IV. 6. 1. 1: "The sacrificer is born with his whole body in yonder world." (*SBE*, vol. 26, p. 424.) Cf. also *ŚB*, XII. 8. 3. 31.
51. Cf. *ŚB*, X. 1. 5. 4. Indeed a major purpose of the fire altar sacrifice is to secure subsistence for this world and the next. The same Brāhmaṇa goes even so far as to maintain: "There is only one foundation, only one finale to the sacrifice—even heaven." *ŚB*, VIII. 7. 4. 6 in *SBE*, vol. 43, p. 146.
52. *ŚB*, VI. 2. 7. 33 in *SBE*, vol. 44, p. 45. The goodness is here not so much of moral, but of ritual nature; in this context see Keith, *The Religion and Philosophy of the Veda and the Upaniṣads*, pp. 473-75.

53. Zaehner, *Hinduism*, p. 39.
54. Cf. *ibid.*, p. 51.
55. S. Radhakrishnan, *The Principal Upaniṣads* (London: G. Allen & Unwin, 1953), p. 74.
56. Cf. *ibid.*, p. 73.
57. "Whoever knows thus, 'I am Brāhman,' becomes this all." Bṛhad-Āraṇyaka Upaniṣad, I. 4. 10, trans. Radhakrishnan, *The Principal Upaniṣads*, p. 168. That same Upaniṣad (II. 5. 12) joyfully identifies the knowing person (*puruṣa*), not only with totality (*sarvam*), but with immortality (*amṛtam*).
58. *Ibid.*, p. 277: "Knowing that immortal *Brahman* I am immortal." (Bṛhad-Āraṇyaka Upaniṣad, IV. 4. 17.) Cf. also IV. 4, 20, 22 and Chāndogya Upanisad, VII. 25. 2, VII. 26. 2.
59. Cf. Chāndogya Upaniṣad III. 14. 4. See also Jan Gonda, *Veda und älterer Hinduismus*, Die Religionen Indiens, vol. 1 (Stuttgart, 1960), pp. 203 ff. (an excellent up-to-date presentation).
60. The idea of grace (prasāda) is rather an exception; cf. Śvetāśvatara Upaniṣad, III. 20. See also Gonda, *Veda und älterer Hinduismus*, p. 205.
61. Cf. Bṛhad-Āraṇyaka Upaniṣad IV. 4. 5. and III. 2. 13. Chāndogya Upaniṣad V. 10. 7. Cf. also Gonda, *Veda und älterer Hinduismus*, p. 207.
62. Maitrī Upaniṣad I. 3., trans. Radhakrishnan, *The Principal Upaniṣads*, p. 796.
63. Bṛhad-Āraṇyaka Upaniṣad IV. 4. 5-7., *ibid.*, pp. 272 f.
64. *Ibid.*, p. 569. See also Gonda, *Veda und älterer Hinduismus*, p. 209.
65. Bṛhad-Āraṇyaka Upaniṣad I. 3. 28, trans. Radhakrishnan, *The Principal Upaniṣads*, p. 162.
66. Cf. *ibid.*, IV. 3. 8.
67. The following quotations are in Radhakrishnan, *The Principal Upaniṣads.*
68. Cf. Sten Rodhe, *Deliver Us from Evil* (Lund: Gleerup, 1946), p. 101.
69. From the Upaniṣadic viewpoint the immortality in question can only be a relative immortality. "Compared to the life of the people on earth, the life [in heaven] is very long; yet it is very short from the standpoint of Brahman." (Swami Nikhilānanda, ed., *The Upanishads*, 3 vols. (New York: Harper, 1949-1956), vol. 1, p. 121.) The ultimate worthlessness of rites in the pursuit of absolute immortality is expressed in the beautiful dialogue between Yājñavalkya and his wife Maitreyī, where the husband wants to renounce the world. She withholds her consent until he has instructed her in the road to knowledge (*vidyā*) leading to true immortality. In her concern for this immortality she asks him: "If . . . this whole earth filled with wealth were mine, would I be immortal?" Whereupon he replies: "No . . . like the life of the rich even so would your life be. Of immortality, however, there is no hope through [rites performed by means of] wealth." Brhad-Āranyaka Upanisad II. 4. 2., trans. Radhakrishnan, *The Principal Upaniṣads*, p. 195.
70. Radhakrishnan, *The Principal Upaniṣads*, p. 616.
71. Cf. Nikhilānanda, ed., *The Upanishads*, vol. 1, p. 157.

II
Tradition

Section 1. Sūtras and the Mahābhārata Epic

F. H. HOLCK

Leaving the Vedic Period and Indian literature classified as Śruti or revealed, we shall deal in this part of our investigation with some quite different early literary works. These will include two of the ancient Sūtras or manuals on law, conduct, and religious duties. The Sūtras are also known as Smṛti or memorized tradition and are closely related to the Vedas. In addition, we will look at the great epic [1] Mahābhārata as well as the Purāṇas.

The Sūtras and the epic literature began to take shape, though not all in final form, as early as the second part of the first millennium B.C., whereas the Purāṇas probably date from the earlier part of the first millennium A.D. We have combined these works under the heading of tradition, not only because of lack of a more appropriate common classification, but also because this designation alludes to the historical content of and the high esteem for this literature. However, referring to historiography, it must be kept in mind that history in Hindu civilization should not be understood in Western terms. Historical events and facts, especially of early India, are so closely intertwined with myths, poetry, and legends that their historicity can only rarely be ascertained.[2]

Death and the Sūtras

The Sūtras,[3] being basically concerned with practical things such as domestic religious ceremonies, legal questions, and customs related to the caste system and the four stages in the life of the "twice-born" Hindu, contain little original speculation. They do not attempt to interpret. What little they do reveal about attitudes towards death is related either to rituals for the householder as in the Gṛhya Sūtra of Hiraṇyakeśin, a domestic manual, or to the conduct of the forest hermit and ascetic as in the Manu-Smṛti, the Laws of Manu. Moreover, they do not generate many new ideas on our theme, but adopt thoughts and attitudes as we have met them in our encounter with the Vedic literature. In the Gṛhya Sūtra we detect the same desire for happiness in this world, long life for oneself and one's offspring, and the same hope for immortality as in the Ṛg-Veda Saṃhitā. In conjunction with a house-building ceremony several gods are implored. "Vāstoṣpati! Be our furtherer; make our wealth increase in cows and horses, O Indu (i.e., Soma). Free from decay may we dwell in thy friendship; give us thy favour, as a father to his sons." An incantation follows in which the god Yama, lord of the dead, is conceived in his benevolent aspect: "May death go away; may immortality come to us. May Vivasvat's son (Yama) protect us from danger. May wealth, like a leaf (that falls) from a tree, fall down over us." Then death, as the destroying force, is directly conjured: "Go another way, O death, that belongs to thee, separated from the way of the gods." After this the invocation to Vāstoṣpati, the lord of the building site, continues: "To thee who hears us, I speak: do no harm to our offspring nor to our heroes." [4]

The Manu-Smṛti, an ancient code of law for the "twice-born" named after the legendary sage Manu, yields somewhat more on our subject than the Gṛhya-Sūtras. It is the literary product of a Brahmanic school identified as the Mānavas in the northwestern part of the Indian subcontinent.[5] It originated in its present form somewhere between the second century B.C. and the second century A.D. Its twelve chapters reflect the influence of previous contemporaneous religious and intellectual developments. The religio-philosophical movements as they began to arise in the principal Upaniṣads also found entrance into the Manu-Smṛti. This especially becomes apparent in the first, sixth, and last chapters where Saṃkhya, Yoga and Vedānta principles can be detected.[6]

In its rules for forest hermits and ascetics, the Manu-Smṛti takes up the Upaniṣadic notion of final liberation (*mokṣa*) and the means to achieve this goal.[7] A "twice-born" Hindu in his pursuit for immortality of his soul is to practice harsher and harsher austerities until his mortal part is dried up; and "in order to attain complete (union with) the (supreme) Soul, (he must study) the various sacred texts contained in the Upaniṣads (Manu VI. 24,29). A way to hasten the death of that which is mortal, and by the same token to prepare one's immortal part for the sorrow-free world of Brahman, is to start, fully determined, a journey "in a northeasterly direction, subsisting on water and air, until his body sinks to rest." [8] This is in effect a form of suicide by starvation, a permissible, even a meritorious act as it was widely practiced at that time in Jainism. It reflects the detachment from worldly or transitory objects and pleasures as well as a general fearlessness which also pertains to the death of the body. This attitude rests upon the conviction that the true self of the ascetic is not affected by suffering, death, and decay.

To be sure, it is a long arduous process leading to this mental state of equanimity. The Laws of Manu recommend Yogic exercises and meditation as appropriate means. "By the restraint of his senses, by the destruction of love and hatred, and by the abstention from injuring the creatures, he becomes fit for immortality" (Manu VI. 60). On the other hand, the horrors of death, suffering, and hell for those who are attached to this world are vividly portrayed:

"Let him reflect on the transmigrations of men, caused by their sinful deeds, on their falling into hell, and on the torments in the world of Yama . . . on their being overpowered by age and being tormented with diseases . . . on the departure of the individual soul from this body and its new birth in (another) womb, and on its wanderings through ten thousand millions of existences" (Manu VI. 61-63).

Death and the Mahābhārata

The general feeling in Hindu epic literature is eloquently expressed in the most extensive Indian Sanskrit work, the Mahābhārata: "There is no doubt that there is more sorrow than joy in life." [9] This pessimistic feature can be traced back to the Upaniṣadic doctrine of Saṃsāra. Whereas in general the earlier Vedic scriptures display a life affirming, optimistic outlook, we encounter in the Sanskrit poetry a widespread *Weltschmerz* attitude.[10] This great epic which consists of eighteen books (*parvas*) or over 100,000 double verses contains a wealth of material: myths, legends, and various episodes dealing with the fate of individuals and families. It also contains many moral, legal, didactic, and religio-philosophical expositions.

During its long history of development, these parts were combined with the nucleus of an ancient heroic poem about a mighty battle between two related families of the warrior caste, the Kauravas and the Pāṇḍavas. The original secular piece of Indian poetry changed gradually into an entire branch of religious literature because of Brahmanic manipulation and the literary activity of ascetics. The priestly caste, especially those serving the kings, by incorporating their ideas and doctrines into the popular epic extended their sphere of influence among all classes of the Hindu society. They accomplished this through the interpolation of legends about the lives of ancient sages and the enormous powers they gained with the help of sacrifices and self-mortifications. There were also the increasing number of highly respected forest hermits and ascetics who in their diverse writings advocated renunciation, contempt for this transitory life, and compassion for all living beings. A considerable part of this literature, too, found its way into the epic.

Considering these factors that played a role in the formation of the epic as it has been in existence since at least the fourth century A.D., it is not surprising to meet side by side heroic battle songs, priestly elaborations, philosophic reflections, and the gentle wisdom of ascetic narratives. It is just because of this many-sidedness, which so aptly reflects the spirit of Hindu civilization, that the Mahābhārata has been cherished to the present day by all Hindus. Although it is a poetical piece (*kāvya*), it is at the same time regarded as tradition (*śmṛti*) which carries with it indisputable authority.[11] Since the Mahābhārata is such a complex work, we may expect, therefore, a diversity of thoughts pertaining to death.

Man has always wondered about the origin of death. From the ideas expressed in various myths of primitive man, we may conclude that mortality was not considered to be an inevitable feature of man's nature. Rather, death was understood to be the result of a divine intervention.[12] The Mahābhārata contains such a myth which deals with the question of the origin of death and which offers a conclusion similar to those found in other civilizations.

The question arose with King Yudhiṣṭhira on the occasion of

the death of his brother's son Abhimanyu, killed in battle. In response to the king's lamentations, the seer, Vyāsa, explains that death takes all without exception. Looking around with grief in his heart, he recognizes the bodies of many great heroes lying on the battlefield, and he cannot but wonder about the mystery of death: "Whence is Death? Whose (offspring) is Death? What is Death? Why does Death take away creatures?" [13] And here Vyāsa, the legendary author of the epic, recounts an ancient story which the sage Nārada once told King Akampana who had lost his own son. To underline the significance of the story, Vyāsa promises miraculous consequences for the listener, including freedom from sorrow and grief and an extended lifespan and health for both the listener and his offspring. Listening to it is even equated with the study of the Vedas.

The story goes as follows: When god Brahma created the living beings, they were all immortal. But they multiplied too rapidly and the entire universe was in danger of becoming overcrowded.[14] To remedy the situation, the creator decided to decimate the population, but he could not determine the means by which his decision was to be carried out. His ensuing anger began to manifest itself in destructive fires issuing from his body. Immediately, the flames covered the quarters of the universe, threatening all life. In his compassion the god Śiva approached Brahma, interceding for the creatures, whereupon the creator replied: "I had no desire of destroying the universe, I desired good of the earth, and it was for this that wrath possessed me. The goddess Earth, afflicted with the heavy weight of creatures, always urged me for destroying the creatures on her." Brahma, then, controlling his wrath, reabsorbed into himself the devastating energy after having acknowledged Śiva's counsel to let all living beings return into the world through repeated births and deaths.

As the powerful lord of creation suppressed the destructive fires in his heart, there suddenly emanated from the openings of his body a beautiful woman with dark eyes. She was ornate with brilliant jewels, dressed in robes of black and red, and adorned with a lotus crown. Looking at the two gods, she smiled and was about to set out for the southern region, the realm of the dead, when Brahma addressed her by the name of Death, commanding her to slay all his creatures, the fools and the wise alike, irrespective of anything at all. Thereupon the goddess Death began to weep bitterly, while the creator caught her tears with his hands. She implored him to release her from this dreadful duty, saying:

"I shall not be able to cut off living creatures—infants, youths, and aged ones,—who have done me no injury. . . . I shall not be able to cut off dear sons and loved friends and brothers and mothers and fathers. If these die, their surviving relatives will surely curse me. I am filled with fear at the prospect of this. The tears of the sorrow-stricken survivors will burn me for eternity."

But Brahma in his attempt to convince her of the necessity of carrying out his command, replied: "O Death, thou has been intended for achieving the destruction of creatures. Go, destroy all creatures, thou needest have no scruples. Even this must be. It cannot be otherwise. . . . Nobody in the world will find any fault in thee." Still refusing to hurt the living beings, she underwent exceedingly long periods of most severe austerities in the Himalaya mountains, remaining motionless like a stone, fasting, living only on air and water, and finally suspending her life breath.

Moved by her ascetic vigor on behalf of the beloved creatures, yet without changing his decision, Brahma promised the goddess that she would not incur any sin or demerit by doing her duty with equanimity, and that the god Yama and diverse diseases would become her helpmates. At last, realizing the inevitability of the creator's decree, she accepted her assignment; yet, not without having been first assured by him that it is "covetousness, wrath, malice, jealousy, quarrel, folly and shamelessness, and other stern passions" by which the creatures are destroyed. And then he added: "Those tear-drops of thine that are in my hands, even they will become diseases, springing from living creatures themselves. They will kill men when their last hours come." Thereupon the obedient goddess "casting off desire and wrath, began to take the lives of living creatures when the time came (for their dissolution)."

The story as told by Nārada concludes with the understanding that "death has been ordained by the Creator himself for all creatures." Therefore, the wise, knowing of the inevitability of death and of the return of the creatures, should never grieve for the dead. This, then, constitutes Vyāsa's answer to King Yudhiṣṭhira's question about the origin and nature of death. It is a very ancient myth which becomes apparent in the still exalted position of the god Brahma and the subordinate rank of the god Śiva. It is also an unusual myth as death is personified as a female; the only other case of a goddess Death appears to be in the Purāṇic literature.[15]

The myth has several significant, though not always consistent, features:

1) In both versions the point is made that the idea of destroying the life of his creatures did not originate in the mind of the creator; mortality is presented rather as a logical necessity arising from dangerous circumstances, such as the overburdening of the earth and consequently the hazard of sinking into the waters.

2) Since the destruction of the constantly increasing number of living beings is necessary for preventing a cosmic catastrophe, the Lord of the universe is expected not only to act as the creator, but also as the destroyer. On the one hand he does not agree that

"the created beings should cease to exist," and on the other hand, he is responsible for order in the universe. He therefore delegates the task of killing to another being, one who emanated from him. This removes him from the immediate act of killing, but the relationship between his authority and the execution is nevertheless maintained. The ambivalent attitude of the creator is symbolically expressed in the person and behavior of the goddess Death: (a) She is depicted as a mysterious woman, beautiful and gentle; though her name is Death, her attire and jewels are not symbolic of destruction. (b) Her duty is to kill, yet she refuses to take the lives of the creatures. (c) Instead of frightening the people with her destructive powers, she feels guilty, is afraid of being cursed, and sheds tears.

3) In the attempt to clear the gods of any wrongdoings or cruelties, the myth finally arrives at the position where man himself is held responsible for his destruction. "Creatures kill themselves" by their own passions. Thus, the goddess Death, when discharging her duty without emotional involvement, is not guilty of killing.

4) Fear of death and grief for the dead is mitigated by the prospect of rebirth. The beings shall come back to this world. Fear of repeated deaths (*punarmṛtyu*) is not expressed.

Man has wondered not only about the origin and nature of death, but also about the ultimate cause of it. Who or what force is responsible for the destruction of a being? Who or what determines the time of one's death? These questions are raised in an episode which reveals the guilt feelings of the Pāṇḍava prince, Yudhiṣṭhira, who considers himself the cause of the death of many friends. Since he cannot find peace of mind, he prefers death to life. The mortally wounded hero, Bhīṣma, tries to console the prince by telling him an old story about the conversation between

Gautamī, a fowler, a serpent, Death, and Time. The story begins with the sad fact that the son of Gautamī is found dead after he has been bitten by a poisonous snake. Pursuing the serpent, a fowler by the name of Arjunaka finds the reptile and suggests to Gautamī that it be destroyed as the cause of her son's death. The mother, endowed with great compassion and understanding, rejects Arjunaka's intention as a foolish act. She cannot accept his reasoning or that the killing of the snake could remove her grief. Neither would such an act restore her son's life. Rather, she accepts his death as an inevitable destiny, saying: "The death of the boy was predestined. . . . Why should we not forgive this serpent and try to acquire merit by setting it free." [16]

When the fowler is not persuaded, the serpent speaks up in self-defense: "O foolish Arjunaka, what is my fault? I have no will of my own and am not independent. Death sent me on this work. By his order have I bitten this child. . . . Therefore, if there be any sin in this, . . . the sin is his." Again, the fowler is not convinced and holds the snake as much responsible for the killing, as a "potter's wheel and rod and other things are all considered as causes" in the forming of an earthen vessel. Unwilling to take the full blame, the serpent finally admits only a combination of causes. At this point of the conversation Death (*mṛytu*) appears in order to clarify the issue. He exonerates himself from the charge and points at Kāla (Time, Fate) as the true cause of the boy's death, stating: "As the clouds are driven hither and thither by the wind, I am . . . moved by Kāla. . . . The whole universe is permeated by this same influence of Kāla." Whatever happens is due to the creative and destructive power of Kāla. Though neither the serpent nor Death is free and accountable for the boy's death, the fowler curses and threatens to kill them both. In this predicament Kāla arrives, not only to give moral support to the serpent and to Death, but also to vindicate himself and to offer the ultimate answer to the problem. According to him no one is guilty, no one is the true cause of the child's death. "We are merely the immediate causes of the event. O Arjunaka, the Karma of this child was the exciting cause of our action in this matter. There was no other cause by which this child met its death. It was killed by the result of its own Karma."

This profound explanation of each individual's ultimate responsibility for his own death is readily accepted by Gautamī and the fowler. Yudhiṣṭhira, for whose comfort the story is told, finds peace of mind as he learns about the true cause of death. The role of Death is of particular interest in this story. Death is not a free agent, neither does he determine the fate of living beings; Death is simply an instrument like others in the service of Karma.

The noble Bhiṣma tells of the following episode in response to Yudhiṣṭhira's question, whether any mortal was ever restored to life.[17] The story reveals the widespread attitude of pessimism, and related to it, gives advice on how to cope with the fact of death.

The only son of a Brahmin family has succumbed to a severe illness. Overcome with unspeakable grief, the parents and relatives carry the body of the boy to the crematory, lamenting loudly as they go. A vulture, attracted by their cries, accosts them, telling them of the futility of their grief: All that are born are subject to death "in consequence of their own acts [*karma*] when the allotted periods of their own lives run out. . . . No one ever comes back to [this] life having once succumbed to the power of Time [*kāla*]." [18] The vulture advises them to cast off their affection for the deceased child, to accept the inevitable, and to return home. As they depart, a black jackal appears and charges them with lack of affection for leaving the son's body behind. There could still be a chance that he may come back to life. Touched by his words, they return only to be confused by the remarks of the vulture who scolds them for mourning for a lifeless body instead of grieving for their own selves. It would be better to cleanse oneself from sin by the practice of austere penances than to mourn for the dead. After all, each individual's weal and woe would depend on his own deeds [*karma*]. Nothing could be gained by sorrow or affection for the dead. "Wise or ignorant, rich or poor, every one succumbs to Time, endued with acts, good and bad . . . in pride of youth or in helpless infancy, bearing the weight of years or lying in the mother's womb, every one is subject to be assailed by Death. Such, indeed, is the course of the world." Continuing their argument, the vulture and the jackal for very selfish reasons increase the confusion of the mourners who do not know whether they should stay or leave. Overhearing the argument, the goddess Umā in her compassion urges her spouse, the god Śaṃkara (Śiva), to come to their aid. "Taking up a quantity of water in his hands [he grants] unto that dead child life extending for a hundred years." Then the explanatory statement is added: "Through persistent hopefulness and firm resolution and the grace of the great god, the fruit of one's acts are obtained without delay."

Doctrinally related to the preceding episode, this story wants to show that time and circumstances of an individual's death are determined by his Karma. It is, therefore, of no use to lament the death of a beloved one, or to maintain affection for the dead. It is wiser to accept calmly the inevitable fact of death which lies ahead of everyone, and to be concerned about one's own actions that affect one's fate. The revival of the boy has no bearing on the real lesson of the story. In fact, the conclusion of it, where hopefulness, firm resolution, god's grace and one's Karma are combined, is intrinsically inconsistent.

Perhaps the most beautiful episode in the Mahābhārata dealing with death is the very ancient story of Sāvitrī. It is at least as old as the myth of the goddess Death since here, too, the god Brahma is referred to as Lord of the Universe. In this story death appears in the person of the god Yama who, as in the Upaniṣadic Naciketas episode, grants several boons to a most remarkable woman. After having scrutinized many eligible bachelors, Sāvitrī, a beautiful and virtuous princess, chooses prince Satyavāna, who lives with his parents in a forest hermitage, to be her husband. He is described as "possessed of self-restraint, meek, heroic, truthful, of subdued senses, faithful to his friends, free from malice, modest and patient." [19] He has, however, one defect which surpasses all his merits. According to the prophecy of the seer Nārada, he will die within one year. Despite this sad news Sāvitrī is firm in her resolve, and the two get married. They settle in the parental hermitage where Satyavāna's blind father who has lost his throne undergoes ascetic exercises. In all her actions Sāvitrī proves to be an ideal wife and daughter-in-law, though whether asleep or awake, she cannot forget Nārada's prophecy. Shortly before the day destined for Satyavāna's death arrives, Sāvitrī observes the Triratra vow of fasting and penance for the sake of his life. On the fateful day itself she clings to her husband and unwilling to leave his side as he prepares to enter the woods with his hatchet, she says: "You should not go alone. I will go with you. I do not feel inclined to be separated from you." In the woods she watches all his movements, "but remembering what the sage Nārada has said, she considers him as already dead." Then suddenly Satyavāna complains: "I have a headache on account of this exercise. And, O Sāvitrī, my limbs and heart are aching . . . I feel unwell. It seems (to me) my head is being pierced by arrows . . . I feel inclined to sleep; for I am quite unable to stand." Sitting down on the ground, she rests his head on her lap.

At this moment there appears "a person attired in red garments, wearing a diadem, of an enormous structure, having the splendour of the sun, of a dark and yellow complexion, endued with red eyes, with a noose in his hands, dreadful to look at, standing beside Satyavāna, and gazing at him." Realizing the presence of Death she places her husband's head on the ground and fearfully approaches the stranger. He identifies himself as Yama and tells her of his intention to take the life of her husband. Sāvitrī is surprised that Yama is personally involved, since it is normally his emissaries that come to take away people. To explain his presence he says: "I have come here personally considering that my emissaries are not fit to bring such a devotional and handsome person, endued with qualities, vast as a sea." Thereupon Yama draws out of Satyavāna's body the soul in form of a thumb sized person, fettering it with a noose. Leaving the lifeless body behind, he moves in a southerly direction toward the land of the dead.

Sāvitrī with a broken heart follows him despite Yama's repeated advice to stay behind and perform the last rites for the dead. Still, the faithful wife is determined to have her husband restored to life again. Impressed by her virtuous behavior, her ascetic observances, her devotion and beautiful words of wisdom, Yama grants her a variety of boons excluding, however, the restoration of Satyavāna's life. In a prudent way, she first asks for three gifts: that her father-in-law may see again, regain his kingdom, and have one hundred sons to perpetuate his family. As Yama complies with her request, she continues following him despite his plea to retrace her steps. While walking along, she succeeds in fascinating him with her words to the extent that he offers her additional boons. Shrewdly she begs him now for "one hundred strong and powerful sons, born of Satyavāna's loins and begotten of both of us, who will perpetuate our line." Again he grants her wish, obviously without realizing its logical implication. "Lady, you shall have one hundred strong and powerful sons who will cause your delight. Princess, do not take any further trouble; go back; indeed you have come a great way." Sensing her advantage, Sāvitrī resumes her words of wisdom delighting Yama immensely. Finally, when the right moment has come, she addresses the touched god: "The boon that you have (just) given me cannot bear fruit (without my union with my husband). Therefore, O bestower of honour, among other boons (that you have already granted me) I crave this boon that Satyavāna may be brought back to life." And so it happens that Yama, who is also called here the lord of justice, releases Satyavāna's soul and promises the couple freedom from disease and a happy life of four hundred years. As the husband regains his consciousness and wonders about his long sleep and "that dark complexioned person who was dragging me away," the god returns to his own realm.

This, in essence, is the tale of the virtuous Sāvitrī who by her ascetism, love, and words of wisdom is able to wrest her husband's soul from Death. Yama in this story appears both as Death and the god of justice. He radiates what Rudolf Otto calls the *mysterium tremendum* and the *mysterium fascinans,* appearing "an object of horror and dread, but at the same time it is . . . no less something that allures with a potent charm." [20] This ambivalent attitude toward Death is clearly expressed in this story, where the manifestation of Yama is described: Sāvitrī "saw a person attired in red garments, wearing a diadem, of an enormous structure, having the splendour of the sun." This part reflects the element of fascination, whereas the *tremendum* is contained in the continuation of the quotation: "Of a dark and yellow complexion, endued with red eyes, with a noose in his hands, dreadful to look at, standing beside Satyavāna, and gazing at him." Though Yama is a dreaded executioner carrying out his assignment relentlessly, he is also the god of justice who rewards and punishes the people according to their deeds by leading them either up to the heavenly sphere of the Fathers or to hell. This is not explicitly stated in the Sāvitrī story, but can be inferred from Yama's words. The story also reveals that his relentlessness is not absolute. There are the hidden traits of mercy and emotion in Yama which become apparent in the dialogue with Sāvitrī. She does not outsmart the god in her fourth request as has been suggested;[21] rather, he softens his sternness as he becomes more and more touched by her words of wisdom and determination.

The event of death itself is another interesting feature of the tale. The cessation of life occurs when Yama removes from the unconscious prince the soul which he binds with a noose. This immortal life principle, called Puruṣa, is conceived of as a small person the size of a thumb. During sleep it is believed to leave the body temporarily, whereas at the moment of death it is separated from a body for good. This soul idea can also be found in the Upaniṣads: "A person of the measure of a thumb is the inner soul, ever seated in the heart of creatures. Him one should draw out from one's own body like an arrow-shaft out from a reed. . . . Him one should know as the Pure, the Immortal." [22]

The four episodes we have encountered so far mainly deal with aspects of the phenomenon and person of death. We shall now investigate a dialogue between a father and a son where the attitude towards life and death is the main topic. Their conversation is of special interest as each of them holds a different world view: The father represents the established Brahmanic ideal, whereas the son propagates an ascetic, world-denying way of life as it was widely shared at that time by many Hindu, Buddhist, and Jaina ascetics.[23]

There is a priest, well educated in the Vedic tradition, living the life of a householder. He has a very intelligent son, Medhāvin, who has knowledge of both the liberating truth (*ātman-brahman*) and the various aspects of life in the world. He asks his father to tell him about the duties of a wise man faced with the fact "that the period of human life is passing away so very quickly." [24] As might be expected, the father recommends the usual stages of life (*āśramas*) for the "twice-born" Hindu: as a youth, the study of the Veda; then, as a householder, the procuring of sons and the performing of prescribed sacrifices and rituals; and finally, as a hermit, contemplation in the forest. Medhāvin cannot agree with this answer since he feels his father has failed to take into account the "irresistible things of fatal consequences" that fall upon the world.

In a discourse which clearly reveals the ascetic movements as its source, the son now elaborates on the world as he sees it. According to him the world is surrounded and assailed by death. As each night passes, the length of one's lifetime is shortened. The truly wise man, realizing the steady approach of death, finds no happiness in this world. Before a man can satisfy all his desires, death carries him away. And so it is with his duties. "The acts of tomorrow should be done today, those of the afternoon in the forenoon." Death does not wait to see whether the acts of its victim have all been accomplished or not. "Who knows that death will not come to him even today?" Only the ignorant man is interested in sons and wives; the wise know that "as soon as a creature is born, decrepitude and death pursue him for (effecting) his destruction." The only way to overcome this predicament is to overcome attachment of any kind. So saying, Medhāvin recommends that his father practice detachment and noninjury of living creatures by thought, word, or deed because with that attitude dangerous consequences can be eliminated. He tells him he has no need for sons to rescue him by means of sacrifices because he knows: "I have sprung from *Brahma* through *Brahma*. I shall devote myself to

Brahma, though I am childless, I shall return to *Brahma.*" He ends the conversation by asking, and at the same time advising, his father: "What use hast thou . . . of wealth or kinsmen and relatives, of wives, when thou shalt have to die? Seek thy Self (*ātman*) which is concealed in a cave."

When we said that the general feeling in the epics is pessimistic since they find "more sorrow than joy in life" (see note 9), we were thinking especially of passages such as this father-son conversation. Both know about the inevitability of death. The father appears not to be troubled too much by it. The place he yields to death is at the end of the career of a "twice-born" without even mentioning it. For the son, however, whose way of thinking is heavily influenced by the Upaniṣads, the thought of death affects his entire life-style. To him, death is the great enemy who lies in wait to snatch away everyone. Only the fools ignore him for a limited time over the few fictitious pleasures in life. The wise realize the predominance of sorrow. "There is no sorrow equal to (that involved in) attachment." To cope effectively with the horror of death and with sorrow, one has to change one's attitude and outlook on life. By doing so one overcomes fear of death. The general pessimism is transcended by the knowledge of the immortality of the true self.

While the preceding story is designed to propagate the philosophy of the ascetics at the expense of the second stage of life, the householder stage; the following episode emphasizes the adequacy of the householder for dealing with death, although death is not exactly the main issue in it. Again, it is in the didactic books of the Mahābhārata, where Yudhiṣṭhira inquires from Bhīṣma: "O king, tell me if any householder has ever succeeded in conquering Death by the practice of virtue." [25] In answer to his question Bhīṣma tells him the story of King Sudarśana and his wife Oghavatī. "This intelligent prince of fiery energy took the vow . . . of conquering Death by leading the life of a householder." As such, one of his main duties was to observe the rule of hospitality to guests, which he impressed upon his wife as being the highest virtue. "You should ungrudgingly welcome the guests, even if you have to offer your own body." When Death (*mṛtyu*) became aware of this vow, he decided to outwit the royal householder and began to watch his every step in order to trap him.

One day when the king was collecting firewood in the forest, a Brahmin approached his residence asking for hospitality. Oghavatī welcomed and served him according to ancient custom, whereupon the guest asked for her body. The faithful wife tried to dissuade him by offering him various other things only to find out that he was determined. Recalling her husband's command, she gave herself to the Brahmin, fulfilling her duty as a virtuous hostess. "Meanwhile (Sudarśana) having collected fuel, returned to his home. Mṛtyu [Death] with his dreadful and inexorable nature, was always by his side." When he repeatedly called his wife, still in the Brahmin's arms, and filled with shame, she did not reply. Finally, the Brahmin answered on her behalf from within the chamber, explaining exactly what had happened. Suppressing all jealousy and anger of any kind Sudarśana responded by saying: "Enjoy yourself! . . . It is a great pleasure to me! A householder acquires the highest merit by honouring a guest. . . . [Everything is] dedicated to the use of my guests! This is the vow that I have taken. . . . By that . . . I shall acquire the knowledge of Self." Thereupon, the guest came out of the house, revealing himself as the god Dharma. Congratulating the virtuous host, he said: "You have controlled and conquered Death who always has pursued you, seeking your shortcomings." Then, following the bestowal of certain privileges, he added: "You will acquire with [Oghavatī] all the worlds that are acquired by penances. You will acquire even in this material body those eternal and everlasting worlds from which none return. You have conquered Death, and acquired the highest happiness. . . . You have conquered your passions, desires and anger." Then Bhīṣma concludes his story with the remark that to a householder "the blessings of an honoured guest are more fruitful than the merit of a hundred sacrifices."

This story has several significant features. There is the virtuous Oghavatī who by her absolute obedience to her husband's command exemplifies the ancient Hindu ideal of a devoted wife. Next, and equal to it, there is the great Vedic ideal of hospitality. As to the wife the husband is like a god, so to the householder there is "no greater god than the guest." The virtue of hospitality is brought here into relation to the conquest of death to emphasize the extraordinary importance of this particular virtue for this stage in life. The episode expresses the conviction that a householder by living a moral life according to Dharma, the universal law of conduct and duty, will find it possible to conquer death. Death appears here to be both a person with a "dreadful and inexorable nature" and a kind of tempter who tests the "steadfastness and faithfulness" of the couple, as well as the god of justice, Dharma,[26] manifested as the visiting Brahmin who rewards their virtue. The conquest of death does not imply an endless life in the present form, but pertains to repeated deaths as a consequence of repeated births. The way these householders have fulfilled the great command of hospitality with the detachment and control of their senses and emotions brings them to the same goal as the forest dwellers and ascetics: knowledge of the true self, and with that, highest happiness.

Although most didactic passages are found in Books XII and XIII of the Mahābhārata, there are discourses dispersed throughout the epic which touch upon the theme of our investigation. One of them deserves to be included as it expresses a more philosophical approach than the others we have recounted. It concerns the question that the blind king Dhṛtarāṣṭra asks of the sage Sanatsujāta who holds the opinion that there is no death. If this were true, wonders the king, why, then, would the gods practice ascetic exercises for the prevention of death. The sage explains to the king that both are true. The wise men believe that death is the result of ignorance. His own position is that "ignorance *is* Death, and so the absence of ignorance (Knowledge) *is* immortality."[27] In Upaniṣadic fashion Sanatsujāta rationalizes when he says: "Death doth not devour creatures like a tiger; its form itself is unascertainable." He even tries to demythologize, saying that for him Death is only an imaginary god. Ignorant people, subject to passions, "cast off their bodies and repeatedly fall into hell. They are always followed by their senses. It is for this that ignorance receives the name of death." He advocates the familiar Karma-Saṃsāra teaching that ignorant people "are obliged to sojourn in a cycle of re-births . . . [and that] the desire of enjoyments, lust, and wrath, lead foolish men to death. They, however, that have conquered their souls, succeed by self-restraint, to escape death. . . . Ignorance, assuming the form of Yama, cannot devour that learned man who controlled his desires." In other words, for the wise and self-controlled, death is not real. He compares death to a tiger made of straw and therefore not to be feared. The essence of his thoughts on death is perhaps best summed up in his own words: "Indeed, as the body is destroyed when brought under the influence of death, so death itself is destroyed when it comes under the influence of knowledge."

A unique position in the epic is held by a theistic religio-philosophical poem known as the Bhagavad Gītā, or Song of the Lord

(VI. 25-42). It is probably the most widely read book in India and cherished by every Hindu as a source of inspiration and edification, irrespective of his sect. In its importance it can be compared to the Bible for Christians. There are many translations, and numerous books and commentaries have been written in an attempt to interpret the meaning of this poem to Hindus as well as to Western readers. In its present form it may have originated in the second or third centuries A.D. as a Vaiṣṇava text. The poem exalts the god Viṣṇu, identifying him with the Upaniṣadic Ātman-Brahman. By the same token Viṣṇu manifests himself through self-limitation in the person of the hero Kṛṣṇa who becomes the charioteer and spiritual adviser of prince Arjuna.

The Bhagavad Gītā consists of a dialogue between the divine hero and the Pāṇḍava prince who is depressed over the thought of fighting his close relatives in order to gain an empire. As he looks at the battle lines, he drops his bow and arrows, wondering whether it would be better to conquer or to be conquered. In his bewilderment he asks his divine charioteer for advice. Kṛṣṇa's answers to his questions reflect the diverse religious and philosophical movements of the time. Because of this diversity, there have been a good number of conflicting interpretations as to the "true" teaching of the poem. Although it is not within the scope of this investigation to deal with these diverse interpretations, the very important fact must not be overlooked that it offers three distinct roads leading to final liberation. There is first the Upaniṣadic way of knowledge (*jñāna mārga*) as it also appears in the philosophic systems such as Sāṃkhya, Yoga and Vedānta. Next, there is the way of works (*karma mārga*) which comprises the entire system of Dharma, according to which all duties are to be performed without attachment and desire. And finally, there is the way of unconditional love or devotion to god Kṛṣṇa (*bhakti mārga*). The story of the royal householder, Sudarśana, and his wife Oghavatī has shown that liberation is within the reach of dedicated householders. This liberation becomes even more apparent in the Bhagavad Gītā. "In all earlier systems release was possible only for those who gave up the ordinary life of man and became professional ascetics. In the Gītā release is made available for the layman and his wife while they . . . take part in the business of the world." [28]

For Arjuna, the issue at hand is whether to fight or not. He is not interested in victory, kingdom, or joy. He does not want to destroy life. He feels compassion for his enemies, and yet he is aware of his responsibilities. He is confused. Kṛṣṇa criticizes this weakness as unbecoming for a Kṣatriya, but at the same time he helps him understand the issue of life and death. For Kṛṣṇa, the truly wise do not grieve for the living or the dead, because all have been, all are, and all shall be. Neither the condition of death nor that of life affects one's true being. The soul occupies a changing body and experiences at death a new incarnation. Death pertains only to the body. The soul is indestructible; no one can annihilate it. Therefore, he advises the prince to fight. If one should consider him a killer, and another a potential victim, they both would thereby reveal their ignorance. There is no slayer, and there is no victim. What people call death can be compared to a person who "puts on new garments, giving up old ones; similarly, the soul accepts new material bodies, giving up the old and useless ones." [29] Since the true self cannot be injured by weapons or the elements, there is no reason for grief when a body dies. Man has to accept the natural order that each birth is followed by death and death by birth. In view of the meaning of death, Kṛṣṇa urges Arjuna to overcome his sorrow and hesitation and to perform his caste duty as a good soldier, yet without selfish desire.[30] If he should refuse to fight in a just war such as the present one, he would not only violate his duty, but also dishonor his name which would be worse than death. In case of death he could be sure to enter heaven; in case of victory, he would rule the earth (cf. II. 37).

In most instances the Bhagavad Gītā does not deal with death apart from discussing the roads to liberation. The poem's main purpose is to offer each searching soul a suitable way to overcome the cycles of life and death and to find eternal life in the divine being. To this end the god Kṛṣṇa advises Arjuna to set his mind on him alone. By doing so the prince would live in him hereafter.

> But if thou art unable to rest thy mind on me, then seek to reach me by the practice of Yoga concentration. If thou art not able to practice concentration, consecrate all thy work to me. By merely doing actions in my service thou shalt attain perfection. And if even this thou art not able to do, then take refuge in devotion to me.[31]

An individual may choose the way which fits his personality best. If the way is pursued in the right manner, he will reach his goal. No fear of death will disturb his peace of mind. "Even in the last hour of his life upon earth [he] can reach the Nirvāṇa of Brahman [and] can find peace in the peace of God" (II. 72; IV. 9). On the other hand, men of selfishness, lust, wrath, greed and hate have to face death with the frightful expectation not only of being thrown down the path of hell, but also of recurrent deaths and births (Cf. XVI. 17-22; VIII. 26). Those who tread the path of works (*karma mārga*) are reminded to do their duty "even if it be humble, rather than another's, even if it be great. To die in one's duty is life: to live in another's is death" (III. 35; XVIII. 42-44). Those who follow the path of devotion (*bhakti mārga*) are told: "Having come to this world of sorrow, . . . love thou me."

Their reward will be "everlasting peace. For this is my word of promise, that he who loves me shall not perish" (IX. 33).

What kind of god is he who makes those promises? He reveals himself as the all-encompassing totality, and as the *coincidentia oppositorum*. "I am life immortal and death, I am what is and I am what is not (IX. 19). Of the spirits of the fathers I am Aryaman, and of rulers Yama, the ruler of death (X. 29). I am death that carries off all things, and I am the source of things to come" (X. 34). In a grandiose vision Arjuna sees him manifested as the *tremendum:* "When I see thy vast form . . . with wide open mouths, with vast flaming eyes, my heart shakes in terror: my power is gone and gone is my peace, O Viṣṇu! Like the fire at the end of Time . . . I see thy vast mouths and terrible teeth. As roaring torrents of waters rush forward into the ocean, so do these heroes of our mortal world rush into thy flaming mouths" (XI. 24-25,28). And yet, here, too, the "element of fascination" is present in Arjuna's vision: "I adore thee, O god supreme: be gracious unto me. I yearn to know thee, who are from the beginning: for I understand not thy mysterious works" (XI. 31). In a panentheistic conception Kṛṣṇa is understood as comprising the entire universe with all movable and immovable things within himself (Cf. XI. 7). These include, of course, the universal laws, especially the law of Karma. Therefore, in his capacity as the destroyer of physical forms he can say to Arjuna: "I am all-powerful Time [kāla] which destroys all things, and I have come here to slay these men. . . . Through the fate of their Karma I have doomed them to die: be thou merely the means of my work" (XI. 32-33). Thus, the god Kṛṣṇa is seen as the gracious god of eternal life by those who devoutly pursue any one of the recommended roads to liberation. At the same time he is feared by selfish, attached, and evil characters as the terrible god of death and destruction who devours their physical manifestations, only to see them subjected to new cycles of births, suffering, and deaths.

Section 2. Death and the Purāṇas

L. D. SHINN

The Purāṇas, or legends, belong to the most popular writings in Indian literature. Traditionally, the stories and admonitions of the eighteen Mahāpurāṇas or "Great Purāṇas," most of which were composed during the first thousand years of our era, have been passed on by storytellers, mothers, temple priests, and poets. Some of these stories will be retold in this chapter as they have influenced greatly the attitude of many Hindus toward death.

Each Purāṇa centers its attention on one Indian deity while mentioning other deities in a subservient role. Śiva and Viṣṇu stand above all other gods in importance and attention given. In fact, many local or regional deities receive wider exposure and devotion by weaving their legends into those of the two better-known deities. It is because of the prominence of Śiva and Viṣṇu that stories from the Bhāgavata Purāṇa, one of the six Viṣṇu Purāṇas, and the Śiva Purāṇa have been chosen to exemplify this oral and literary contribution to the attitude of most Indians toward death.[1] Since this multifaceted tradition places an extreme emphasis on devotion (*bhakti*) as the only way to solve the problems of living and dying, the attitudes toward death have to be seen in that framework. Simply, the view of death in the Purāṇas can be found in two contrasting destinies: that of the deluded nonbeliever and that of the devotee.

A Spinning World Leads to the Jaws of Hell

Saṃsāra as an endless trap. At some time during the early interaction of the Aryan invaders and the indigenous people of India, the positive evaluation of the world which supported the Vedic rituals gave way to the pessimistic belief that man was caught up in a life (and cosmic) process that never ended. Birth followed birth, and death followed death except for the few persons who could, by various paths, escape the vicious cycle of Saṃsāra. The Purāṇas reflect this ancient belief in stories like that of Puramjana, as recorded in the Bhāgavata Purāṇa:

Once there was a powerful king named Puramjana who roamed the world looking for a place fit for his rule. Being a king among kings, Puramjana desired a kingdom which would provide not only the riches of land, animals, and subjects appropriate to his station, but also a woman who would be a worthy queen. While wandering in the foothills of the Himalayas, he came upon a beautiful city with nine gates. The houses were made of precious jewels and the land bore rich and plentiful harvests. Entering this city, Puramjana saw approaching him the most beautiful woman he had ever seen, attended by hundreds of female companions. Introducing himself as the greatest of kings, Puramjana learned of the beautiful lady's fear for her city's safety. Being more than mildly attracted to each other and after a short speech by Puramjana concerning the virtue of the householder's life, perfect man and perfect woman were united.

The married life of this ideal couple went on for one hundred years with physical enjoyments being the focus of their lives. Puramjana followed his wife around like a fawn follows its mother. Only after tiring of their amorous sport did the king decide to embark upon a hunt of great magnitude. Leaving his wife and city, Puramjana and his warriors entered the forests where game was to be found in abundance. Captivated by the joy of the hunt, the king forgot about his duties as a husband and engaged himself fully in the killing of the animals of the forest. Killing deer, boar, and any other beast that crossed his path, the king grew deaf to the cries of the beasts who were mercilessly destroyed. Finally, Puramjana wearied of the hunt and returned to his city and his queen.

After relieving himself of his weariness and hunger, the king was overcome with desire and sought out his wife for sport. Following the directions of the queen's maidens, the king found his wife lying on the bare ground. Although being disappointed that his wife displayed no loving anger, Puramjana caressed her until she surrendered to his loving advances which resulted in the birth of 1100 sons and 110 daughters who populated the region known as Pañcāla country.

Being occupied with procreation and the pleasures of the beautiful world around him, Puramjana forgot about all else except that which could satisfy his desires. Then there came into his kingdom Kāla (Time) under the guise of Chanda (Pleasure or Delight). With her, Chanda brought 360 Gandharvas and their spouses. Puramjaṇa sent out his warriors to combat this threat to his city. But after 100 years of fighting the 720 Gandharvas, Puramjana and his soldiers grew weak and tired. The experience of witnessing his men fall before Chanda and her forces was new and frightening for Puramjana. Overtaken by the daughter of Kāla named Jara (Decrepitude) and her husband Bhaya (Fear), the king lost his beauty, power and, finally, his city and his life.

Just before he died his thoughts were of his wife and the unfortunate circumstances his death would provide for her. As a result of thinking last upon his wife, Puramjana was reborn a woman—after 100 years in hell where he suffered at the hands of the animals he abused on his merciless hunt.

In his new form, Puramjana was the daughter of the king of Vidarbha and, thus, was called Vaidarbhī. Given in marriage to the greatest of heroes, Malayadhavaja, Vaidarbhī bore her husband seven sons and one daughter. After a lengthy reign, King Malayadhavaja sought through learning and austerities the spiritual truth of his highest Self (*paramātman*). Having achieved a calm mind and an awareness of the transiency of the world and its pleasures, the king retreated to the forest with his wife to seek ultimate wisdom. One day while deep in meditation, the king died. However, his wife continued to worship him as a god and provide fuel for the fire. When she realized that her husband was dead, Vaidarbhī prepared a funeral pyre and was about to throw herself upon the fire with him when a Brahmin stopped her. This Brahmin recalled for Vaidarbhī that in a former birth she was Puramjana the king, and before that a swan friend of his who lived for 1000 years on a lake near the city where Puramjana ruled. At that moment, the former Swan-Puramjana-Vaidarbhī remembered his true nature, his Paramātman, and was freed from Saṃsāra's clutches.

W. Norman Brown in a recent book indicates the content of one of his chapters with the title, "Time is a Noose." [2] He begins with the assumption that "the Puranic conception of time is the most widely accepted among tradition-minded Hindus today." [3] He describes the Yuga (literally, "a yoke or team" which, by use, connotes the ages or long time periods of the world) theory of classical India as the central notion of time in the Purāṇas. Of this cyclical concept of time he says:

> The thought of the unnumbered, in fact the innumerable existences each one of us has experienced in the innumerable billions of years embraced by the past, and the expectation of an equally incalculable number of billions of years in the future, is a grim, disheartening, terrifying prospect. It is a prospect of perpetual motion with never a moment of rest. The commonest word in India for the process is *saṃsāra,* which means the wandering.[4]

The story of Puramjana demonstrates the notion of Saṃsāra as cyclical time. The Bhāgavata Purāṇa devotes one whole chapter to an interpretation of this story by its teller, the divine sage Nārada (*Bhāgavata P.,* IV. 29). Nārada says that the city of Puramjana symbolizes the body with its nine gates being "the two eyes, two nostrils, two ears, mouth, [and the] organs of generation and excretion, through which the person having those organs goes out" (*Bhāgavata P.*, IV. 29. 8). Using an ancient analogy, the Bhāgavata Purvāṇa likens the body to a chariot:

> The car is the body, the senses are the horses, the speed is the time, the two wheels are virtue [*dharma* and *adharma*], the qualities of goodness, energy and ignorance are the three qualities; and the five vital breaths are the five ties or fetters.
>
> The mind is the rein, the intellect is the charioteer, the heart is his seat, the two poles are sorrow and ignorance, into which five objects of senses are thrown, and the seven metals constitute the coat of mail. Gifted with the power of desire, he goes out on hunting excursions in pursuit of desire; the eleven senses constitute his army and by five senses he enjoys objects of desire.[5]

Chanda (a euphemism for Kāla, Time) represents the year, while the 360 Gandharvas and their 360 consorts represent the 360 days and nights of the year respectively. The daughter of Kāla, Jara, represents the aging process which people do not welcome. Therefore, a Jīva (an embodied self) is born again and again according to its actions of the past existence. Just as a leech does not entirely leave one blade of grass before it attaches itself to another, so, too, the Jīva assumes one body after another. Nārada concludes, "So long as action exists there is ignorance, too, and so long as ignorance exists, bodies are tied to actions" (*Bhāgavata P.*, IV. 29. 78).

The Purāṇas organize time by the four Yugas or ages which are progressively shorter. The Satya (Truth) or Kṛta (Perfect) age lasts 4,000 divine years, the Tretā lasts 3,000 divine years, the Dvāpara, 2,000, and the Kali only 1,000. Since each of the Yugas has a period of dawn and twilight, the full Caturyuga (Four Ages) or Mahāyuga (Great Ages) equals 12,000 divine years in length.

Because one divine year equals 360 human years, the length of a Mahāyuga (one cycle of the four Yugas) equals 4,320,000 human years.

A Kalpa is 1,000 Mahāyugas in length and equals a *day* in the life of Brahma so that another Kalpa equals a *night* in the life of Brahma. In each Kalpa there are fourteen Manus or "Primal Men" who rule the different dynasties during this period. The length of the abode of Brahma, called Maharloka or Great Sphere, equals his lifetime in duration so that the destruction of the three worlds (heavens, earth, hells) does not touch the home of Brahma except once in 100 Brahma years (*Bhāgavata P.*, III. 2; III. 10. 7-10). According to this time-reckoning scheme:

> Brahmā is now in the first *kalpa* of his fifty-first year. Six Manus of the *kalpa* have passed away. We are living of the Kaliyuga of the twenty-eight four-age period (*caturyuga*) of the seventh manvantara [age of manus] of Brahmā's fifty-first year. The Kaliyuga began on February 18, 3102 B.C.[6]

Often when time is personified, it is equated with Viṣṇu or Śiva. In one place the Bhāgavata Purāṇa states that the discus of Bhagavān (Viṣṇu) is identical with Kāla and in its mighty path makes waste of all living things (*Bhāgavata P.*, V. 14. 27). This allows the comparison of Viṣṇu to a terrible snake which represents the destructive Kāla (*Bhāgavata P.*, IV. 7. 28). In commenting on the relationship between Kālī (the terrible consort of Śiva), Kāla (Time) and Kali (the Yuga), M. Eliade says:

> Regardless of the etymology, the association of *Kāla,* Time, with the goddess Kālī and the Kali Yuga is structurally justified: Time is black because it is irrational, hard, pitiless; and Kālī, like all the other Great Goddesses, is the mistress of Time, of the destinies she forges and accomplishes.[7]

The Śiva Purāṇa in the midst of the story of Śiva's defeat of the Man-lion form of Viṣṇu identifies both deities with destructive Kāla. An admonition directed at Viṣṇu says:

Lord Śiva manifests himself in between heaven and earth . . . in the heart of darkness and in the light of the moon.

You are Kāla but lord Śiva is Mahākāla and Kālakāla. Hence you will be death of death only through Śiva's digit.
(*Śiva P.*, Śatarudrasaṃhitā, II. 58. 59)

While both deities are identified with Kāla in their respective Purāṇas, tradition more often relates Śiva, the cosmic destroyer, to the dark and terrible aspects of time. The miseries of man deepen when he feels himself in the hands of Kāla, experienced as fate, destiny or the destructive aspect of Viṣṇu or Śiva. Time is an inexorable wheel and man is caught in its terrible rotation.

Yama and the Abode of Death. While time is the ultimate destroyer, it is the thoughts and actions of a man's past life which determine the quality and status of his present life. Karma, the moral law of cause and effect, lies at the basis of the operation of Saṃsāra. Each man is bound by caste and other duties (*dharma*) and is judged against those standards. Because Puramjana killed animals mercilessly, he suffered in hell accordingly. Likewise, because his last thoughts (as well as lifetime obsession) were of his wife, he was born a woman. The law of Karma and its consequences is impersonal and nearly mechanical. Even accidental misdeeds bear their appropriate fruits as the story of King Nirga demonstrates.

Once while playing near a dried well, some boys found a beautiful lizard, which, in the presence of Kṛṣṇa, assumed its true form as a celestial king named Nirga. When asked why he had been so unfortunate to be born a lizard, King Nirga replied that he had accidentally affronted two Brahmins. King Nirga made it a habit to support all the sages and priests by giving them large numbers of his cattle. One day the cow of a renowned Brahmin wandered into Nirga's cattle pen and by mistake the king gave the Brahmin's cow to another Brahmin. Seeing his cow being given away, the first Brahmin protested by calling the king a thief. While offering many cattle to both Brahmins, King Nirga was called a thief by one and a false giver by the other. The king died a few days later and chose before Yama to suffer first for his evil deeds. Consequently, he was born a lizard on account of the accidental abuse of the Brahmin's cow.[8]

Yama (guardian of the dead) appears differently according to a man's merit (good *karma*) or unrighteousness (bad *karma*). Virtuous men see Yama with a gentle face, but the Śiva Purāṇa gives the following description of Yama as seen by the unrighteous man:

> His face is terrible with curved fangs. His eyes are cruel with knit eyebrows. The hairs on his head stand lifted up. He has a big moustache. His lips are pouted and they throb. He has eighteen hands. He is furious. He resembles black collyrium. His uplifted hands hold all weapons. He threatens with punishment. He is seated on a great buffalo. His eyes resemble blazing fire. He wears red garlands and garments. He is as tall as the mountain Mahā Meru. His voice resembles the rumbling sound of the clouds at the time of dissolution [of the universe]. He appears ready to drink up even the big ocean and to swallow even great mountains. He appears to vomit fire. Very near him is Death (*mṛtyu*) whose lustre is like that of black fire.
>
> (*Śiva P.*, Umāśaṃhitā, 7. 49-53)

While pictured in the grotesque garb of Death, "Yama as Dharma [Righteousness] is a fair and impartial judge."[9] The Purāṇas assume that the nondevotee is caught up in the cycle of existence which is governed by the law of Karma and impartially ruled by the king of Dharma, i.e., Yama. Bhatacarji puts it this way: "This [i.e., dispensing rewards or punishments according to a man's accumulated *karma*] is the special province of Yama as Dharmarāja whose code of justice is immutable and infallible. Thus Karmavāda (theory of Karman) is shown to be the only irrefutable truth regarding life, death, and after-life." [10]

What is frightening about the process of Saṃsāra is not that death brings the possibility of man's being born in a heaven where he can enjoy the fruits of his past good deeds, but that it allows no escape from enduring punishment for his misdeeds. While King Nirga was predominantly a righteous king, his one accidental mistake had to be recompensed after his death. This means that every person will eventually see the terrible face of Yama. It also means that every person will experience one of the seven levels of Yama's abode that can only be described as hell.

At the moment of death, Yama's attendants claim the soul of the deceased. The Śiva Purāṇa identifies the dead souls as naked ghosts who hunger, thirst, and experience a burning sensation all over. Wailing and screaming, the naked ghosts are dragged to the underworld along a torturous path.

At places the path is strewn with sharp thorns, at places it is full of sand, elsewhere it is full of pebbles sharp like the razor-edge.

In other places it is full of deep irregular chasms and canyons, elsewhere, of rugged lumps of clay; of burning sands here and sharp spikes there.

Different places are infested with different terrible beasts of prey such as lions, wolves, tigers and huge pythons or terrible mosquitoes or huge leeches.

The persons who go that way are tortured and harassed by big boars digging and butting against the path with their sharp fangs, buffaloes with sharp horns, all sorts of beasts of prey, terrible evil spirits like Dākinīs, horrible Rākṣasas and pernicious diseases.

They go on, burnt and scorched by lightning falls and pierced through by heavy showers of arrows.

They cry when heavy showers of dust envelop them. They tremble with fear ever and anon at the terrible rumbling sounds of massive clouds.

They shrink and wither when oppressed by the rough and chill wind all round.

(*Śiva P.*, Umāsaṃhitā, 7. 9-25)

The path to Yama's abode is only the beginning of the horror for the dead man. While each man suffers punishments suited to his particular evil deeds, the stories all have a familiar, disheartening ring. Just as a piece of wood burns until there is no energy left in it, so, too, a man suffers until all his bad Karma is spent. The Śiva Purāṇa puts it this way:

Just as metals are melted in fire to remove their impurities so also sinners are put in hells in order to remove their sins.

The hands are tightly tied and the men are battered. Then they are suspended from the branches of tall trees by the attendants of Yama.

Then the sinners are beaten with goads of fiery colour and terrible iron rods by the terrible servants of Yama.

Then they are again smeared with glowing acid more unbearable than fire.

Their limbs are cut and smothered, gradually torn and severed and smeared with molten metal. They are then roasted like brinjal in red-hot iron cauldrons. They are then cast into wells full of filth, swarms of worms or in tanks full of putrid fat and blood. They are eaten by worms and crows with beaks strong as iron.

Dogs, mosquitoes, wolves and tigers of terrible and hideous faces also devour them. They are roasted like fish over glowing heaps of coal.

(*Śiva P.*, Umāsaṃhitā, 9. 2-12)

Not only is Saṃsāra an endless trap for the man who is born again and again (with Time the ultimate pursuer and destroyer), but also at each death the emissaries of Yama take the naked soul to its appropriate punishment and hell. According to the Purāṇas, this fate awaits every nondevotee. Even if a man achieves a high birth (e.g., as a Brahmin) and lives a life in full accord with his Dharma, or caste duty, unless he is totally devoted to Śiva or Viṣṇu (depending on the sectarian bias of each Purāṇa), he will still suffer pain and another birth and consequently view death as a terrifying event. But the person who sets his mind and actions in the context of devotion (*bhakti*) may expect happiness; he is not afraid of death.

Devotion Leads to the Abode Beyond

The logic of the Purāṇas can be observed in their claim that the fate of a devotee is release (*kaivalya*) from Saṃsāra and attainment of the abode of the supreme deity. If Time (*kāla*) is the symbol of the destructive life process, then it follows that it must be subsumed under the deity's power. Likewise, only the supreme deity, according to the Purāṇas, has the capability of granting release from the clutches of Time. The Bhāgavata Purāṇa states:

> Kāla (Time) is the mightiest of the mighty ones, Kāla is the undecaying eternal Iśvara [Lord]. As though in sport Kāla collects all creatures of the world as the king of beasts does the beasts. May good betide you. Do you now beg of us [lower deities] any boon except emancipation [*kaivalya*]. Because only the one, unchangeable Viṣṇu is capable of granting the boon of emancipation.[11]

With this final declaration that only the supreme deity can grant deliverance from the wheel of births, the logic of the Purāṇas unfolds even further. If only the deity who resides beyond all hells, heavens, and the earth can grant release, then devotion to that deity is the only activity of man which can produce a favorable outcome at the moment of death. In other words, devotion (*bhakti*) is the only path to deliverance from Saṃsāra. Likewise, it is the release coming from devotion which enables the devotee to develop a positive attitude toward death.

This path is open to women and "outcasts" as well as to the traditional religious elite (the three upper castes). The most extreme statement of the inclusiveness and supremacy of Bhakti occurs in the following Śiva Purāṇa passage:

> A master of four Vedas is not dearer to me than a Cāṇḍāla [an outcast who "eats dogs"] devoted to me. . . . He shall be worshipped like me. I am not lost to him nor is he lost to me who offers unto me with devotion even a leaf, a flower, a fruit or mere water.[12]

One consequence of Purāṇic devotionalism is that it alters the traditional attitude toward Saṃsāra. Rather than a terrifying place, Saṃsāra is experienced by the devotee as a gratuitous realm. The story of Nārada's mother demonstrates this notion.

> In one of his births, Nārada was the son of a woman who was a servant in the home of a Brahmin family. Even though she was wholly dependent upon her master for all of life's needs and pleasures, Nārada's mother attempted to give her son all the attention and care a king's son would receive. She fondled her five year old son so much that he knew no hardships or cares. Then one night, Nārada's mother went out to milk the cow and stepped upon a snake on her way to the cowpen. Even though she barely touched the snake, it bit her, and she died immediately.
>
> (*Bhāgavata P.*, X. 15)

Within the context of Karma-theory, one would expect some

comment about an incident from a previous life to explain this unfortunate occurrence. One might even expect some comment about the evils of the Kali-yuga or a fate which acts beyond the understanding of mortals. Instead, Nārada comments concerning his mother's death: "I was not a bit sorry for the sad death of my mother. On the contrary, I looked at the incident as a gracious dispensation [*anugraham*] of the Lord" (*Bhāgavata P.*, X. 15. 52).

The devotee's altering of the Karma-Dharma notion with the idea of a supreme deity who acts graciously and independently of any law is well stated by J. Estlin Carpenter:

> The law of the Deed was thus incorporated in religion. On the one side its operation was stern and unbending; as a calf could recognize its mother among a thousand kine, so the deeds of the past would not fail to find out the doer. On the other, its operation might be qualified on rare occasions by divine grace (*prasāda*). . . . The Moral Order is at length formally ensphered in God.[13]

A second consequence of Purāṇic devotionalism is the devotee's positive attitude toward death. The supreme deity encompasses not only the human sphere, but also the realms of death (both the traditional heavens and hells). What this means is that Yama becomes a subordinate deity to either Viṣṇu or Śiva, and his right to punish a dead man's soul is challenged by them. Neither Death (i.e., Yama) nor his abode (hells) is feared by the devotee. On the contrary, it is the heavenlike abode from which no man is born again that a devotee anticipates after death. Viṣṇu's heavenly abode is called Vaikuṇṭha and Śiva's sphere is called Kailāsa. Therefore, whichever sectarian Purāṇa one reads, the outcome is the same: Yama's messengers are defeated by the soldiers of the supreme deity, and the naked soul of the devotee is carried off to that deity's heavenly abode.

The Śiva Purāṇa claims that even an accidental hearing of its sacred verses will free a man from the effects of his evil deeds and mark that person for heaven. One obvious implication inherent in this claim is that Yama will be denied the opportunity to recompense such a sinner for his evil ways. In short, full release from the clutches of Kāla and Yama is achieved by even accidental devotional practices—such as hearing the deeds of Śiva recorded in his Purāṇa. The story of Devarāja exemplifies the remarkable power of devotion—even accidental devotion.

In the small city of Kiratas lived a poor Brahmin named Devarāja who was unusually ignorant for someone of his social and spiritual rank. Opposite to the demands of his profession, he worshipped none of the gods and engaged in selling forbidden liquors.

Devarāja forgot his daily prayers, deceived the persons with whom he dealt and gained an immense fortune through his deceitfulness in business. Furthermore, being ignorant of his duty, he did not use any of his wealth for virtuous causes.

Once while bathing in a lake, Devarāja was sexually aroused by a prostitute named Sobhavatī who had also come to bathe. Mistaking his infatuation for love, the wealthy Brahmin Devarāja asked Sobhavatī to be his wife. Recognizing the increased status and wealth such a marriage would afford her, Sobhavatī agreed.

Engaged in amorous play for days on end, the newlyweds flaunted all conventions ascribed for a householder Brahmin. They drank, ate, slept and played together. All the while, Devarāja spurned the admonitions of his first wife, his mother and his father. Devarāja became so enraged one night that he killed his first wife, his mother and his father and took their possessions. At the same time he gave to his harlot-wife all that he stole or had gained before her arrival. Devarāja was the most degenerate of all Brahmins.

While traveling in an unfamiliar place, Devarāja, just by chance, passed a Śiva temple where men were congregating for daily instruction and prayer. Feeling ill, Devarāja stopped and was treated for a fever which had gripped him. While lying in a feverish state, Devarāja overheard a discourse on Śiva by a temple priest.

After a month of suffering, Devarāja died from the fever. At the moment of death Devarāja was bound with nooses by Yama's attendents and forcibly dragged toward Yama's abode. Meanwhile, Śiva's army, gleaming white from the sacred ashes of the burial grounds, with tridents in their hands, rushed to Yama's city and intercepted Yama's attendents and took Devarāja from them.

Placing Devarāja in a celestial chariot they were about to depart for Kailāsa (Śiva's heavenly abode) when Yama, the King of Dharma, came out of his palace. Perceiving what had transpired, Yama did not question Śiva's servants. Instead, Yama honored Śiva's name and offered his adoration. Receiving Yama's blessings, Śiva's army with Devarāja in their midst, departed for Kailāsa where Devarāja was received by the merciful Śiva.[14]

The Śiva Purāṇa comments concerning the story of Devarāja:

Blessed indeed is the story of Śivapurāṇa, the holiest of holy stories, a mere hearing of which qualifies even the greatest sinner for salvation. . . . Devarāja the base Brahmin, addicted to wine, enamoured of a vile harlot, slayer of his own father, mother and wife and who out of greed for money had killed many Brahmins, Kṣatriyas, Vaiśyas and Śudras and others became a liberated soul instantaneously on reaching that supreme Loka [sphere].[15]

The Bhāgavata Purāṇa also tells several stories which extol the power of devotional acts—even those done by chance.

Ajamila began his married life with an act vigorously denounced by others of his caste. He was a Brahmin and took for his wife a lowly servant girl. Being ostracized, Ajamila resorted to *adharmic* means of livelihood such as playing dice and stealing. Living eighty-eight years he fathered ten sons, the youngest of whom was called Nārāyaṇa. Considering his son Nārāyaṇa to be the choicest of sons, Ajamila focused his attention and wealth on him. When death (Yama) approached in the form of three messengers, Ajamila became frightened and called out for his favorite son, Nārāyaṇa. On the basis of his calling out the name of Nārāyaṇa (another name for Viṣṇu), even though it was his son and not the deity he had in mind, he was delivered from the messengers of Yama and taken to Viṣṇu's realm, Vaikuṇṭha.

(*Bhāgavata P.*, VI. 1-2)

Conclusion

The stories of Devarāja and Ajamila are extreme examples of the power of devotion. Lest every man wait until his deathbed to turn to Viṣṇu or Śiva, there are also many stories which tell of devoted men who at the last moment of their life have a lapse in their devotion to their deity and end up suffering the fate of a nondevotee. What never varies in the Purāṇic accounts is the notion that the realms of life and death are ensphered by the supreme deity and, therefore, man is freed from the fetters of the world and death only by the gracious action of the supreme deity.

As stated earlier, the Purāṇic attitude toward death can be exemplified in the fates of the devotee and nondevotee. The Purāṇas look at life in the cyclical world of Saṃsāra and death in the abode of Yama from a devotee's point of view. Death is a terrifying phenomenon to the man who is burdened by unbelief and whose future is bound up in birth after birth. Hounded by Time (*kāla*) and the messengers of Yama, the nondevotee can anticipate only one hell to be followed by another. But for the man who is devoted to the supreme deity (Viṣṇu or Śiva), the world is a gratuitous realm, and death is the door to the abode of eternal bliss.

Notes for Section 1

1. Contrary to earlier views, it is incorrect to speak of an epic period as such. Cf. Louis Renou, *Indian Literature* (New York: Walker, 1964), p. 11.
2. This weakness is a consequence of the Indian outlook on life which is not conducive to the development of a sense of history. The sequence of historical events was considered ephemeral and too insignificant to be recorded. Also the authors, mostly Brahmins, were preoccupied with their own caste affairs. Cf. Benjamin Walker, *The Hindu World,* 2 vols. (New York: Praeger, 1968), vol. 1, p. 453.
3. For detailed information on the Sūtras consult Arthur A. Macdonell, *A History of Sanskrit Literature* (1900; reprint ed., New York: Haskell House, 1968), pp. 245-64.
4. Gṛhya Sūtra of Hiraṇyakeśin I. 8. 28. 1, in *SBE,* vol. 30, p. 206. Cf. also *RV* X. 18. 1.
5. Cf. Gowen, *A History of Indian Literature,* p. 165. See also E. W. Hopkins, *The Ordinances of Manu* (London: Trübner, 1884).
6. Cf. Moriz Winternitz, *History of Indian Literature,* Scientific Literature, (Delhi: Motilal Banarsidass, 1967), vol. 3, pt. 2, p. 552. A brief survey of these philosophical systems relative to our investigation will take place in the third part of our analysis.
7. "Austerity and sacred learning are the best means by which a Brāhmaṇa secures supreme bliss; by austerities he destroys guilt, by sacred learning he obtains the cessation of (births and) deaths" (Manu XII. 104, in *SBE,* vol. 25, p. 508). The following quotations are from the same translation.
8. Manu VI. 31. This action in order to serve its purpose must not be motivated by Karma-producing desire: "Let him not desire to die, let him not desire to live; let him wait for (his appointed) time, as a servant (waits) for the payment of his wages" (Manu VI. 45).
9. XII. 331. 16, quoted in E. W. Hopkins, *The Great Epic of India* (New York: Charles Scribner's Sons, 1901), p. 85.
10. Cf. Macdonell, *History of Sanskrit Literature,* p. 277 f.
11. Cf. Moriz Winternitz, *Geschichte der Indischen Litteratur* (Leipzig: C. F. Amelang, 1908), vol. 1, pp. 265 ff. Both epics offer a comprehensive survey of man in an unsystematic way to all segments of Hindu society. See P. T. Raju, "The Concept of Man in Indian Thought" in S. Radhakrishnan and P. T. Raju, eds., *The Concept of Man,* 2nd ed. (London: Allen & Unwin, 1966), pp. 286 f.
12. Cf. Jacques Choron, *Death and Western Thought* (New York: Collier Books, 1963), p. 14. Even if death appears to be natural to man, as in the Gilgamesh epic, the cause of death results, nevertheless, from the divine will. See S. G. F. Brandon, "Origin of Death in Ancient Near Eastern Religions," *Religious Studies,* 1 (April, 1966): 223.
13. VI. 52-54, trans. P. C. Roy, *The Mahābhārata,* 10 vols. (Calcutta: 1884-94),

vol. 6, pp. 104-11. The following quotations are from the same translation. The myth appears also in XII. 256-58, *idem.*, vol. 9, pp. 239-45.

14. This "Myth of the Overcrowded Earth" is found in the tradition of many primitive peoples. It expresses the necessity for replacement of the old generation by the new. Reproduction implies succession. See S. G. F. Brandon, "Origin of Death," p. 227. See also H. Schwarzbaum, "The Overcrowded Earth," *Numen,* 4 (1957): 59-71.
15. Cf. Winternitz, *Geschichte der Indischen Litteratur,* vol. 1, p. 339.
16. Mahābhārata XIII. 1, trans. M. N. Dutt, *The Mahābhārata* (Calcutta, 1905), vol. 13, pp. 1-4. The following quotations are from the same translation.
17. Indian literature contains numerous stories of revival of the dead. Cf. H. V. Glasenapp, "Unsterblichkeit und Erlösung in den Indischen Religionen," *Schriften der Königsberger Gelehrten Gesellschaft,* 14. Jahr, Geisteswissenschaftliche Klasse (Halle: 1938), Heft 1, p. 2.
18. Mahābhārata XII. 153, trans. Roy, *The Mahābhārata,* vol. 8, pp. 359-66. The following quotations are from the same translation.
19. Mahābhārata III. 293-97, trans. Dutt, *The Mahābhārata,* Vana Parva, pp. 419-29. The following quotations are from the same translation.
20. Rudolf Otto, *The Idea of the Holy* (Galaxy Books; New York: Oxford University Press, 1958), p. 31.
21. Cf. Winternitz, *Geschichte der Indischen Litteratur,* vol. 1, p. 341.
22. Kaṭha Upaniṣad VI. 17, trans. R. E. Hume, *The Thirteen Principal Upanishads,* 2nd. ed., rev. (1934; London: Oxford University Press, 1971), p. 361.
23. Cf. Winternitz, *Geschichte der Indischen Litteratur,* vol. 1, p. 360. Like most of the other didactic chapters of the twelfth and thirteenth books, so is this discourse told by Bhīṣma for the edification and instruction of Yudhiṣṭhira.
24. Mahābhārata XII. 175, trans. Roy, *The Mahābhārata,* vol. 9, p. 6. The following quotations are from the same translation.
25. XIII. 2, trans. Dutt, *The Mahābhārata,* vol. 13, pp. 4-7. The following quotations are from the same translation.
26. Cf. Mahābhārata III. 296. 55 and VII. 54. 41 where Death and the god of justice are also identical.
27. V. 42, trans. Roy, *The Mahābhārata,* vol. 4, pp. 95 ff. The following quotations are from the same translation.
28. J. N. Farquhar, *An Outline of the Religious Literature of India* (Delhi: Motilal Banarsidass, 1967), pp. 87 f.
29. Bhagavad Gītā II. 22, trans. A. C. Bhaktivedanta, *The Bhagavad Gita as It Is* (New York: Collier Books, 1968), p. 73.
30. "On action alone be thy interest,/ Never on its fruits;/ Let not the fruits of action be thy motive,/ Nor be thy attachment to inaction." (II. 47, trans. Franklin Edgerton, *The Bhagavad Gītā,* 2nd ed. [1952; reprint ed., New York: Harper, 1964], p. 14.)

31. XII. 9-11, trans. Juan Mascaro, *The Bhagavad Gītā* (Baltimore: Penguin Books, 1963), pp. 96 f. The following quotations are from the same translation.

Notes for Section 2

1. All stories and texts are taken from: *The Śiva Purāna* [*Śiva P.*] edited by J. L. Shastri (Delhi: Motilal Banarsidass, 1970), vols. 1-4 and the *Srimad-Bhagavatam* [*Bhāgavata P.*] trans. J. M. Sanyal (London: Luzac & Co. 1929-39, vols. 1-5. Any revisions by this author are based on the Sanskrit texts and noted by brackets. All stories used are abridged retellings.
2. *Man in the Universe* (Los Angeles: University of California Press, 1966), pp. 68-87.
3. *Ibid.*, p. 79.
4. *Ibid.*, p. 81.
5. *Bhāgavata P.*, IV. 29. 18; compare the *Kaṭha Upaniṣad* 3. 3-6.
6. Brown, *Man in the Universe*, p. 80; see also Achut D. Pusalker, *Studies in the Epics and Purāṇas*, 2nd ed. (Bombay: Bharatiya Vidya, 1963), pp. 105-6 and J. F. Fleet, "The Kaliyuga of B.C. 3102," *Journal of the Royal Asiatic Society of Great Britain and Ireland* (1911), pp. 479-96 and 675-98.
7. "Time and Eternity in Indian Thought" in *Man and Time*, Bollingen Series XXX, 3 (New York: Pantheon Books, 1957), p. 179.
8. *Bhāgavata P.*, X. 64; see also I. 13. 46-50 and V. 26. 38; and compare *Gītā*, I. 40-44.
9. Sukumari Bhattacarji, *The Indian Theogony* (Cambridge: The University Press, 1970), p. 57.
10. *Ibid.*, p. 61.
11. *Bhāgavata P.*, X. 51. 19-20. See also IV. 11. 15-18 and XI. 7. 48.
12. *Śiva P.*, Vāyavīyasaṃhitā, 10. 71-72; see also *Bhāgaavta* P., X. 81. 4 and the Bhagavad Gītā, IX. 26-27.
13. *Theism in Medieval India* (London: Constable & Company, 1926), pp. 159-60.
14. Cf. *Śiva P.*, Introduction 2. 15-36.
15. *Ibid.*, 2. 37, 39-40.

III

The Orthodox Philosophical Systems

K. R. SUNDARARAJAN

In this section we shall attempt to study the significance of the phenomenon of death in what has been traditionally called the Āstika systems in Hindu tradition. The orthodox Indian philosophical schools (*darśanas*) are known as the Āstika Darśanas by the Hindus in contrast to Buddhism and Jainism which have been designated as the Nāstika schools. The terms Āstika and Nāstika for our purposes can be translated as orthodox and heterodox systems respectively. Here the orthodoxy or the heterodoxy is primarily based on the acceptance or the nonacceptance of the scriptural authority of the Vedas. In a broader sense we could identify the Āstika systems as those which accept the validity of the tradition that has come out from the Vedic circles and Nāstika systems as those which reject the efficacy of this tradition, claiming that they are not meaningful to one's religious life. However, we should note that both groups of systems share certain common views, especially in regard to the painful nature of man's present existence, his involvement in the cyclic process of Karma and the consequent birth-death-rebirth sequence as well as the need to be liberated from this kind of existence.

The development of the six orthodox philosophical systems can be broadly viewed in two ways: (1) They emerged as critiques of the heterodox systems, especially Buddhism, and (2) they emerged as attempts to systematize the teachings within the Hindu tradition.[1] Though the roots of some of these philosophical schools are pre-Buddhist,[2] their systematic development, through the Sūtra form of writing and the commentaries on these Sūtras (*bhāṣyas*),[3] is post-Buddhist. One can presume that they came in the face of Buddhist critiques of the Vedic tradition. But they also played an important role within the tradition itself by systematizing the teachings and also by developing certain aspects of the tradition that needed formulation. In this sense we may say that the philosophical system of Nyāya developed the Hindu logic, Vaiśeṣika, that may be called the "Hindu Physics"; Sāṃkhya, the theory of evolution of matter; Yoga, the codes of practical discipline; Mīmāṃsā, the canons of the interpretation of the scripture; and Vedānta, the metaphysics. But there is obviously some oversimplification in this classification. It should be kept in mind that each of these systems is complete in itself, containing to some extent all the necessary elements that make a philosophical school complete; i.e., metaphysics, cosmology, epistemology, etc. Despite interaction, they also function at times as critiques of each other, pointing to the difference in their interpretation of the same traditional material. Relative to the subject of our investigation, we should note that the problem of death belongs to a group of issues which all Indian schools share in common.

Death is part of the transmigratory process with birth as its counterpart. All the orthodox philosophical schools accept the doctrine of Karma-Saṃsāra, and their philosophical endeavor is directed towards release from the apparently endless cycle of birth-death-rebirth. Although they hold this basic doctrine in common, they may differ considerably in their understanding of the phenomenon of death. Keeping in mind both the differences as well as the similarities, we have decided to treat the subject matter of this section collectively while emphasizing divergent positions. However, before discussing the problem of death in these schools, it is necessary to elaborate on some key ideas.

All schools view the transmigratory state of existence as a state of bondage. This description comes from the understanding of the nature of the soul. Though there are significant differences in the soul concept, it is held by all that the soul *per se* is free from transmigratory existence. Saṃsāra is the result of the association of the soul with the body, or in broader terms with the world of matter. The cause for this association is the soul's ignorance (*avidyā*) of its true nature.[4] This process of birth-death-rebirth operates on the principle that all human actions are directed towards the achievement of desired goals; the fruits of action in their turn lead to further actions and thus to an endless chain of actions.[5] Birth leads to death and death in its turn results in birth. Liberation, then, is the cessation of one's involvement in this cyclic process. As to the method leading to this cessation, the schools offer different answers in accordance with their particular emphases.

In this perspective the following two points should be noted:

1. The state of bondage is an unnatural state of existence. This unnaturalness is due to the fact that the soul, which is free and detached from matter and also in some sense changeless, is associated with a body and, therefore, subject to the feelings of pleasure and pain, like a prince who lives among the poor forest dwellers not knowing his princely state, to use one of the metaphors of the schools. Liberation (*mokṣa*) is realizing the true nature of the soul, the prince knowing he is a prince and not a poor forest dweller. There are certain equations which may be useful to keep in mind: (a) the natural is the real; the more a thing is natural the more real (ontologically) it is, and (b) simplicity is correlated with reality; unity is more real than multiplicity or diversity. From the

above point of view Saṃsāra has some unreality and limitedness about it.

2. The state of bondage (*saṃsāra*) is the state of ignorance (*avidyā*), an unnatural condition. On the other hand, Mokṣa is knowledge, self-knowledge primarily. It may be more appropriate to call it realization than knowledge, keeping in mind the vagueness involved in the expression "knowing." Mokṣa does not arise when one merely intellectually *knows* the nature of the self, but when one in a sense *sees* the self in its naturalness. This is a state transcending discursive thought. This is perhaps best illustrated from the Advaita school of Vedānta. There one should not only know that reality is nondual, but should see no multiplicity whatsoever.[6] This characterizes liberation in this school of Vedānta.

These considerations enable us to see that for the philosophical schools the relation between Saṃsāra (bondage-state) and Mokṣa (liberated state) is one of opposition.[7] This opposition is generally seen in two ways. The first from an existential point of view and the second from a logical point of view. It is from the latter point of view that Saṃsāra and Mokṣa are considered "contradictory" to one another. The existential or the actual aspect of this opposition is seen in the description of Saṃsāra as painful ultimately, though interspersed with pleasure, and Mokṣa as cessation from this pain.[8] These two kinds of descriptions, however, freely intermingle when schools attempt to elaborate on Saṃsāra and Mokṣa.

The existential dimension seems to serve two purposes for the philosophical schools. It shows that liberation is not merely a matter of epistemology. It is an inescapable existential problem. This could serve as a critique of the materialistic Cārvāka system by pointing out that worldly pleasures are not worth seeking, since they are invariably accompanied by pain; and that perhaps the true pleasure consists of being liberated from bondage. For the Hindu schools the emphasis on the existential dimension could have also served as a critique of Buddhism. Both accept the common premises of human sorrow and yet arrive at different conclusions as to the means for achieving liberation, the nature of the soul, God, world; thus, building different doctrinal structures on the same premises.[9]

In general the opposition between Saṃsāra and Mokṣa in both existential and logical dimensions can be expressed in the following ways: (1) Saṃsāra is a process going on continually through the binding nature of human actions. Mokṣa, on the other hand, is a state where the soul is free from involvement in the cyclic process.[10] (2) Saṃsāra is a state of existence characterized by the association of the soul with a body (or, to use the Sāṃkhya terminology, by the association between Puruṣa and Prakṛti respectively).[11]

Mokṣa, in contrast, is where this association is broken. Body here is of two kinds: gross or physical and subtle; both of which are material and like other material things constituted by three qualities (*guṇa*), i.e., intelligence (*sattva*), activity (*rajas*), and inactivity (*tamas*). In the event of birth there is association of the soul with a gross body, and at the moment of death there is dissociation from this gross body. However, the subtle body is being continuously associated with the soul in bondage (*saṃsāra*). During the state of death, characterized as an "experiential" prebirth state of existence, the soul has been described as living in some kind of celestial region.[12] The idea seems to be that a body is essential for any kind of experience, even in the state of death. In fact, the subtle body provides the continuity in the transmigratory process of the soul. It carries all the residual impressions that human actions leave and determines the nature of the gross body which a soul will receive at the time of rebirth. These residual impressions also determine the kind of experiences a soul would be subjected to before being reborn.

In contrast, the Mokṣa state is a state of existence where the soul shines in its pristine purity, free from association with gross and subtle bodies. Even where the Mokṣa state is described as blissful, it is not a bliss arising out of active interaction, but a bliss that results from the cessation of action and the restoration of the soul to its natural state. In the Vedānta systems where active interaction and participation even in the liberated state is emphasized, as in Viśiṣṭādvaita, the liberated soul assumes a body, though not the same kind as of this world. It is described as a body of pure intelligence or goodness (*sattva*), assumed of one's own accord, without being forced upon one by the principles of transmigration (*karma*).[13]

Thus far we have emphasized the contrast between Saṃsāra and Mokṣa. But there is another important angle to this relation which mitigates this opposition. It is the usefulness of Saṃsāra in the pursuit of liberation. For the schools, Saṃsāra is not irrelevant to the "salvation history," in spite of being opposed to Mokṣa. The emphasis has been laid on the individual effort, using the techniques and tools available in the world of Saṃsāra to overcome Saṃsāra. In other words, Saṃsāra serves as a kind of springboard for Mokṣa. In this sense the whole Saṃsāric life can be structured for the leap into Mokṣa. The emphasis is laid on "acquiring" rather than on "receiving" through grace. This seems to make the Saṃsāra state relevant to some extent in terms of Mokṣa. Nevertheless, it should be noticed that the relation between Saṃsāra and Mokṣa is a dialectical one, for in these schools Mokṣa is not Saṃsāra transformed.

It is in this overall perspective of opposition as well as of a kind of springboard relationship between Mokṣa and Saṃsāra that we need to study the concept of death and assess its significance. Death is part of Saṃsāra with its counterpart, birth. Both originate from the association of the soul with a body, gross and subtle. This association is caused and sustained by ignorance (*avidyā*). In this context we shall initially study the significance of death and then explicate the concept of death in the light of its significance.

The significance of death should be ascertained from the angle of Mokṣa, as all these schools are Mokṣa oriented. To what extent death contributes to Mokṣa is, however, broadly tied up with the positive as well as negative relation between Saṃsāra and Mokṣa. The negative significance of death is apparent when death is viewed as part of Saṃsāra, and Saṃsāra itself is viewed in its opposition to Mokṣa. As such, the entire cyclic process is futile. The sentiment like the one expressed by Śaṃkara, in his *Bhaja Govindam*, "of repeated births and deaths" amply illustrates the attitude of one who is tired of the Saṃsāric life, like a person who has journeyed long and is eager to find a resting place.[14]

There is another side to this relationship which could be viewed as very significant in terms of Mokṣa. It is the weariness of the traveler that makes him seek a resting place. In that sense the journey itself contributes to his seeking. Similarly, it is Saṃsāra itself which impels one to seek Mokṣa; or, to put it in terms of death, it is mortality that forces one to seek immortality. In this sense there is an existential dimension to Saṃsāra to death, being a part of Saṃsāra. But there is also a kind of irony involved. The entanglement of the soul in the process of Saṃsāra is said to be ancient; it is even said to be beginningless, to emphasize a very long association. This has resulted in an attachment to Saṃsāra, keeping the soul within its fold, in spite of pain and sorrow, in spite of an existential pull to transcend.

From this existential dimension of death and of Saṃsāra in general we can move to the study of the second aspect of the significance of death, which is in terms of its role within the Saṃsāric cycle itself. Here we need to determine how death has been viewed in these schools both as a phenomenon as well as a death-state or "afterlife." As a phenomenon, death is a break from life (or the life-state, to be more precise), a break occurring as the result of the dissociation of the soul from the gross body. In terms of the cyclic process, it is a state caused by the exhaustion of the deeds which have governed that particular life-state (i.e., the *prārabdha karma*). But when death is viewed in terms of afterlife (or death-state), there is some kind of continuity between death and life since the former is as much caused by the fructification of deeds as is the latter.[15] In both the above aspects we intend to show that death occupies a significant place as contributing to Mokṣa in some way.

The phenomenon of death is considered a preliminary ground for liberation.[16] According to the schools, death is a signal point for liberation, for here the association with a (gross) body is dissolved. It is in fact a signal point for two kinds of destinations. One destination is towards liberation and the other is towards bondage. At the point of death, deeds which are responsible for the "present life" are exhausted. Whether one would be liberated or again be bound through other deeds depends upon the kind of "present life" one has led. This aspect of death being the signal point for two directions is stressed in the Vedānta systems. They point out that in the process of dissociation from the body, souls to be liberated or "destined" to bondage follow the same route in the body until they reach the nerve points (*nādi*) after which their routes bifurcate.[17] The subtle body still continues to be associated with the liberated soul, as in the case of the unliberated one, but only up to a certain point after which it also separates from the soul.[18]

A Vedāntist like Rāmānuja routes the journey of the freed soul through the place of the ancestors, i.e., the moon. Then while the bound souls stay there and are subsequently reborn, the freed souls continue their upward journey until they reach the abode of God.[19]

The importance of death as a signal point for the two kinds of destinations becomes clear from another angle too. The Vedāntist Rāmānuja views life as preparing the ground for death. He points out that the object of meditation during one's lifetime as well as the final thoughts at the point of death are of utmost importance, as they determine the future existence: one becomes what he contemplates.[20] As a part of religious discipline, Rāmānuja suggests contemplation of the path that a liberated soul will take in its journey towards the abode of God.[21] Such contemplation will enable an individual to discipline his mind and at the point of death to direct his thoughts toward the path leading to God. For him there is no Saṃsāric involvement anymore.

Death is understood here as an event which provides the possibility for liberation. For many this possibility is not open due to the still unexhausted deeds (*karma*) which "take over" when Karma responsible for the "present life" is exhausted. Taking into consideration the recommended mental discipline during one's lifetime and the thoughts at the moment of death as determinative of "afterlife," one could say that the deeds responsible for the present life, though exhausted at the point of death, determine to some extent the kind of deeds (*karma*) that "take over" and govern the "afterlife." In this sense there is continuity between this life and "afterlife." The larger dimension of this continuity is, however, part of Saṃsāra. Just as birth is determined by the fructification of deeds, so is the death-state. According to these deeds, one's "afterlife" is structured and experienced. We find some descriptions of the "afterlife" in the philosophical schools. In the Vedānta system, as we have pointed out, there are some discussions about the path the soul takes after being released from the gross body. The moon is said to be the place where the ancestors live until they are reborn. However, not all the departed bound-souls need go to this place. Some of them are reborn almost immediately, depending on their actions in the previous life and on the kind of deeds responsible for their death-state.[22]

There is some difference in the manner in which the deeds are exhausted in the present life and afterlife. In the present life there are two kinds of activities: (1) the experiencing of these deeds when fructified, and (2) the accumulation of new deeds as the result of the first process. The binding nature of deeds lies precisely in a type of action which leads to further actions and so on. Thus, Saṃsāra cannot be exhausted by merely living a number of lives; for in the process of exhausting accumulated Karma, one acquires fresh deeds at the same time. The exhaustion of these deeds in the death-state is different, since there is no accumulation of new deeds.[23] The death-state has been described as an unconscious state and compared to a deep sleep experience, where one knows nothing.[24] These descriptions seem to show that it is a state which is negative in character, where one cannot perform positive, motivated, and responsible actions as one does in the life-state, or even in the liberated state in the case of the theistic Vedāntic schools. But it is no doubt a state of experience, since deeds can be exhausted only by way of experience. This leads to the following position: the death-state is significant from the viewpoint of Mokṣa, since it provides an opportunity to exhaust some of the accumulated deeds without gathering new Karma. In this sense the transmigratory process may not be futile. It may be conceived as not merely cyclical, but in some sense spiral, i.e., developmental. This implies maturation as the soul passes from one birth complex to the next;

in this context death contributes more to liberation than birth by providing a situation where one merely spends without getting any "returns."

The emphasis on the orientation of life towards death is central to the understanding of death. This becomes apparent in the very importance of death as a preliminary ground for liberation and also as a signal point for two directions. It has some interesting consequences in regard to attitudes towards death. It presents life and death as related events with a high degree of dependence on each other. The Mokṣa significance of death is dependent on life, since death provides the opening for Mokṣa only to those whose life has been properly oriented. From one point of view, therefore, death is not to be feared; it is even to be welcomed. But from another point of view, death is undesirable without preparing oneself for it. It can be a blessing as well as a curse. Each point of death in the transmigratory process is a "judgmental point" where one could be "saved or condemned."

How does one properly relate to death in these schools? By relating to Mokṣa one has to die in some way before one can be liberated. The means for liberation enunciated in the different systems can be viewed as orientation towards death *immediately* and towards Mokṣa *mediately*. Part of this orientation includes the imitation of death as exemplified in some forms of Yogic discipline such as the withdrawal of the senses, or while remaining in the world, not being of it. The former may be considered imitation of the phenomenon of death where the sense organs are being withdrawn and one loses the awareness of the outer, gross world. The latter is the imitation of the death-state, which is experiential, but not motivated. Known as the *jīvan mukta* state, it is to be understood in terms of its relation to the world as a condition where the death-state has in a sense been realized, even while alive, and where the *mukta* is dead to the world though living in it. Here the death-attitude seems to be more stressed than the physical occurrence of death.[25] The emphasis on the need to develop detachment and on the performance of desireless (unmotivated) actions (*niṣkāma karma*) are part of the imitation of the death-state and are efforts to cultivate some kind of death-state attitude.

Death, however, is not to be equated with Mokṣa. It is only a gateway, a springboard for the leap into Mokṣa. The descriptions of the Mokṣa state are positive, and death is still viewed in these schools in terms of association with the subtle body. Yet death has certain features which are most relevant from the viewpoint of Mokṣa. It has an important lesson to teach and—in the context of Hindu spirituality—also an important exercise to perform: death points to the tension between Saṃsāra and Mokṣa and the need to break away from Saṃsāra to resolve this tension. As an exercise it offers a method for breaking down the tension, either by way of a Yogic withdrawal of the senses from the phenomenal world or by a detachment from the world-process.

Summarizing our findings, we may define the concept of death in the orthodox philosophical systems as follows: death is part of Saṃsāra with its counterpart, birth. Death is the cessation of the current mode of existence. Life ceases when there is dissociation of the soul from a gross body. By the same token there is also some sort of continuity in the state of death as death is a point in the Saṃsāric process. The soul is associated with a subtle body which acts as the repository of residual impressions of actions performed in the life-state. These actions determine the nature of a person's death-state experience as well as rebirth by determining the kind of gross body with which an individual will be reassociated.

Death has to be understood both in its aspect of break as well as continuity. This alone makes explicit the meaningful relation between death and Mokṣa on which this section has attempted to focus. The orientation of life towards death, and the orientation of death in its turn towards Mokṣa can be understood in the light of these two aspects. Again, the springboard relationship on the one side and some kind of general depreciative insignificance of death as part of Saṃsāra on the other can best be appreciated in the same perspective. Thus death is both an event of anxiety as well as of joyful expectation in the understanding of these schools.

Notes

1. These twofold functions are evident from the writings of the philosophical schools themselves. Probably one could more precisely describe the first function as that which emerges in the context of the second function, namely, systematization of the doctrine within the systems. However, the incentive for this systematization arises in the context of the Buddhist critique of the Vedic tradition and also in the context of philosophical developments within Buddhism itself.
2. Sāṃkhya, Yoga and Mīmāṃsā are considered pre-Buddhist.
3. Sūtras can be translated as aphorisms, a concise summary of the teachings of the different systems. To explain these aphorisms, *Bhāṣyas* came to be written. These *Bhāṣyas* are commentaries essential to the understanding of the philosophical systems. Then there are subcommentaries on these commentaries. In addition we find independent treatises, summaries, and dissertations sometimes in verse form called *Kārikās* and *Vārtikas*. There are six *Sūtras* corresponding to the six philosophical systems, *Nyāya Sūtra, Vaiśeṣika Sūtra, Sāṃkhya Sūtra, Yoga Sūtra, Mīmāṃsā Sūtra* and *Vedānta Sutra*. In addition there are a number of commentaries on the basis of which subschools have been formed. This applies especially to the case of Vedānta, where we have three major Vedānta schools: Advaita (nondualistic), Viśiṣṭādvaita (qualified nondualistic), and Dvaita (dualistic).
4. This idea is very important for the understanding of Hindu spirituality. The insistence on contemplation or meditation is based on the *knowledge-ignorance* perspective. The knowledge which is sought is the knowledge of the self,

and hence there is an inward search. *Mokṣa* or liberation is essentially knowledge and all the means for liberation emphasized in the different schools result in knowledge.

5. The binding nature of actions is due to an invisible potency each of the actions produces. This potency is termed *adṛṣṭa* (invisible). These actions settle in the subtle body, as it were, and fructify in course of time or even immediately, depending on the nature of the potency registered. They are classified as: (1) white or virtuous (*śukla*), (2) black or wicked (*kṛṣṇa*), (3) white-black, partly virtuous and partly wicked (*śukla-kṛṣṇa*). However, there is a fourth kind which is *not* of binding nature, neither black nor white (*aśuklākṛṣṇa*). There are acts of self-renunciation or meditation which are not associated with desires for the fruits of action. We shall see that actions in the death-state (the experiences between death and rebirth) are also of the same kind.
6. Three steps are said to be involved in this "realization" according to Advaita Vedānta: (1) One should learn from the teacher the true nature of reality, which is nondual. This is called learning (*śravaṇa*) by way of listening. (2) One should strengthen his conviction about the nondual nature of reality through arguments which are favorable for this purpose. It is called independent thinking or reflecting (*manana*). (3) Then one should try to meditate on these arguments and reflections trying to realize the truth. This is called profound meditation (*nididhyāsana*). *Nididhyāsana* is the attempt to "see the truth" having been intellectually convinced of its nature.
7. Cf. Boris Vysheslawzeff, "Two ways of Redemption: Redemption as a Solution of the Tragic Contradiction" in Joseph Campbell, ed., *The Mystic Vision,* Bollingen Series, XXX, vol. 6 (Princeton: Princeton University Press, 1970). The author demonstrates this opposition between *Saṃsāra* and *Mokṣa* in a comparative context, though not without oversimplifying. "The solution of the basic contradiction is impossible in so far as we hold fast to oppositions. The only solution and redemption is the dissolution of opposition in identity or indifference or a radical annulment of opposition itself." This opposition may be illustrated from a passage in Vātsyāyana's commentary on the *Nyāya Sūtra,* 1. 1. 2: ". . . Death-Rebirth is without beginning, but ends in final release,—Death-Rebirth, having a cause is caused by activity (merit and demerit),—Death-birth is connected with the soul and operates through disruption and restoration of continuous connection of such things as body, the sense organs, the consciousness and sensations . . ." ". . . with regard to final release, it is in the form 'Final Release' involving dissociation from all things and cessation from all activity . . . ," trans. by Ganganatha Jha, *Gautama's Nyāya Sūtras* (Poona: Oriental Book Agency, 1939), pp. 14 f.
8. "Finding everything to be mingled with pain, when one wishes to get rid of pain, he finds that birth (or life) itself is nothing but pain and thus becomes disgusted with life and being disgusted he loses all attachment and

being free from pain, he becomes released." Vātsyāyana's commentary on the *Nyāya Sūtra,* 1. 1. 21. *The Sarva Darśana Saṃgraha* compares this aspect of pleasure mixed with pain to honey mixed with poison. Cf. E. B. Cowell and A. E. Gough, trans., *The Sarva Darśana Saṃgraha,* Chowkamba Sanskrit Series, 6th ed. (Varnasi, 1961), pp. 170 f. The existential and the logical aspects of Saṃsāra separated above for our understanding are often considered together, as for instance in the following passage from the *Nyāya Sūtra:* "There is cessation of each member of the following series—Pain, Birth, Activity, Defect and Wrong Notion: the cessation of which follows bringing about the annihilation of that which precedes it: and this ultimately leads to the Highest Good." (1. 1. 2)

9. Kumārila-bhaṭṭa of the Mīmāṃsā school writing in the context of the heterodox systems points out that milk, though by itself pure and useful, becomes useless and unacceptable when poured into a bag of dog-skin; similarly even if the heterodox systems contain something valid in their doctrinal structure, they get vitiated in the midst of other wrongly held notions. Cf. P. V. Kane, *History of the Dharma Śāstra* (Bhandarkar Oriental Research Institute, 1962), vol. 5, pt. 2, p. 1263 f.
10. ". . . the body that belongs to the soul in one life is not the first that the soul has had; nor is it the last; in fact there can be no first in the previous bodies the soul has had (as we cannot trace the beginning of the worldly process); and as for its subsequent bodies there can be an end to these only when the ultimate good is attained." Vātsyāyana's commentary on *Nyāya Sūtra,* 1. 1. 9.
11. One has to be careful in understanding the word association here. In some of the philosophical schools there is no real association; it is only apparent. This is true of Sāṃkhya and Advaita Vedānta. For Sāṃkhya, the soul is like a spectator watching the play. However, it is moved by feelings that the actors express in the play. In reality these feelings or the sufferings that the actors express do not belong to the soul, which is only a spectator. To be liberated is to realize one's true nature as a detached spectator. In Advaita, however, Saṃsāra is not ultimately real, since the nondual reality "has always been." Therefore, multiplicity and the soul's involvement in it are only apparent. When the true knowledge dawns, they disappear like a snake which disappears when one realizes his mistake of having seen a rope as a snake. For other schools the association in a sense is real. The soul undergoes changes and afflictions in its bound-life. But these are contrary to the true and natural state of the self.
12. Some discussion on heaven and hell can be found in *Vedānta Sūtra,* III. 1. 12-19. Descriptions of the path of the soul after death are contained in chapters IV and V of the same Sūtra and in various commentaries. These descriptions are more for meditative purposes. In the theistic Vedānta systems (Viśiṣṭādvaita and Dvaita) the liberated state is described as a heavenly life in immediate proximity to God. This Heaven has to be distinguished

from the heaven which a soul reaches as the result of its meritorious deeds, one which is a counterpart of hell.

13. "As, moreover, the released soul has freed itself from the bondage of karman, has its powers of knowledge fully developed, and has all its being in the supremely blissful intuition of the highest Brahman, it evidently cannot desire anything else nor enter on any other form of activity, and the idea of returning into *saṃsāra,* therefore, is altogether excluded." Śrī Bhāṣya of Rāmānuja, IV. 4. 11-14, trans. by V. K. Ramanujachari, *Śrī Bhāṣyam* (Kumbakonam, 1930).
14. This illustration is used in Śaṃkara's *Pañcadaśī* though in a slightly different context. Cf. T. M. P. Mahadevan, *The Philosophy of Advaita* (London: Luzac & Co., 1938), p. 262.
15. The term life-state is used to signify "present life" or what we usually designate as life in contrast to death. This life is occasioned by an unexhausted deed (*karma*) according to the Hindu doctrine of Karma. This deed is designated as the Prārabdha Karma. Once this Prārabdha Karma is exhausted, death occurs. This is shown by dissociation from a gross body which is associated with the soul at the time of birth. What has been described as the death-state is the state of existence of the soul after death, before being reborn. Life and death are to be understood in terms of association or dissociation of the soul with the gross body. As far as the soul is concerned it always "is."
16. The dissociation from the gross body is essential for liberation. Whether one will also be freed from the subtle body depends upon the spiritual disciplines one has practiced in his "life."
17. Cf. *Vedānta Sūtra,* IV. 2. 7. It should be noted that in Śaṃkaraś Advaita Vedānta School for the knower of *Nirguṇa Brahman* there is no departure at all, since Reality (Brahman), which he realizes, is forever nondual.
    When truth is realized, one attains Mokṣa which is "not merely knowing Brahman but *being* Brahman." M. Hiriyanna, *The Essentials of Indian Philosophy,* 6th ed. (London: 1967), p. 173. The rope-snake analogy which is extensively used in this school of Vedānta may be useful in explaining this aspect here. One mistakes a rope for a snake due to insufficient light. As long as one sees a snake, the snake exists. But as soon as there is light, one realizes it is only a rope, and the snake disappears. Similarly, when one realizes Brahman, the ultimate nature of Reality which is one without a second, all multiplicity disappears, since multiplicity is as unreal as the snake.
18. Cf. *Vedānta Sūtra,* IV. 2. 9; also Rāmānuja's Commentary, *Śrī Bhāṣya* on the same passage, p. 865.
19. Cf. *Śrī Bhāṣya,* IV. 2. 20.
20. Rāmānuja cites the following passage from the Chāndogya Upaniṣad: "What one meditates on that he becomes when he departs from here," *Śrī Bhāṣya,* III. 3. 51.
21. Cf. *ibid.,* IV. 2. 20.

22. Cf. *Vedānta Sūtra,* III. 1. 12 f.
23. Cf. *ibid.,* III. 1. 8. Here the Sūtra speaks of a remnant Karma as being responsible for rebirth. In fact, all three states, i.e., life, death and rebirth, are caused by different deeds. When one deed exhausts itself, another deed "takes over." There is a continuity, however, as previous deeds determine prior to their exhaustion the choice of the succeeding deeds.
24. Cf. *ibid.,* IV. 4. 16. See also *Śrī Bhāṣya* on the same passage.
25. A *Jīvan mukta* is also a *saṃnyāsin* (mendicant). A mendicant is one who is "dead to the world." Though "living *in* the world, he is not *of* it. . . . To his synoptic vision there is neither action nor agent, neither enjoyment nor enjoyer. He has transcended the temporal process; and temporal categories have no meaning for him. He revels in the bliss of non-difference that has not come to be, but which was, is and will ever be." Mahadevan, *The Philosophy of Advaita,* p. 262.

IV
The Heterodox Philosophical Systems

R. C. AMORE

The religious pluralism in North Central India in the sixth century B.C. fostered not only the development of Upaniṣadic speculation *from within* the Vedic schools of thought, but also the development of several ascetic movements *outside* the Brahmanic Vedic tradition. Numerous wandering teachers arose who formulated innovative doctrinal systems and gathered followers around their charismatic leadership. These later movements were by no means united under any common doctrinal or practical banner; indeed, each tended to look upon the others as its main rivals. But from the point of view of Brahmanic Vedism these diverse movements had a common, heretical characteristic; they denied the sacrality and authority of the Vedas believed to have been revealed through the ancient seers. Hinduism has been noted for its tolerance toward divergent sectarian movements through the centuries, but the movements in this period which denied the authority of the Vedas and undermined the class distinctions came to be denounced as Nāstika, "Deniers." The word Nāstika consists of the parts *na-asti-ka,* which would translate literally as "no-is-ists," meaning "deniers," or "those who say 'there is no. . . .' "

Many scholars have pointed to the role that non-Brahmins, especially members of the ruling (Kṣatriya) class, had in the rise of the Nāstika movements. Long ago Jacobi suggested in the introduction to his translation of the *Jaina Sūtras* that because of the exclusivism practiced by the Brahmins, the non-Brahmin ascetics came to be a separate movement inclined to dissent. Jacobi believed that among ascetics of the era there was a tendency not only to omit doing the householder sacrifices, but also to omit recitation of the Vedas. This latter omission is tantamount to becoming a Śudra, says the Vasiṣṭha (X. 4).

Among the numerous Nāstika leaders of the era, the reputation and influence of seven have extended far beyond their area and era. Four of them founded movements which survived over a thousand years in India, and two of those four movements survive today as major world religions. In this chapter we will consider death and the thought of four of the Nāstika systems dating from this era, the sixth century B.C.

Buddhism will be dealt with first and at greatest length because it has played such an important role, not only in India, but throughout Asia and to a lesser extent throughout the world. Then turning to the other major Nāstika movement, Jainism, we shall call attention to ways in which this living Indian religion diverged from Buddhism in certain respects concerning death. Finally, we will briefly consider the place of suicide in the strongly ascetic Ājīvika movement and the rejection of all but material reality among the Cārvāka thinkers.

Death and Buddhist Thought

The Buddhist commentator Buddhaghosa gives this explanation of how all men feel the anguish of death and dying: "The evil man who sees the ripening of evil deeds, the good man who cannot bear to be separate from those he loves: they both, on nearing death, feel mental pain. All things in general, through wear and tear, are physically undergoing pain, insufferable, irreparable, as the cutting off of joints and bandages. Since of such ill, death constitutes the base, so death has been declared the same as ill." [1]

We shall consider how important death was in Gautama's career, how Nirvāṇa is the theoretical opposite of death, and finally how Buddhist thought concerning death relates to Buddhist practice.

Death and Gautama's Career

The Bodhisattva's Career. The mature Gautama, after he had become a fully enlightened Buddha, believed that he had lived many previous lives in various types of animal and human bodies. He realized that during the course of his Bodhisattva career spanning more than five hundred lives he experienced suffering from getting old and dying again and again. But by developing and perfecting his spiritual qualities, he had been able to come to his last life. Having waited in a heaven until the proper time, the Bodhisattva was miraculously born into a royal family in a small kingdom in the foothills of the Himalayas. The legendary accounts of his birth are similar to those told of other Indian saviors and make the point that even as a baby the life of the Bodhisattva was imbued with magical power and holiness. An ascetic prophet gave a "psychic reading" of the infant Bodhisattva and announced to the king that his infant son was destined to be a supreme person in either the worldly or the spiritual realm; he would become either a universal monarch or a fully enlightened Buddha.

According to the legends, Gautama's father greatly preferred that his son's prophesied potential be directed toward the worldly rather than the spiritual path, and to lessen the risk of Gautama's departing from the world the king attempted to maximize his son's enjoyments and eliminate all unpleasantness from his youthful life. For our purposes the important part of this story is that the overprotective father attempted to shelter Gautama from learning about sickness, old age, and death. The king is thought to have been remarkably successful in this endeavor, and so it was not until Gautama was in his twenties that he learned of life's inherent maladies. His instructions came not from the courtiers, who had been prohibited from discussing such matters with the youth, but rather from the unexpected sighting of four men.

The first three men seen—a sick man, a decrepit old man, and a dead man—brought the young Gautama into shocking awareness of suffering and death. Then the sight of a meditating monk suggested the possibility of pursuing a spiritual path aimed at overcoming the anxiety arising from sickness, old age, and death. The decision to "renounce the world" and undertake the life of a wandering ascetic was, then, an attempt to resolve the existential problem of "being toward death." [2] The renunciation of the normal desire to pursue worldly pleasure, which is the implication of the phrase "renouncing the world," involved the resolve to become dead to the world. This symbolic death to worldly desires was ritually acted out when Gautama, having left behind his beloved wife and son, cut his long hair, traded his princely clothing for the rags of a hunter, and dismissed his horse and servant. These acts functionally corresponded to the rituals of symbolic death characteristic of puberty initiation such as having a tooth chipped off, being "buried" in the earth like a corpse, or being submerged in water.

Having died to the world, Gautama took up the life of a student ascetic. The significant aspect of this phase of his life as far as our purposes are concerned is that though Gautama's drive for liberation led him to severe ascetic torment of the body, to the point of starvation or madness, Gautama rejected suicide itself as a means toward liberation. His goal was to conquer death within life, stimulated by the belief that those who die unliberated will always be born again, no matter how earnestly they may have struggled.

Māra as Death's Counselor. Like the Christian Devil and the related Islamic Iblis, the Buddhist Māra in part plays the role of accuser of man. Such devil figures accuse humans or humanity in general of being unqualified for the life of spiritual purity to which they aspire. In Buddhism, Māra—the word means "death"—appeared before Gautama at dusk on the night of enlightenment, after Gautama had seated hmiself in meditation on the seat of enlightenment beneath the Bodhi tree with the firm resolve to achieve full enlightenment then and there. Māra protested that Gautama was not qualified to occupy this seat of enlightenment, saying instead that he, Māra, was its rightful occupant on that auspicious night. Māra called upon his army of demons as witnesses to his fraudulent claim to the Bodhi-seat. Gautama, having no equivalent army to witness on his behalf, called upon the earth "herself" as his witness.

In struggling against Māra, Gautama increased his resolve to do the opposite of what Māra had counseled, for Māra advocated a course which would have meant the death of Gautama's spiritual career. Later Māra again counseled a deadly path when he advised Gautama not to teach Dharma to people, whom he accused of being incapable of spiritual attainment. Just as death is the opposite of life, so Māra's counsel was consistently the opposite of truth.

Shedding Light on the Wheel of Death. During each of the three watches of the night of enlightenment, Gautama gained an ever deepening insight into the nature of death. During the first watch he recalled the numerous births which he himself had undergone in the long course of his career as a Bodhisattva. This insight led to an understanding of how spiritual perfections accumulate throughout the course of birth after birth. In the second watch of the night Gautama saw how all beings come and go; that is, he was able to see before him the parade of beings suffering over and over again through birth, old age, and death. In the third watch he achieved a knowledge of the flux of the whole universe. He comprehended that all things, except for Nirvāṇa and space, arise and pass away, and that the existence of all things is dependent upon a number of causal conditions. These insights provide the basis for a number of important Buddhist doctrines, including the famous "four noble truths" and "dependent origination" formulations as well as the Buddhist understanding of reincarnation.

The "four noble truths" is a formulation in four steps which begins with the problem of death and ends with a complicated prescription for its cure. Just as Gautama's spiritual quest was launched by a sudden awareness of human ills, so the awareness of the *suffering* caused by such factors as old age, sickness, and especially death is the first of the four truths. "One thing only do I teach/Sorrow and its end to reach,"[3] Gautama explained. The second truth is the prognosis that suffering has a *cause*—craving. The third truth, following the Buddhist logic of causation, is the diagnosis that if craving could be stopped there would be a cessation of suffering. The final truth, the *path* of eight right practices, is the cure which puts an end to old age and death and thereby eliminates suffering.

Gautama also saw with his expanding awareness that all things arise if and only if certain conditions are present. This far-reaching insight into reality was the basis of the important doctrine of "dependent origination" (or "conditioned genesis"). From this fundamental doctrine it follows, according to Buddhist thought, that everything which has come into existence (since it is conditioned and dependent) is subject to decay or death. All things are impermanent by nature, and attachment to them will lead to suffering (*dukkha*) when they eventually do decay or die.

The insight that all things originate dependently led to the famous formulation of a twelvefold chain of dependent origination. The standard order of presentation of the twelve links of the chain reflects the progressive compiling of the factors which sustain Saṃsāra, the unending wheel of death after death. However, the logic of the system is clearer when the links of the chain are considered in reverse order, beginning with the subject of this study, death. In brief, the logical steps of the analysis are as follows.

Old age and death currently exist and are important causes of suffering, but they could not exist without the prior condition of birth. (So if birth were eliminated, old age and death would disappear as causes of suffering.) *Birth,* in turn, could not exist without the prior condition of gestation. *Gestation* itself is dependent upon indulgence for its occurrence, and *indulgence* is conditioned by craving. Psychologically speaking, *craving* is conditioned by emotional feeling. *Feeling* is brought about by *sense contact,* which is based upon the *sensual system,* and that is inherent in the structure of the human body (*nāma-rūpa*). However, the *human body* in question would not have arisen in the first place except for the karma-laden "consciousness" (*vijñāna*) which migrated from a previous existence. That *consciousness* was conditioned by its motivations (or habituations), and that which allowed the *motivations* to be oriented toward rebirth in the first place was *ignorance,* the lack of spiritual insight.

The fine points of interpretation of dependent origination led to many doctrinal disputes among the various schools of Buddhist thought, but the thrust of the doctrine is clear. Death, along with old age, is the beginning of Buddhist thought, in this context at least.

With reference to the intriguing Buddhist notion of "reincarnation" it should be understood that Buddhist thought takes a middle position concerning soul-theory. On the one hand Buddhism denies the existence of an eternal soul, and on the other it denounces the materialistic view that there is no afterlife. Buddhist thought affirms that after the death of an individual a nonmaterial force known as Vijñāna karmically influences the nature of the destiny of a new birth. Buddhists, however, insist that Vijñāna is not the same as the Upaniṣadic Ātman or the Christian soul. The exact nature of this distinction has been differently stated, but in essence the Vijñāna is not an Ātman or soul because it is neither eternal nor substantial. Perhaps having in mind the concept of Ātman as conceived in sixth century B.C. folk belief and not the much more subtle conceptions of the Upaniṣads, the Buddhists denied that a "subtle self" or Ātman existed anywhere in the body or mind. And, perhaps, having in mind the Jain "Life" (*jīva*) or the Upaniṣadic Ātman, the Buddhists denied that the transmigrating entity was eternal. Saṃsāra, the wheel of births and deaths, involves the seemingly endless migration of the Vijñāna from body to body through destiny after destiny, but the saint puts an end to death and Saṃsāra because at death his purified mind does not produce any Vijñāna to bring about a new birth.

The Yogācāra school of Mahāyāna Buddhism developed the notion of the transmigrating Vijñāna into a "storehouse consciousness" (*ālaya vijñāna*), which underlies regular conscious awareness as the water of an ocean underlies its waves. Critics of Yogācāra said the "storehouse consciousness" was just a Buddhist term for the Upaniṣadic Ātman, but in fairness it should be mentioned that the Ālaya-Vijñāna was not thought of as eternal. Like the older notion of the transmigrating Vijñāna, the storehouse consciousness was said to come to an end when death was conquered by Buddhas, saints, or advanced Bodhisattvas.

Gautama's Death and the Stupa Cult. Having become the fully enlightened Buddha at the age of thirty-five, Gautama undertook a teaching career according to the traditions of Indian holy men. Traveling in northern India, he instructed many Indians in the doctrines of dependent origination, the analysis of suffering, and the path which puts an end to the wheel of death. At the age of eighty his own aging body surrendered to an attack of food poisoning, and the Buddha died his final death in a grove while the trees dropped flowers and gods came to honor him. Death had conquered him physically, but the Buddha had conquered death because he died peacefully, confident that Death's angels would have no control over him (for reasons to be discussed in the next section).

Gautama's famous final instruction to his disciples consists of four words which summarize Buddhist thought on death: "Compounded-things decay; strive earnestly." The phrase "compounded-things" (*saṃkhārā*) calls attention to the Buddhist view that everything is in flux, that all existing entities have arisen due to various causes—they are compounded, not self-perpetuating. The characteristic of existing things is that they are subject to decay—sooner or later all things, even mountains, die. The Buddhist doctrine of the "three signs of existence" elaborates upon the same insight with its threefold formulation that all existing things are *impermanent,* lead to *suffering,* and have *no eternal soul.* With regard to the subject of death and Buddhist thought, it should be appropriate to interpret Gautama's final instruction as "Death conquers all, so conquer death."

After his cremation Gautama's remains were divided and enshrined as holy relics in several burial mounds (*stupas*); and as Buddhism spread, new stupas were built which contained secondary relics such as the remains of a saint or a canonical text. Buddhists circumambulated the mound, placed flowers and other offerings upon an altar, and dedicated themselves to perfecting the qualities of the Buddha in their lives. Over the course of five or six centuries the practice of going to venerate the Buddha at his stupa became the normative spiritual endeavor for Buddhist laymen. In the era in which devotional movements (*bhakti* cults) were sweeping across North India, a new Buddhology formulated from a devotional point of view took shape and gradually came into predominance. The stupa cult was a main contributor to the development of devotional Buddhism which in turn contributed to the rise of the "Great Vehicle" (Mahāyāna).[4] Whereas early Buddhism had thought of the stupas as honorific shrines containing relics of a Buddha who was beyond contact (in the state of *nirvāṇa*), Mahāyāna talked of saving Buddhas and gracious Bodhisattvas.

Death was no longer thought of as something that had to be faced alone, with the fruits of one's own deeds meeting him after death. Rather, the heavens were filled with savior figures dedicated to pouring out grace for the aid of those who sincerely turned to them with devotion. Pious laymen continued in their meritorious practices, but with a new confidence that Bodhisattvas, like guardian angels, were looking down upon them with compassion. Avalokiteśvara, "the Lord who looks down" was extremely popular throughout the Mahāyāna world, from Kashmir to Indonesia. And in China, where this Bodhisattva of compassionate mercy was especially popular, he came to be looked upon as feminine and fulfilled the function of a goddess of mercy.

Nirvāṇa as Deathlessness

Heaven and Beyond Heaven. All the Nāstika systems shared the Brahmanic view that one could win for oneself a heavenly world by the performance of good deeds. The concept of winning a *Loka,* "world," by good deeds may have originated in the old motif of the victorious warrior gaining territory by his heroic efforts, and the notion that the warrior who dies in battle goes immediately to Indra's heaven is similar to the belief that the one who sacrifices to a god will be welcomed to that god's heavenly abode after death. "This idea, viz. the possibility of sharing the loka of a divine being whose presence is so characteristic of that loka that it is called after that deity, gained in importance. It is at the root of the doctrine according to which one may, after death, attain to communion of 'world' with that god with whom one has identified oneself in love and reverence.[5]

In this context, the Vedic concept "world" means a sacred space or location which one's good deeds generate. Although usually conceived of as in the heavens, the Loka was not thought of as a physical location but rather as a sacred place "which, being qualitatively different from any other place or from homogeneous space in general, has a specific and independent value of its own." [6]

The world which one creates for oneself by good deeds lies in waiting until one goes to dwell in it after death. One's heavenly world represents his treasure of merits which have been accumulated through a lifetime of good works. For example, the Muṇḍaka Upaniṣad declares that the three Vedas contain the truth and exhorts lovers of truth to faithfully perform the sacrifices prescribed in the Vedas, for "this is your path to the *loka* made by good deeds." [7] After warning that the person who does not perform the sacrifices properly destroys his Loka, the Muṇḍaka promises the faithful sacrificer that his offerings, having gone to the Brahma-loka, call back to him "come, come" and carry him there (from the funeral pyre[8]) via the rays of the sun and pay homage to him when he arrives with the pleasing words, "This is your Brahma-loka well created by merit." [9]

In some other religious traditions, especially in Iran, it is said that the righteous man is welcomed to heaven by his meritorious deeds personified as a beautiful maiden, and conversely the unrighteous man is escorted to hell by the old hag generated by his evil works. Similarly, a Vedic passage states that those who die pure go to the bright world where they have plenty of women.[10] Buddhism follows this line of thought as closely as its ethic will allow, but avoids the symbolism of the young maiden. For example, the Dhammapada promises that "one who has done good works and then has gone beyond this world is welcomed by his merits, as a returning loved one is welcomed by his relatives."

However, at the time of the origin of Buddhism there was a growing tendency among both the Upaniṣadic and Nāstika teachers to criticize the ideal of winning a heavenly world. The change in belief which led to this critique of the old ideal involved the growth of the idea that the pleasures of heaven were short-lived. Upaniṣadic thinkers warned of the possibility of "re-death," and eventually the Indian concept of Saṃsāra took shape. Gonda's study of the concept Loka in the Vedic literature reveals this downgrading of Loka as a religious goal in the later period:

> The term under discussion now that the belief in recurrent death and transmigration has taken a firm root is used in passages dealing with the course of the soul in its various incarnations clearly to denote those "places," "states" or "situations" in which to enjoy, while transmigrating from one existence to another, the fruits of merits—or to expiate the sins committed—until these are ex-

hausted and, generally, the intermediate stations on the way from one rebirth to another in which Karman is produced and cleared off.[11]

Those who reduced the desire to win a heavenly world to a second-rate goal held out to their hearers the promise of an (new) ultimate goal, one that would be eternal bliss and completely beyond death. For example, the Kaivalya Upaniṣad exhorts persons to follow a path higher than sacrificing. Rather one should seek to know Brahman, to identify with the one who can say, "There is neither merit nor demerit for me." [12] The person who attains this wisdom crosses over the ocean of births and deaths to liberation (*kaivalya*).

Similarly, Buddhism and the other Nāstika systems looked upon attaining heaven as an inferior goal and directed their followers instead toward the ultimate liberation from Saṃsāra known variously as release (*mokṣa*), liberation (*kaivalya*), and Nirvāṇa. The Buddhist disciple who is truly well advanced is said to be beyond the generation of merit as well as demerit, according to some texts. For example, in one passage Gautama listens approvingly to the verses sung by the gods in praise of good deeds, but adds a verse of his own which indicates that there is something higher than what comes from meritorious karma; namely, the Nirvāṇa which comes from spiritual insight.[13]

Other Buddhist passages are even more explicit in their view that the liberated man who has overcome the bondage of death after death is characterized by a state of consciousness which is active, but generates neither good nor bad Karma. What motivates this desire to avoid generating even good Karma is the view that good Karma causes one to be reborn—in a pleasant destiny of course—but the holy man seeks to put an end to rebirth in any form.

For example, a mendicant once asked Gautama if there were really any difference between himself, a practicing Brahmin, and the mendicant Gautama. Gautama emphasized that there was a very important distinction between himself and the Brahmin concerning whether or not Karma-producing consciousness had been put aside: "Whoever in this world, having put aside merit and demerit, wisely leads the Brahmacarya life is accurately called "Mendicant" (*Bhikkhu*)." [14] Similarly, an often quoted Buddhist passage redefines the Brahmin as one who has overcome Karmic bondage leading to rebirth: "Whoever in this world has escaped from the bondage of both merit and demerit, who is free of sorrow and corruption, who is pure; him I call 'Brahman.' " [15]

Buddhist thought, having begun with death, understands the realm of death to reach from the lowest hell to the highest heaven. This line of analysis has led some critics to label Buddhist thought as pessimistic, negative, or world denying, but to be fair we must see Buddhist thought as a whole. It begins with death but optimistically points toward a realm of Nirvāṇa beyond death and suffering.

Nirvāṇa. The answer to death is Nirvāṇa, the state of deathlessness. According to Buddhist thought most people, after suffering death, are reborn according to their Karma in one of the six destinies: in a hell-body, demon-body, ghost-body, animal-body, human-body, or heavenly-body. As we have seen, life in each of these six destinies is only temporary and death will follow, and so on endlessly. However, there is the possibility of putting an end to this wheel of death: "Some persons are reborn on earth, while evil-doers go to hell and good-doers go to heaven, but those who are free from the causes of rebirth achieve Nirvāṇa." [16]

A popular Buddhist simile for Nirvāṇa compares the going out of the consciousness-which-is-reborn with the extinction of an oil lamp: "Wise men go out (*nibbāna*) like a lamp."[17] The state of Nirvāṇa is indescribable, it is said, just as the state of an extinguished fire is indescribable.[18]

Besides the figurative comparisons of Nirvāṇa and the extinguishing of fire, Buddhist thought more commonly employs the straightforward statement that Nirvāṇa is the extinction of the three evil root causes (deep-seated mental complexes): lust, hatred, and delusion. Once, a wandering ascetic questioned the learned disciple Sariputta as follows: "'*Nirvāṇa, Nirvāṇa,*' it is said, Sariputta. Tell me, sir, just what is this *Nirvāṇa?* Sire, the destruction of lust, hatred and delusion is what is called '*Nirvāṇa.*'"[19] Contemporary Buddhist interpreters often lament the way many Western[20] books talk of Nirvāṇa as extinction of the self rather than extinction of the three evil roots and the suffering they cause. For example, after criticizing the entry of the *Oxford Dictionary* on Nirvāṇa as confusing the Buddhist Nirvāṇa with the Vedāntic Nirvāṇa as absorption into the ultimate, one writer stresses that the Buddhist Nirvāṇa is the culmination of the path which leads to the end of the suffering of birth, old age, and death:

> "The world is aflame" says the Buddha; (S.I. 31.), and according to the Commentator, it is aflame with the fire kindled by lust, hatred and delusion, and also by birth, decay and death, pain, lamentation, sorrow, grief and despair. (A.I. 15.)
>
> There is the full meaning of extinction explained as "blowing out," the blowing out of the fire of lust, hatred and illusion, and this Nibbāna consists of the Fruit of the Path, the actual attainment of the blowing out of the fire from the heart that was burning with it.[21]

Another modern Buddhist expresses the understanding of Nirvāṇa as an extraordinary mental state in similar words: "*What is*

Nirvāṇa? It is a condition of heart and mind in which every earthly craving is extinct; it is the cessation of every passion and desire, of every feeling of ill-will, fear, and sorrow. It is a mental state of perfect rest and peace and joy, in the steadfast assurance of deliverance attained, from all the imperfections of finite being." [22]

Buddhist thought distinguishes between the Nirvāṇa attainable during embodiment and that attainable upon the dissolution of the body. This distinction goes back to the life of Gautama Buddha himself, who is said to have achieved provisional Nirvāṇa during the night of enlightenment (which continued during the remaining forty-five years of his life) and final Nirvāṇa at the time of his death.

The provisional Nirvāṇa which characterizes the Buddha as well as the saints is known in Pali as *sa-upādi-sesa-nibbāna,* "*nirvāṇa with* the life-complexes[23] remaining." This Nirvāṇa-while-still-embodied is characterized by the full extinction of the defiling mental states; that is, the state of complete purity of mind which generates no Karma leading to rebirth. The Buddhist canon recounts a dialogue between Gautama and a Brahmin named Jānussoni, who asks the Buddha to explain further the meaning of this Buddhist teaching which he has heard, "*Nirvāṇa* is visible in this life." Gautama answers that to the extent that one has reached a state of mind in which he is no longer ablaze with lust, hatred, or delusion, to that extent one sees Nirvāṇa: in this way the wise realize Nirvāṇa for themselves.[24]

The final Nirvāṇa which takes place at the death of a Buddha or saint is described as *an-upādi-sesa-nibbāna,* "*nirvāṇa without* the life-complexes remaining." Final Nirvāṇa is said to be everlasting, for unlike a rebirth on earth or even in a heaven, this state is free from rebirth and, therefore, from redeath. But exact description of final Nirvāṇa is avoided. Nirvāṇa remains a mystery to be entered into rather than described. He who partakes of Nirvāṇa never again tastes the suffering of birth, old age, and death.

The question which arose among the Buddha's disciples and remains today is, What happens to a Tathāgata after death? Gautama himself was asked about this by Vacchagotta and responded with the fourfold denial which is often employed in Buddhist thought:

> "A Tathāgata *is* after death,"
> "A Tathāgata *is not* after death,"
> "A Tathāgata *both is* and *is not* after death,"
> "A Tathāgata *neither is nor is not* after death"
> —to take any of these positions would be view-going,
> . . . . A Tathāgata has set aside view-going.[25]

One simile for the Tathāgata after death is that he is like an extinguished fire in the sense that one cannot meaningfully state where the fire has gone. Gautama also said this matter is unfathomable like a deep ocean. Gautama, this time speaking without simile, said that one cannot discuss the whereabouts of a Tathāgata after death because every aspect by which a person is known has been dissipated. The life-complexes—feeling, ideations, Karma-complexes, consciousness, and body—have each been dissolved away without the possibility of arising anew. Therefore, one cannot meaningfully predicate anything about the state of a Tathāgata after death.[26]

Just as ordinary men cannot intellectually get hold of the saint who is in the state of Nirvāṇa, so Death (Māra) himself cannot discern where the saint has gone. Death's sphere has been transcended, as Gautama taught his disciples on the occasion of the death of the saint, Godhika. Gautama took his disciples to the rock where Godhika had committed suicide[27] and pointed out to them the hazy areas of smoke here and there around the spot, saying that was Māra vainly looking for the reborn consciousness of Godhika and thinking: "Where has the consciousness of Godhika, son of a good family, become established?" Gautama then explains to the disciples why Māra's task is futile: "Bhikkhus, Godhika, the son of a good family, is completely liberated (*parinibbuto*) with an unestablished consciousness." [28] Elsewhere it is said that the King of Death cannot see the man of insight who understands that the world is impermanent and that one has no eternal soul.[29]

Death and Buddhist Practice

In Buddhist thought there are two meditational contexts in which death is the subject. One of these contexts involves the development of mental awareness or "mindfulness" (*sati*) of the inevitability of one's own death. The other context involves the objects of meditation, for ten of the forty prescribed objects of meditation are corpses. Both the mindfulness of death and the corpse meditations are dealt with at length by Buddhaghosa in his *Path of Purity*, and we shall follow his account.

Mindfulness of Death. Buddhaghosa begins by explaining that in this context "death" has its usual meaning of the coming to an end of the life faculties. He classifies death according to its three causes. Death by "loss of merit" refers to death in which the underlying cause is that the good Karma (merit) which brought about the birth in the first place has been exhausted, regardless of the age of the person. Death by "loss of life" refers to death brought about by the completion of man's lifespan, which is approximately one hundred years in the case of present-day men living in a period of declining morals, intelligence, and physical endurance. Loss of life and loss of merit may cause death independently or conjunctively. In addition to these two "natural" causes of death, there are two types of "untimely" deaths; those which occur as a result of violence, and those which are brought about by the ability of the psychic power of certain individuals to depart instantly from the body.[30]

The practice of mindfulness with reference to death involves finding a secluded spot and then expanding one's awareness that death is inevitable for all beings, including oneself. One should say to oneself, "Death will take place," or perhaps simply, "Death, death." An appropriate awareness of death may be attained in this manner, but if this proves insufficient, the person should enhance his awareness of death by meditating in eight ways on the inevitability of death.

(1) One should imagine oneself as facing an executioner or murderer, and then reflect on the fact that death *always* follows upon birth. "Just as a mushroom springs up carrying soil on top of it, so beings are born carrying old age and death." [31] All persons stand before death like a condemned criminal before the executioner.

(2) One should recall that no achievement is immune from the possibility of a reversal, that prosperity is always subject to loss, and that no ordinary means can conquer or avert loss or death. One cannot wage war against death even with a full army of elephants, chariots, and infantry. Nor will magic spells or great wealth[32] be of any use.

(3) A third approach is to reflect on the death of others and then infer one's own mortality. In order to give this approach power, one should recall that even the seven types of superior persons had to suffer death: these include men of great pomp such as

King Mahāsammata, men of great merit, men of great strength such as the wrestler Cānuroya, men with great magical power, men of great insight such as Sāriputta, nonteaching Buddhas, and even Supreme Buddhas such as Gautama.

(4) A fourth approach is to reflect on the fact that the human body is not exclusively one's own, but is shared with "the eighty families of worms." In addition to the threat of parasites, the body is also open to attack from without by snakes, insects, etc., any of which may cause death.

(5) Furthermore, one may reflect on the contingency of bodily life, recalling that it is weak because it is dependent upon air, water, heat control, etc.

(6) Complicating the whole matter of death and giving rise to anxiety concerning death is the fact that there is no sign or means by which one can know when one will die.[33]

(7) In this meditation one reflects upon the very limited life-span of men in this era, for whom one hundred years is considered a very long life.

(8) A reflection on the momentariness of consciousness makes one aware that the actual "life" of an individual is only a single moment, at any one time. The past moments of consciousness are dead and gone, and the future is not yet real, leaving only the fleeting present moment. This typically Buddhist understanding of consciousness as a stream of individual moments leads one toward an awareness of the transitoriness of life.

The benefits which derive from the development of mindfulness of death are that one becomes zealous, one breaks away from domination by sensual pleasure seeking, one denounces what is evil, and one neither hoards nor is stingy. His realization of the impermanence of existence is enhanced, which in turn gives rise to the perception of the suffering and soulless nature of existence. When death approaches the man who has developed his awareness of death, he is not afraid of death and may attain a state of deathlessness, or, failing that, at least attain rebirth in a happy destiny.[34]

Meditations on the Dead. Besides the reflections on dying intended to increase one's mindfulness of death, there are *meditations on corpses* which are intended to eliminate lustful states of mind. These corpse meditations are only one of the several types of meditations in Buddhism; indeed, they have seldom been practiced by a very large percentage of monks. Corpse meditation is much less used than the meditations on the ten devices of different colors or the four divine ethical states; yet, from early Buddhism to the present, corpse meditation has been a part of the instruction in concentration (*samādhi*) and certain monks have found it useful.

Essentially, the corpse meditations, known as the "meditations on the foul," involve seating oneself near corpses in various states of decay in order to increase one's feeling of disgust at the body and conversely decrease one's eagerness to take delight in bodily appearances. Buddhaghosa explains that the meditator should find an appropriate corpse—it should be of one's own sex and in the proper state of decay—seat oneself nearby (but not downwind) and begin to reflect upon the nature of embodiment.

The ten foul states and the benefits derived from each are as follows according to Buddhaghosa.[35] (1) Meditating on a *swollen* corpse, with its distorted figure, is a corrective for anyone who tends to lust after bodily forms. (2) Meditating on a *discolored* corpse, with its ugly skin tones, is a corrective for the tendency to lust after bodily complexion. (3) Meditating on a *festering* corpse, with its horrible stench, is a corrective for the tendency to lust after pleasant bodily smells produced by perfumes, flowers, etc. (4) Meditating on a corpse which has been *cut in two,* which reveals the hollows within the human body, is a corrective for those who think of their bodies as solid and full. (5) Meditating on a *mangled, gnawed* corpse, with its features so distorted, is a corrective for those who lust after the fullness of flesh in the breasts or other parts of the body. (6) Meditating on a *dismembered* corpse, with the limbs lying every which way, is a corrective for those who lust after graceful limbs. (7) Meditating on a corpse which has been *cut and dismembered* is a corrective for those who lust after the way the bodily joints, etc., are combined. (8) Meditating on a *bloody* corpse, with blood smeared all over it, corrects the lust for bodily ointments. (9) Meditating on a *worm-eaten* corpse, which makes plain the fact that one's body is coinhabited by many types of foul creatures, helps correct the tendency to think of one's body as "mine." (10) Meditating on a *skeleton,* which shows the wretched state of the body's bones, helps overcome the lust for having perfect teeth.

Buddhaghosa explained that these ten types of corpses have a common character; they are foul, stinking, and ugly. Furthermore, the wise man knows that the living body is as foul as the corpse. The only difference is that the living body is covered over with skin and kept relatively free from odor, but even a king's body would become wretched if he had to live like the outcasts, Buddhaghosa added.

Doing Merit and the Fear of Death. The meditations on death were practiced primarily by monks, whereas the laymen turned to deeds of merit as a refuge against the fear of death. For example, in a canonical story of an encounter between Gautama and two elderly Brahmins, the Brahmins described themselves as men who have not done any good works which would lead to fortune, happiness, and refuge against the fear of death. Gautama recommended that they should practice restraint in body, speech, and thought; that is, they should take refuge in a purified mind. The man who has a purified mind goes to a good destiny after death. Gautama summed up his teaching by telling the two Brahmins to do meritorious deeds, which make for happiness in the face of death.[36]

A very clear expression of the belief that a pure mind leads to a good destiny occurred in Gautama's sermon employing the simile of the cloth. Gautama instructed some monks that just as a dirty cloth turns out badly when dyed, but a clean cloth dyes nicely, so "a bad destiny is to be expected when the mind is tainted" and conversely "a good destiny is to be expected when the mind is untainted."[37] He then explained that the deep-seated motivations which taint the mind are greed, hatred, anger, ill will, etc.

"Just as among ripe fruit there is a fear of falling, so among mortals there is a constant fear of death," according to an often quoted simile.[38] The solution to this fear is to lead a meritorious life. One of the "good omen" stanzas teaches, "Living as instructed and having formerly made merit, with right resolve about oneself, that is the best omen."[39] The popular Dhammapada text sums up this teaching with its usual succinctness, "Merit is pleasant at the time of death."[40]

The theory that doing meritorious deeds would lead to happiness in this life and especially to a happy rebirth after death was an important reason for the central role that merit practices had among lay Buddhists. In later Theravada Buddhism a list of "ten means of merit" had become standard: merit could be made by practicing charity, by keeping the precepts, by mind development, by showing respect to one's superiors, by assisting others, by listening to a sermon, by sharing merit with others, by rejoicing in another's meritorious deeds, and by righting wrong views.

These ten means of merit are elaborations upon the very ancient

Indian concept of defilement. The archaic concept was that evil actions (*pāpa karma*) defile the soul with a sticky, material substance which must then be burnt off by acts of purification. The Buddhists, and many other Nāstika systems, reinterpreted defilement along more psychological lines, locating defilements with the person himself, with his outward actions (*karma*) being expressions of the inner evil. Buddhaghosa, for example, explained that the ordinary man, in the grip of spiritual ignorance, kills and otherwise generates evil actions by harming, although it gives him no lasting satisfaction because of the continuing fire of his evil passions; and when he dies, an evil destiny awaits him.

In keeping with the ancient tradition of looking upon killing as the paramount evil action—a notion which was taken to extremes by the more severe ascetics—Buddhist ethics denounced all acts of injury ranging from harsh speech to actual killing. The Brahmanical sacrifices which involved killing animals were denounced under this rubric, as were such occupations as hunting and fishing.[41]

Late canonical stories[42] greatly elaborated upon the ancient concept of Karmic retribution and taught that a single Karmic act could lead to a *corresponding, multiple* retribution after life. For example, a single red lotus offered to a holy monk or to a Buddha image might cause the offerer to be reborn in a heavenly mansion surrounded by ponds of beautiful red lotuses. Conversely, a single act of greed such as refusing to share one's food with a hungry monk might cause one to be reborn as a miserable ghost and suffer severe hunger for many years. Although the degree of reward or punishment was exaggerated in such stories, the motif remains constant: meritorious deeds are one's hope in the face of death.

The Moment of Death. Folk belief in India and in other areas looked upon the state of one's mind at the moment of death as especially relevant in determining one's destiny after death. The time of the year and the location in which the death occurs were also thought to be significant for happiness after death. Put simply, people prefer to die in holy places at holy times and with their minds peacefully fixed upon holy subjects.[43]

Similarly, Indian Buddhists preferred to die in a state of mind characterized by peaceful reflection on the spiritual qualities of the Buddha, Dharma, or Saṅgha. Buddhists tended to disapprove of using last moment magical practices or appeals to savior deities, and instead, sought to deepen the confidence in taking refuge in the Triple Gem. When properly practiced, the hour of death was to be a time for further purifying the mind and not a last-minute repentance, but through the centuries the moment of death was sometimes emphasized above all else. A number of textual passages in the later layers of the canon[44] reveal the belief that one's consciousness at the moment of death was of critical importance.

The Vimānavatthu ("Stories about Heavenly Mansions") and Petavatthu ("Stories about Miserable Ghosts") abound in instances of the determination of destiny according to the state of consciousness at the time of death. Again and again we have stories about persons who attained a heavenly mansion because they passed away with their minds joyfully fixed upon the Buddha, Dharma, or Saṅgha. In one such story a miser's son was at the point of death when the Buddha visited him out of compassion. The boy arose, made respectful veneration to the Buddha, and immediately died mindful of the Buddha.[45] The boy's state of consciousness at the moment of death led to his being reborn in a heavenly mansion.

In another story a young man heard the Buddha preaching and was killed by thieves shortly thereafter, while still in a state of being mindful of the Buddha and Dharma.[46] His state of mind at the time of death enabled him to be reborn in a heavenly mansion.

Even a frog gained rebirth in a heavenly mansion because he was stepped on and killed while listening to a sermon by the Buddha.

The importance of the mental attitude at the time of death is also apparent in stories about persons who miss being reborn in a heavenly mansion because their joyous attention to the Buddha was disturbed at the last minute. One such story concerns a "prodigal son" who turned to thievery after squandering his inheritance. He was apprehended and sentenced to death. Mogallana, a saint and leading disciple of the Buddha, out of compassion allowed the man to do an act of merit by giving him his last meal. The condemned man wisely did the meritorious deed and a joyous consciousness arose in him, but he lost his serene state of mind when, at the last minute before execution, his attention was diverted toward a young girl among the crowd of spectators. So he died with lustful rather than meritorious thoughts and was reborn as a miserable ghost rather than as a resident of a heavenly mansion.[47]

For Buddhists who had long dedicated themselves to meritorious practices, the time of death could be an occasion for the joyous remembrance of a lifetime of good works. One of the pious Buddhist kings of Ceylon at the time of his death became joyful and serene when his ministers read aloud from a book which recorded the acts of merit which he had commissioned during his long reign.[48] Presumably other kings and, perhaps, other laymen kept such "merit-books" as well.[49]

Buddhist thought discouraged reliance upon magical practices, but Buddhists came to feel that it was permissible and desirable to have the more powerful of the canonical passages recited at critical times such as at the hour of death and during the cremation ceremony. This belief in the power of chants to help determine the destiny of the deceased, deriving from folk belief, helped Buddhism compete against non-Buddhist, magical practices.

Some Mahāyāna Developments. Several developments in Mahāyāna practice, in addition to those already discussed, altered Buddhist thought concerning death. The most important of these was the Bodhisattva practice, in which the Buddhist vowed to become worthy of Nirvāṇa but then to postpone his entrance into Nirvāṇa in order to help other, lesser beings. The Bodhisattva who had spiritually advanced to the upper three of the ten levels of attainment was said to have eliminated the Karmic factors which necessitate rebirth, as had the early Buddhist Arhat; but unlike the Arhat, the Bodhisattva could share his store of merit with others. This means that the Bodhisattva voluntarily remained within Saṃsāra, the realm of death, in order to assist those who were still within death's grip. The practice of taking this Bodhisattva vow of compassion toward all beings altered the former Buddhist goal of putting an end to the wheel of death as soon as possible.

Early Buddhism believed that there had been numerous ancient Buddhas for earlier eras, but for this age the only fully enlightened, teaching Buddha was Gautama, the sage of the Śākya family. But some branches of Mahāyāna Buddhism held that there were innumerable Buddhas, each with a "Buddha-field" of heavenly paradise. By worshiping one of these Buddhas, the devotee could be assured of going to that Buddha's paradise after death. By far the most popular of these savior Buddhas was Amitabha (or Amitāyus), the Buddha of Boundless Light, who presided over a "Pure Land" in the West. Those who had faith in this Buddha and had paid homage to him could fearlessly face death confident in a salvation through grace by faith:

Beings are not born in that Buddha country of the Tathagāta Amitāyus as a reward and result of good works performed in this present life. No, whatever son or daughter of a family shall hear the name of the blessed Amitāyus, the Tathāgata, and having heard it, shall keep it in mind, and with thoughts undisturbed shall keep it in mind for one, two, three, four, five, six or seven nights—when that son or daughter of a family comes to die, then that Amitāyus, the Tathāgata, surrounded by an assembly of disciples and followed by a host of Bodhisattvas, will stand before them at their hour of death, and they will depart this life with tranquil minds. After their death they will be born in the world Sukhavati, in the Buddha country of the same Amitāyus, the Tathāgata. Therefore, then, O Sariputra, having perceived this cause and effect, I with reverence say thus, Every son and every daughter of a family ought with their whole mind to make fervent prayer for that Buddha country.[50]

This "Pure Land" Buddhism alters the earlier beliefs that Karma actions determine one's destiny after death, that a person faces death with only his own moral actions as refuge, and that existence in a heaven is temporary.

Another Mahāyāna development concerning death occurred within the important Mādhyamika school of Nāgārjuna, who undertook to harmonize the more recent "Perfection of Wisdom" texts with early Buddhist thought. In so doing he altered the early Buddhist distinction between the realm of flux and death (*saṃsāra*) and the realm of deathlessness (*nirvāṇa*). Nāgārjuna granted that in conventional, relative terms the distinction between Saṃsāra and Nirvāṇa is helpful, but absolutely speaking there is no difference between the two.[51]

The Tibetan Book of the Dead. The final Mahāyāna development which we shall consider had its roots in Indian Buddhism, but took its present shape in Tibet. The Tibetan Tantric Buddhists, whose Buddhism has been heavily influenced by Hatha Yoga, recite a text known as the *Bardo Thödol* to a dying person. *Bardo Thödol,* literally meaning "Liberation by Hearing on the After-Death Plane," has been translated into English under the title *The Tibetan Book of the Dead.*[52] Of the great amount of information on death in this book, a few brief comments may be in order here concerning the ritual function of the text and the nature of its teachings.

Ideally the Buddhist would have studied and memorized the *Bardo Thödol* long before the time of his death so that he could recite it himself as he dies. If he cannot recite it himself, then a priest recites it to him. Like its counterpart, the Egyptian book of the dead, the primary cultic function of this work is to assist the dead person in his journey through the realm of the dead. It is designed to help persons know how to die so as to be "reborn" in a pure state of consciousness. As Eliade has suggested, it has an initiatory function, with the familiar pattern of death and resurrection.[53]

The understanding of death implicit in the *Bardo Thödol* is basically Buddhist, but with important elaborations stemming from Tantric symbolism and ritual. The text describes three divisions of the state of death. The dying person first experiences the Chikhai Bardo, the state at the moment of death. After feeling the symptoms of death coming upon one and building up toward the moment of death itself, one typically swoons, which represents a loss of ordinary consciousness in the sense of the awareness of objects, whether external or imaginary. Then a great, bright, colorless light appears. If it is recognized and approached as the Void (*sūnyatā*), then liberation will be obtained immediately, for this clear light is the Dharma-kāya, the supreme essence of Buddhahood. If one fails to dwell in the light of the Void, a secondary, lesser clear light appears which can dispel the power of Karma. But one's bad Karma may cause one to miss this light too.

After some time in the first division of death, the deceased partially regains object-consciousness and the Chönyid Bardo state begins. Here, in a dreamlike state, one is aware that his own funeral is taking place, though at first he is not aware of his own death. Meanwhile, the priest recites into the ear of the corpse the part of the text which interprets the hallucinations which are about to occur. The text explains that for seven days peaceful deities will appear surrounded by bright lights, then for seven more days wrathful deities will appear in a very frightening manner. The text encourages the deceased not to fear these appearances, for both the good and the wrathful deities are merely manifestations from one's own mind. If these deities are meditated upon as such, liberation into the Sambhogakāya (Buddha Body of Bliss) will occur and the person will break the wheel of Saṃsāra, but voluntarily be born on earth as an enlightened teacher.

The third phase, the Sidpa Bardo, begins when the deceased perceives himself becoming embodied. He should recognize that this is merely a hallucinatory body and take steps to avoid actual reincarnation, for the imaginary body is a foreshadow of the body to come. A judgment by the Lord of Death takes place, with appropriate suffering in hell (temporarily) for those of demeritorious Karma. Then, by the power of one's Karma, the mind becomes fixed upon a certain realm into which one is about to be reborn. But even at this late stage rebirth can be avoided, or at least one's lot can be improved, by meditating on the hallucinations as manifestations of the Lord of Compassion, Avalokiteśvara, for instance. If all the gnostic instruction fails, reincarnation is inevitable and is said to occur on the forty-ninth day following death.

We see in the *Bardo Thödol* the underlying Buddhist conceptions of Saṃsāra versus liberation, of the six destinies or realms into which reincarnation is possible, and of the noble path to deliverance and release from bondage. The Tibetans have taken the Buddhist beliefs that knowledge is important for enlightenment and that the consciousness at the time of death is especially important for determining destiny and have written a cultic text of spiritual instruction for the benefit of the deceased. Despite the repeated attempts of the text to help the deceased make the right choices during his journey through the intermediate state, the fact is acknowledged that the deceased's bad Karma may prevent his taking advantage of the instruction.

Thus, from Gautama to the *Bardo Thödol* we again and again encounter the Buddhist notion of Vijñāna (consciousness) taking up a new destiny and body according to its past deeds, with enlightened liberation from death as the ultimate goal.

Death and Jain Thought

Much of that which has been said concerning death and Buddhist thought also applies to the other heterodox system of major importance, Jainism. Jain thought, like Buddhist, began with the judgment that existence is Saṃsāra and taught that the goal of spiritual achievement was total liberation from the chain of deaths. Like Buddhism, Jainism recognized the value of departing from secular responsibilities in order to practice asceticism and meditation. It, too, talked of previous holy men who had come to teach the path of liberation to earlier generations of Indians and glorified a great leader of the prevailing era who had conquered death.

Mahāvīra, the Conqueror. Jain legends attributed to their great leader, Mahāvīra, many of the same events and accomplishments that Buddhist stories told concerning Gautama. Jain texts[54] relate that Mahāvīra was born into a royal family in Northeast India, grew up in a princely manner surrounded with worldly pleasures, was wise and skillful even as a youth, married and had a daughter, and then at the age of thirty renounced the secular world in search of the enlightenment which would put an end to the wheel of births and its suffering. Mahāvīra practiced severe asceticism and disciplined meditation in quest of enlightenment for a period of twelve years, until at last:

Under a Sal tree, when the moon was in conjunction with the asterism Uttaraphalgunī (the Venerable One) in a squatting position with joined heels, exposing himself to the heat of the sun, after fasting two and a half days without drinking water, being engaged in deep meditation, [he] reached the highest knowledge and intuition, called Kevala, which is infinite, supreme, unobstructed, unimpeded, complete and full.[55]

Mahāvīra then undertook a teaching career and succeeded in bringing numerous followers into his order, which included four divisions consisting of monks, nuns, and male and female adherents. He is the twenty-fourth and last Tīrthaṅkara (pathfinder or founder of a religious order) in this world epoch. Mahāvīra taught his followers a path of ascetic practices and meditation designed to eventually liberate their souls from the bondage of embodiment. It is a foolish man, he taught, who longs for life and is oriented toward worldly pleasures. In contrast to the fool, the wise man is disciplined in spiritual practices and does not desire worldly wealth and pleasures. "Knowing birth and death, one should firmly walk the path. . . . For there is nothing inaccessible for death." [56]

Just as the death of the Buddha was understood to be a final Nirvāṇa, so the death of Mahāvīra was a Nirvāṇa which put an end to Saṃsāra and liberated his soul, freeing it to rise to its state of perfect knowledge and bliss. "In the fourth month of that rainy season . . . the Venerable Ascetic Mahāvīra died, went off, quitted the world, cut asunder the ties of birth, old age, and death; became a Siddha, a Buddha, a Mukta, a maker of the end (to all misery), finally liberated, freed from all pains." [57] Mahāvīra is said to be a *Jina* "conqueror," because he has conquered ignorance and death, and so his followers are called Jaina, "followers of the Jina."

The Jain World View. The Jains hold to a view of the exiled soul. The soul (*jīva*) is thought to be eternal, all-knowing, and pure by nature. However, millions of souls are in exile, in a state of embodiment in one or another of the levels of animate existence. Certain actions (*karma*) are responsible for the soul's continuing bondage. Liberation is possible if and only if this binding Karma can be eliminated. Until then, the soul remains within the material sphere and suffers again and again through birth, old age, and death. "*Sarvadarśanasaṃgraha* very beautifully summarizes the position when it says: 'Āśrava (inflow of *kārmic* matter causing misery) is the cause of mundane existence and Samvara (stoppage of that inflow) is the cause of liberation; this is the *Jaina* view (in short), everything else is only its amplification.' "[58]

These Jain doctrines are quite like those of the Buddhists, with the important exception that the Jains do not share the concept of no-soul (*anātman*). Whereas Buddhism, with its doctrine of no-soul and impermanence, stresses the flux and transitory nature of reality, Jainism holds that the real nature of reality is "permanency in transitoriness."[59] Jainism understands liberation to be the freedom of the eternal soul (*jīva*) from matter (*ajīva*), whereas the Buddhists say that the transmigrating consciousness (*vijñāna*) ceases to exist when liberation occurs. In Jain thought, death can be the occasion which allows the soul liberated from Karmic bondage to rise to the top of the universe. There the soul does not lose its identity, but rather reassumes its primal state of omniscience and bliss.[60]

Karma. Jainism denies the existence of a creating, judging God, as do the Buddhists, and places the responsibility for man's destiny upon man himself. The theory of Karmic determination proves capable of sustaining a systematic world view which, among other matters, accounts for how beings repeatedly suffer birth, decay and death and why there are inequalities among them. In this system Karma, conceived of as the finest material substance, performs the functions ascribed to a judging God in a theistic world view. Merit and demerit operate in such a way as to allow the soul which has done good works to be reborn in better and better destinies and progress toward enlightenment, while evildoers fall lower and lower as a result of each life of evil. The theory of Karma has never been understood as a matter of rigid determinism or fatalism in either Jainism or Buddhism. On the contrary, the Karmic world view looks upon the world as a moral realm which responds to human endeavor. As a contemporary spokesman writes, "Jainism brings us hope of justice in the form of (the) doctrine of Karman. As we sow, so shall we reap. Though there is no God who sits upon judgment on us, there is a law, based on the theory of cause and effect, which works automatically and unfailingly." [61]

Asceticism. It follows from the Karmic world view and the concept of the exiled soul that asceticism is the best spiritual method for achieving liberation, according to Jainism. Ascetic practices generate magical heat (*tapas*) which burns out previously generated Karma, and proper conduct and knowledge lessen the amount of new Karma which is generated. The path from hopeless bondage to complete deliverance has been divided into fourteen stages[62] in Jain thought, with a progressive ridding of Karma at each stage up to the twelfth, where spiritual perfection is such that actions do not produce either good or bad Karma. At the thirteenth stage knowledge is perfected, but the soul is still embodied. The fourteenth stage, the final release of the Jīva at the time of the death of the body, corresponds to the concept of Parinirvāṇa in Buddhist thought.

As in Buddhism, it was thought necessary to depart from the

world in order to pursue ascetic practices in utter seriousness. This may be seen as an initiatory "death," a dying to the world in order to be reborn into the ascetic path which will put an end to the wheel of deaths. The story of the son of Mṛja, whose father at first refused him permission to depart from the world into the ascetic life, reveals the seriousness with which the Jain monks took their task of overcoming Saṃsāra.

> He answered: 'O father and mother, it is even thus as you have plainly told; but in this world nothing is difficult for one who is free from desire.
>
> An infinite number of times have I suffered dreadful pains of body and mind, repeatedly misery and dangers.
>
> In the Saṃsāra, which is a mine of dangers and a wilderness of old age and death, I have undergone dreadful births and deaths.
>
> Though fire be hot here, it is infinitely more so there (viz. in hell); in hell I have undergone suffering from heat.
>
> Though there may be cold here, it is of infinitely greater intensity there; in hell I have undergone suffering from cold.' [63]

Nonviolence. The Ahiṃsā (nonviolence) strain of thought, which has been on Indian soil for centuries, flowered during the era of Mahāvīra and Gautama. Causing death was understood in this thought to be the fundamental sin, and man was tragically caught in a great dilemma, being torn between his physical need for meat and his spiritual need to avoid the impurity which comes upon the killer. Among the many solutions to this dilemma in the era we find a group of ascetics who minimized their demerit by limiting their meat slaughtering to one elephant once a year, and that one was killed by the group as a whole so that the demerit to any one person was not great.[64] Other groups turned to complete vegetarianism, while Gautama allowed his followers to eat meat only if the animal had been killed for others rather than for themselves.

The religious tradition into which Mahāvīra was born already embraced the concept of Ahiṃsā. Under Mahāvīra's leadership the practice of nonviolence received even greater attention. Besides being motivated to avoid killing due to the bad Karma that killing brought upon the killer, there was the other important motivation deriving from the Jain world view which sees an underlying sameness of nature and purpose among all living beings. Each possesses a soul engaged in a struggle upward toward liberation from material bondage. Other orders such as the Buddhists, the Ājīvikas and also the orthodox Brahmanic ascetics practiced Ahiṃsā, but the Jain monks and laymen were noted for being especially diligent concerning nonviolence. The first of the twelve vows for laymen was never to destroy any living creature which has more than one sense. This of course excluded Jains from the orthodox practice of animal sacrifice as well as from such occupations as hunting and fishing. The monk's first vow was even more comprehensive, for he vowed never to destroy any life, however small. For this reason he strained his drinking water and brushed aside any insects lest he might unintentionally crush them.

Jainism built an ethical system upon the Ahiṃsā foundation.[65] Like the Buddhists, the Jains understand Ahiṃsā to prohibit causing harm of any kind. Thus, Ahiṃsā prohibits harming others as well as speaking or acting in such a way as to possibly incite anyone else to violence. And, reasoning that "thought is the father of action," the Ahiṃsā ethic requires the Jain to avoid harmful thoughts stemming from immoderate desire (passion) and immoderate dislike (aversion).[66]

The Ascetic Practice of Dying. Like the Buddhist texts, the Jain sees one's fear of death as a sign of spiritual immaturity. There are said to be two types of death, according to whether or not the factor of anxiety is present: "These two ways of life ending with death have been declared: death with one's will, and death against one's will. Death against one's will is that of ignorant men, and it happens (to the same individual) many times. Death with one's will is that of wise men, and at best it happens but once."[67]

The man who has lived an evil life begins to tremble in the hour of death when he thinks of the suffering in hell and the evil lives he has generated for himself by his bad actions (*karma*). In his hour of death he wishes to turn back. He longs to be on a different course, but it is too late. "As a charioteer, who against his better judgment leaves the smooth highway and gets on a rugged road, repents when the axle breaks; so the fool, who transgresses the Law and embraces unrighteousness, repents in the hour of death, like (the charioteer) over the broken axle."[68] "Then when death comes at last, the fool trembles in fear; he dies the 'death against one's will,' (having lost his chance) like a gambler vanquished by Kali."[69] The text further warns that an outward facade of piety or even a life lived as a monk will not save one from hell and suffering if one has inwardly been following an evil path.

The hour of death is said to be completely different in the case of the wise man who has diligently followed the right path through the years. The wise man will have considered the alternative ways of living and their consequences long before his death and will have chosen to follow the ethical way. Then, when the time of his death approaches, he does not tremble with anxiety, but remains calm with an undisturbed mind. "When the right time (to prepare for death) has arrived, a faithful (monk) should in the presence (of his teacher) suppress all emotions (of fear or joy) and wait for the dissolution of his body. When the time for quitting the body has come, a sage dies the 'death with one's will,' according to one of the three methods."[70]

The principle involved in the death with one's will is that one should conquer death by facing it directly with self-control and serenity. The procedure for doing this in Jain practice is as follows. When a saint senses that death is not far away, he should prepare for it over a period of time as long as twelve years if possible. Knowing that the soul is immortal by nature and that it is miserable while imprisoned in matter, the saint undertakes a death of self-control which will liberate him completely or at least greatly lessen the number of reincarnations through which he will have to live before final liberation is accomplished. Seeking to die the death of a wise man or, perhaps, even the death of a wise man among wise men (*pandita-pandita*), he finds a spot where he will not be unduly disturbed and begins a program of fasting which will eventually bring about his bodily demise. He begins by avoiding milk, curds, ghee, oils, sugar, and salt and eventually reduces his intake of food and drink to the absolute minimum for sustaining consciousness. As the months go by he practices meditation more and more, at first perfecting his control over his body and then practicing mind control. If the desire to eat or drink is disturbing his concentration, he thinks of the amount of food and drink he must have ingested through the course of his innumerable lives and, thus, comes to see that the satisfaction which material food brings is minimal compared to the eternal bliss of liberation.

The saint may choose one of three methods with reference to the care of his body while he slowly dies. The highest and most difficult method does not allow his bodily needs to be attended to, either by himself or by others. The second and slightly less meritorius method permits him to look after his own needs to some extent. A third approach allows other saints and pious laymen to attend upon him while he practices these final penances. If the latter approach is employed, the attendants encourage him by citing the accomplishments of former saints who conquered death in this way.

When death is immediately at hand, he continues his firm resolve, self-control, and meditative attitude to the very end. "Thus filled with the spirit of holiness and *vairāgya*, he recites the great Obeisance *mantram* (auspicious formula) till the mortal coil is shuffled off, and *sallekhanā* terminates in a rebirth in the soul-enrapturing scenery and surroundings of the heavenly regions, the abodes of *devas*," [71] or in the case of final liberation, his soul returns to its primal place at the top of the universe where it eternally dwells in perfect bliss and knowledge.

Both Jainism and Buddhism, then, begin with the judgment that reincarnation repeatedly occurs until death is conquered once and for all times. This attempt to conquer death, thus putting an end to Saṃsāra and its multitude of suffering, is the *raison d'être* of these religious movements. It is for this purpose that the Compassionate Ones build up their perfections, strive, become enlightened, and teach. And with the same goal in mind, millions have followed these two paths to conquer death and win eternal bliss.

Death and the Ājīvikas

A North Indian contemporary of Gautama named Makkhali Gośāla was the leader of a heretical sect of "Ājīvika" ascetics which, though not so influential or well known as Buddhism and Jainism, continued in existence for approximately two thousand years and spread as far as South India. The Ājīvikas held an atomist view of reality and believed in an underlying principle of order known as Niyati which was thought to determine both natural phenomena and human actions. The Buddhist Sāmaññaphala Sūtra ascribed to Makkhali Gośāla the teaching that there is "no human action, no strength, no courage, no human endurance or human prowess (which can affect one's destiny in this life)." [72]

It was this deterministic doctrine which denied Karmic causation that led Gautama Buddha to denounce the Ājīvikas and fear their influence. One passage in the Majjhima Nikāya ascribed to Gautama the extreme statement that in the last ninety-one Kalpas there had been only one Ājīvika reborn in heaven, and he was an *unorthodox* Ājīvika who believed in Karmic causation.[73] Such hostile relations between the Ājīvikas and the Buddhist Bhikkhus seem to have been common, yet Basham also finds evidence of friendly relations between the two groups. The best example of rapport occurs in the Buddhist Vināya (ii. 284) account of how an Ājīvika ascetic, using the most respectful terms of address, informed Mahākassapa of the Parinibbāna of Gautama.[74]

Despite their animadversions, the world-renouncing monks of the Jain, Buddhist, and Ājīvika traditions had much in common. They each seem to have accepted all castes into their orders and to have drawn their greatest support from the mercantile and industrial classes. Likewise, each rejected or at least downgraded the Vedic gods and developed psychologies which differed from the Upaniṣadic speculations on Ātman.

Suicide. Like the Jain ascetics, the Ājīvikas held to the ideal of ending one's life by a spiritually meaningful suicide. But unlike the Jain technique of slow starvation, the Ājīvikas seem to have practiced an agonizing death by thirst. The practitioner of this self-induced death, the ultimate penance, first of all abstained from drinking ordinary water or juices and limited himself to the "four drinks" allowable to one practicing extreme asceticism: (1) water which has fallen from a cow's back (or perhaps the meaning is cow urine); (2) water which has been handled and is dirty, such as the water used in pottery making; (3) stale water which has been exposed to the sun; (4) water which has run over a rock.

Then, in the final days of his dying, the ascetic drank no fluids at all, but rather tormented himself with four "substitutes for fluids": (1) holding an empty metal pot as if it held water, (2) holding an unripe mango or other fruit in the mouth without drinking its juices, (3) holding an unripe Simbali-bean or certain other seeds in the mouth without drinking the juice, (4) drinking the "pure drink" (a vague reference to some final act of penance).[75]

There is an indication that the ritual suicide was to be extended over a six-month period, during which time the ascetic probably developed illnesses such as a fever brought on by bad food and drink. The posture prescribed for the Ājīvika ascetic during this time was to lie for two months each on the ground, on wood, and finally on Darbha grass. When the end was near, two gods would appear to the ascetic, perhaps while he was in a state of delirium produced by the fever. The gods would offer to soothe the fever of the ascetic, but he must refuse the offer lest he lose some of his reservoir of psychic heat.[76]

Finally, by turning his own psychic heat upon himself, the ascetic burned himself to death and achieved liberation. From the Ājīvika point of view this liberation was the ultimate bliss, Nirvāṇa, but both the Buddhist commentator, Buddhaghosa, and the Jain commentator, Mādhavacandra, looked upon the "Nirvāṇa" which the Ājīvika ascetics attained as being merely a rebirth in a high heaven; i.e., as being less than ultimate Nirvāṇic release from the chain of deaths.[77]

The Cārvāka Denial of Afterlife

The last heretical system we shall consider might be called the denier among deniers, for the Cārvākas' dissension from Brahmanic orthodoxy was complete. They not only denied the authority of the

Vedas, the efficacy of Vedic chanting, and the existence of a judging God; they went far beyond the other heretical systems to deny altogether the existence of spiritual realities. The Cārvākas refused to accept any claim which was not based upon empirical evidence and so did not believe in God, a spiritual soul, or an afterlife. Instead, these radical empiricists acknowledged only this world and its values. Unfortunately, the school's principle text, written around 600 B.C., is not extant, so the following information on early Indian materialism and death is based upon polemical references to materialists in works of rival schools of thought.

The question of the nature of the human self or soul was extremely important in early Indian thought, so we shall begin by noting the radical position which the materialists took concerning the Ātman. The Cārvākas held that human life or consciousness arose out of the material elements which combine to form the human body. According to a Jain work, the materialists held that earth, water, fire, and air were the only realities and that consciousness was generated out of these elements as fire is generated by wood and friction or as "spirits" emerge from wine.[78] They denied that the consciousness of man preexists its embodiment. There can be no consciousness in the foetus, they argued, for the foetus' sense organs are not well developed and besides there are no objects to be sensed.[79] In short, "The soul or the self (*ātman*) is born with the body, lives with the body, and dies with the body: it is completely a this-world manifestation, a natural phenomenon." [80]

The Cārvākas' radical denial of the soul was made all the more serious by their total denial of Karma. As a contemporary Jain interpreter writes, "Cārvāka represented a common man's view that either lack of worldly possessions or some mental or physical disability is the cause of misery. This is the first answer that reason afforded to the question." [81] A text in the Jain canon long ago denounced those "fools" who teach as follows: "Everybody, fool or sage, has an individual soul. These souls exist (as long as the body), but after death they are no more; there are no souls which are born again. There is neither virtue nor vice, there is no world beyond; on the dissolution of the body the individual ceases to be." [82] The Cārvākas, then, denied Karmic causation both within one life and from life to life, and they denounced the notions of heaven and hell which gave the doctrine of Karma its homiletical power.

The Cārvāka ethic which followed upon its antispiritual orientation was purely secular. A contemporary critic summarizes their position: "In Ethics the Cārvāka regards sensual pleasure as the *summum bonum* in life. Eat, drink and be merry, for once the body is reduced to ashes, there is no hope of coming back here again." [83] The same critic denounces Cārvāka as a crude individual hedonism which eliminated two of the four traditional goals of Indian ethics, Dharma and Mokṣa.[84] We do not have statements from the Cārvākas sufficient to evaluate their secularism, however. It is apparent, though, that their disparagement of both Dharma and asceticism brought upon them the condemnation of both orthodox Brahmins and the ascetic Nāstikas.[85]

In conclusion, with reference to the understanding of death, the Cārvākas really have nothing in common with the three Kevalin (liberation) systems we have considered. The Kevalins speak of death as the problem from which the soul is to be liberated, while the Cārvākas say that death itself is liberation. The Kevalins fear the wheel of death, whereas the Cārvākas glory in the pleasure of living. The Kevalins call persons to a highly disciplined path of self-denial for the purpose of attaining an ultimate goal after life, while the Cārvākas denounce ultimate goals and their requisite disciplines.

Conclusion

The systems of thought dealt with in this chapter were not regarded as parts of a unified movement, but *in general* the Buddhists, Jains and Ājīvikas shared a common world view concerning death. With the qualification that the following comments are generalizations with regard both to the Nāstika systems and to the Hinduism of early India, some remarks on embodiment and defilement may be of interest.

Embodiment. What distinguished the Nāstika systems from the orthodox strains of Hinduism with reference to death is the comparative absence of the sacrificial theology so important in the Vedic Brahmanism of early India. Brahmanic sacrificial theology held a positive attitude toward embodiment and death. It was precisely because it took embodied life so seriously and with a sense of awe that it offered up life itself to the cosmic powers. Furthermore, sacrificial theology pictured the life-giving powers of the sky as being embodied, though in a heavenly fashion. The sacrificers' gods were themselves eaters, enjoyers of the sacrifice. They desired to feast upon a portion of the fruit of the earth which they themselves had caused to be grown. Man, the creature appointed by the gods to harvest the fruit of the land and sacrificially return a portion of it to the gods, was thought to have an earthly body, but a heavenly purpose. And as his reward for his role in the sacrificial cycle, he was to exchange his body of clay for a heavenly body when he died. Thus, the sacrificial theology provided man with a canopy of meaning under which to live his days, a purpose which gave his life meaning, and a feeling of confidence in the face of death.

When the Nāstika systems denied the Vedas and took exception to the animal sacrifice in particular, they cut themselves off from the traditional means for communicating with the deity, sacrifice. This loss of confidence in sacrifice as the ultimate means of overcoming human finitude in general and death in particular created a vacuum of spiritual means which the Nāstika systems filled by employing ascetic practices long known on Indian soil. In the systems which evolved from this process the grand Brahmanic program of sacrificing the fruit of the earth was changed to the practice of "sacrificial" giving. The role of giving was very important in these systems, therefore, and became the main means for gaining rebirth in heaven. The Nāstika systems, however, reduced the (sacrificial) goal of winning a heavenly world to a position of secondary status and substituted for it the goal of complete liberation from embodiment as the *summum bonum*.

The Nāstika systems, in contrast to the sacrificially based Vedism, did not look upon embodiment positively. They were extremely diligent in respecting life, but not in the same way as sacrificers. The Nāstika ascetics respected life as spirit and so minimized the importance of the bodily dimension of existence. From their point of view the bodily differences between the human and the insect, to take an extreme case, were less important than the similarities in spirit. The sacrificer religiously killed animals because he saw a continuity between the animal's embodied life and his own, while the ascetic religiously avoided killing animals because he saw a continuity between the animal's spirit and his own.

Defilement. Paul Ricoeur's analysis of the symbolism of evil in Western consciousness reveals that a sense of defilement is at the base of all conceptions of evil. He believes that the basic feeling of defilement has become overlaid with a feeling of guilt before others and an awareness of sin before God.[86] Early Indians, like the Greeks and Hebrews Ricoeur considers, also seem to have had the feeling of defilement at the base of their consciousnes of evil.

Given the Nāstikas' negative attitude toward embodiment, it is understandable that defilement was a concept of primary importance in their systems. For them the basic defilement is embodiment itself, and the underlying reasons why such normal human events as birth, old age, and death were looked upon as suffering is, not so much that they cause pain and sorrow, but that they epitomize embodiment, and embodiment gives rise to the anxiety of being defiled. Saṃsāra is embodiment, embodiment is defilement, and defilement produces anxiety. Hence, in the highest conception even good Karma is to be avoided because it leads to further embodiment, and no imaginable state of embodiment (destiny) can contain enough sensual gratifications to overcome the underlying defilement of embodiment.

The orthodox could deal with the threat of defilement through obedience to Dharma and by the performance of purification rituals. The Nāstika ascetics, on the other hand, had cut themselves off from the possibility of justification by purification rituals or by adhering to the Dharma (in the orthodox sense of following the class duties and prescribed sacrifices). The Nāstika alternative was to burn out defilement, especially by mystical heat (*tapas*), and thereby permanently overcome the limitations of embodiment. Once liberated, the person would no longer dwell in the area of materiality and death and would no longer experience a limitation on his knowledge, happiness, or life-span. He, even more than the gods, would have completely conquered death.

Many adherents to the Nāstika systems did not think of themselves as striving in the present life to completely eradicate death. They derived meaning from giving support to the holy ones who were on the highest path. This role distinction, which roughly corresponded to the distinction between laymen and monk, led to a situation in which the average layman had the immediate goal of being reborn (temporarily) in a heavenly world. In this respect the Nāstika lay adherent was not especially distinct from his orthodox counterpart. On the other hand, the Nāstika monk of the sixth century B.C., having taken up a path which was clearly an alternative to the orthodox one, lived in a world of meaning and practice concerning death which made him quite distinct from his traditional counterpart, the Brahmin priest.

Notes

1. *The Path of Purity,* trans. Pe Maung Tin (London: Luzac and Co. for The Pali Text Society, 1923 and 1971), p. 596.
2. I do not mean to imply that Heidegger's use of this term exactly parallels Buddhist thought.
3. Majjhima Nikāya I. no. 22, quoted from Gunaratne, "The Significance of the Four Noble Truths," *The Wheel,* no. 123 (1968), p. 7.
4. Akira Hirakawa, "The Rise of Mahāyāna Buddhism and Its Relationship to the Worship of Stupas," *Memoirs of the Research Department of the Toyo Bunko,* No. 22 (1963), 57-106.
5. Jan Gonda, "Loka; World and Heaven in the Veda," *Verhandelingen der Koninhlijke Nederlandse Akademie van Wetenschappen,* 73 (1966); 114-115.
6. *Ibid.,* pp. 41-42.
7. Muṇḍaka Upaniṣad I. 2. 1. (*eṣa vaḥ panthaḥ sukṛtasya loke*).
8. Compare the description of the path of light in the Chāndogya Upaniṣad v. 10. 1.
9. Muṇḍaka Upaniṣad I. 2. 6. (*eṣa vaḥ puṇyas sukṛto brahmolokah*).
10. Atharva Veda v. 18. 13. All English translations are those of the author unless otherwise noted.
11. Gonda, "Loka," p. 148.
12. Kaivalya Upaniṣad, verse 22.
13. Samyutta Nikāya, I. 22. (Unless noted otherwise, citations of Theravada

Texts refer to the volume and page of the Pali text as published by Luzac and Co. for the Pali Text Society.)

14. Samyutta Nikāya, I. 182.
15. Sutta-nipāta no. 636 and Dhammapada no. 412. The underlying concept here, that of overcoming defilement, will be discussed at length in the section on Jainism and death.
16. Dhammapada no. 126.
17. Sutta-nipāta no. 235.
18. For example, Milindapañha pp. 70-73.
19. Samyutta Nikāya III. 251.
20. The criticism of Western interpretations of Nirvāṇa applies primarily to works written by nonspecialists. For a thorough discussion of Western works see Guy Richard Welbon, *The Buddhist Nirvāṇa and Its Western Interpreters* (Chicago: University of Chicago Press, 1968). Two recent publications, one Western and one Buddhist, provide good discussions of the doctrine of Nirvāṇa according to the Theravada canonical texts: P. Vajirañāna Thera and Francis Story, "The Buddhist Doctrine of Nibbāna," *The Wheel,* publication no. 165-166 (Kandy, Ceylon: Buddhist Publication Society, 1971); Rune Johansson, *The Psychology of Nirvāṇa* (London: George Allen and Unwin, 1969).
21. Vajirañāna Thera, "The Buddhist Doctrine of Nibbāna," p. 21. (The paragraphs are quoted in reverse order.)
22. Subhādra Bhikshu, *A Buddhist Catechism* (New York: Brentano's, 1920), p. 40.
23. *Khandha,* the five "groupings" of which an existent being is composed.
24. Anguttara Nikāya, I. 158-159.
25. Majjhima Nikāya I. 485-486. The term "view-going" (*ditthigatam*) refers to the practice of wasting time on arguing for speculative positions which are not relevant to enlightenment.
26. Majjhima Nikāya I. 486-488.
27. Suicide is not normally advised in Buddhist thought, as will be discussed in the section on the Ājīvikas, but Godhika's case is special in that this seemed to be the only way he could arrange to have a pure mind at the time of death.
28. Samyutta Nikāya, I. 122.
29. Suttā-nipāta no. 1119 and Dhammapada no. 170.
30. Buddhaghosa, Vissudhimagga, p. 229.
31. Visuddhimagga, p. 230.
32. Compare Jesus' parable of the rich man "secure" with his many full barns.
33. An exception would have to be made in the case of a saint who, having developed his mindfulness of respiration, can know how long he will live (Visuddhimagga, p. 292).
34. Visuddhimagga, chap. 8.
35. Visuddhimagga, pp. 193-94.

36. Anguttara Nikāya 1. 155-56.
37. Majjhima Nikāya 1, 36-37.
38. Sutta-nipāta no. 576.
39. Khuddaka-pātha.
40. Dhammapada no. 331.
41. Anguttara Nikāya IV. 39-40.
42. Vimānavatthu and Petavatthu.
43. A good article on this phenomenon, the beliefs in various traditions concerning the time of death, is Franklin Edgerton, "The Hour of Death," *Annals of the Bhandarkar Oriental Institute*, 8 (1926-27); 219-49.
44. This is based on the generally accepted scholarly opinion that the books of the last division of suttas, the Khuddaka Nikāya, such as the Petavatthu and the Vimānavatthu are relatively late compositions.
45. Vimānavatthu, no. 83.
46. *Ibid.*, no. 53.
47. Petavatthu, no. 1.
48. Mahavāmsa, chap. 32.
49. Walpola Rahula, *History of Buddhism in Ceylon* (Colombo: M. D. Gunasena and Co., 1956), p. 254.
50. The Smaller Sukhāvati-vyūha, number 10, trans. by Max Müller, in E. B. Cowell, ed., *Buddhist Mahāyāna Texts*, The Sacred Books of the East, vol. 49, part 2, pp. 98-99.
51. Mūlamadhyamakakārika, XXV. 20.
52. W. Y. Evans-Wentz, ed., *The Tibetan Book of the Dead* (Oxford: Oxford University Press, 1927). The paperback edition (1960) includes informative forewords by Carl Jung, Lāma Anagarika Govinda, and Sir John Woodroff.
53. Mircea Eliade. *Yoga: Immortality and Freedom* (New York: Pantheon Books, 1958), pp. 221, 272, 362.
54. The Jain text I am primarily following here is the Kalpa Sūtra, a work of the Śvetambara School of Jainism.
55. Hermann Jacobi, trans., *Jaina Sūtras,* The Sacred Books of the East, volumes 22 (1884) and 54 (1895), (reprint ed.; New York: Dover Publications, 1968), pt. 1, p. 263.
56. *Ibid.*, p. 19.
57. *Ibid.*, pp. 264-65.
58. Dayanand Bhargava, *Jaina Ethics* (Delhi: Motilal Benarsidass, 1968), p. 11.
59. *Ibid.*, p. 12.
60. *Ibid.*, p. 72.
61. *Ibid.*, p. 222.
62. For details see, for example, A. Guérninot, *La religion Djaina: histoire, doctrine, culte, coutumes, institutions* (Paris: Paul Geuthner, 1926), pp. 266 f.
63. Jacobi, *Jaina Sūtras,* part 2, p. 93.
64. J. C. Jaina, *Life in Ancient India as depicted in the Jaina Canons* (Bombay: New Book Co., 1947).

65. Brahmanic orthodoxy to some extent also built an ethic on Ahiṃsa. Vegetarianism eventually prevailed, of course, and there are references in the Mahābhārata to nonviolence as the supreme Dharma. That epic also contains the famous ethical summary based upon the principle of Ahiṃsa. "Thou shalt not do to others what is disagreeable to thyself." (Bhargava, *Jaina Ethics*, p. 105)
66. Bhargava. *Jaina Ethics*, pp. 62 f. and pp. 106 f.
67. Jacobi, *Jaina Sutras*, part 2, p. 20.
68. *Ibid.*, p. 22.
69. *Ibid.*
70. *Ibid.*, p. 24.
71. Champat Rai Jain, *Sannyāsa Dharma* (Allahabad: The Beledere Press, n.d.), p. 132.
72. Although the Ājīvikas had writings like the Jains and Buddhists, these texts have been lost and thus the reconstruction of Ājīvika thought on death or any other topic is very tenuous. My main source has been Professor A. L. Basham's doctoral thesis, published as *History and Doctrines of the Ājīvikas* (London: Luzac and Co., 1951), which is an excellent scholarly effort to characterize the school based primarily upon a few inscriptions and the numerous (pejorative) references to Ājīvikas made in the texts of rival sects. The reference from the Buddhist Sāmaññaphala Sūtra is cited by Basham on page 13.
73. Basham, *History and Doctrine of the Ājīvikas*, pp. 134-35.
74. *Ibid.*, p. 136.
75. *Ibid.*, p. 128.
76. *Ibid.*, pp. 128-31.
77. *Ibid.*, p. 261.
78. Bhargava, *Jaina Ethics*, p. 47, citing from the Sarvadarśanasangha.
79. J. Sinha, *A History of Indian Philosophy* (Calcutta: Sinha Publishing House, 1956), vol. 1, p. 246.
80. Dale Riepe, *The Naturalistic Tradition in Indian Thought* (Seattle: University of Washington Press, 1961), p. 68.
81. Bhargava, *Jaina Ethics*, p. 53.
82. Jacobi, *Jaina Sutras*, Pt. 2, p. 237.
83. Chandradhar Sharma, *A Critical Survey of Indian Philosophy* (Delhi: Motilal Banarsidass, 1960), p. 46.
84. *Ibid.*
85. For examples of the Buddhist condemnation of materialism, see, for instance, J. P. Abs, "Some Early Buddhist Texts in Relation to the Philosophy of Materialism in India," *Actes du XVIIIe Congrés-international des Orientalistes* (Leiden, 1932), pp. 157 ff.
86. Paul Ricoeur, *The Symbolism of Evil* (New York: Harper and Row, 1967), pp. 3-150.

V

Modern Hindu Thought

K. L. SHESHAGIRI RAO

The phenomenon of death has a perennial fascination to the human mind. It is the most common, yet least understood phenomenon in nature. It is one of the most difficult problems of philosophy. It has exercised the minds of serious thinkers all over the world; poets and philosophers, saints and sages have pondered the theme of death. Indeed man alone can reflect on death; his concern and struggle with death raise for him the question of the meaning of life. Although death is generally feared, dreaded, and concealed, it continues to challenge men to come to grips with life. "The interest in the theme has not yet died, nor will it die so long as human nature exists. Various answers have been presented to the world by various minds. Thousands, again, in every period of history have given up the discussion, and yet the question remains fresh as ever. Often in the turmoil and the struggle of our lives we seem to forget it, but suddenly someone dies—one perhaps whom we loved, one near and dear to our hearts, is snatched away from us—and the struggle, the din, and the turmoil of the world around us cease for a moment, and the soul asks the old question, 'What after this? What becomes of the soul?' "[1]

The present essay attempts to delineate the understanding of death in modern Hinduism as expressed in the lives and thoughts of some of its outstanding representatives and spokesmen—Rabindranath Tagore, Śrī Aurobindo, Mahatma Gandhi, and Radhakrishnan. These modern Hindu thinkers combine in themselves a profound knowledge of their own cultural heritage and a thorough acquaintance with Western thought and culture. Although rooted in their own tradition, they look at the problem of death as a distinctively human problem with universal implications. They recognize the bonds of common humanity and common mortality that bind all men together. However, their attitudes to and reflections on the phenomenon of death are developed in the background of certain fundamental Hindu concepts as discussed in previous chapters (*avidyā, saṃsāra, karma, mokṣa,* etc.). The poet and the sage, the saint and the philosopher go beyond the dichotomy of life and death and bear witness to the fact that there is something deeper than death which integrates both and provides guidance to the practical path of life's fulfillment.

Rabindranath Tagore[2]
Death: The Messenger of God

I was not aware of the moment when
I first crossed the threshold of this life.
What was the power that made me
open out into this vast mystery like a
bud in the forest at midnight!
  When in the morning I looked upon
the light I felt in a moment that I was
no stranger in this world, that the inscrutable
without name and form had taken
in its arms in the form of my mother.
  Even so, in death the same unknown
will appear as ever known to me. And because I
love this life, I know I shall love death as well.
  The child cries out when from the
right breast, the mother takes it away, in the very
next moment to find in the left one its consolation.[3]

Rabindranath Tagore was not a philosopher—in the academic sense of the term—but a poet, first and foremost. To him poetry was more than a craft; it was a worship of the Divine Artist, the creator of the universe. The consciousness of the divine presence in all things was the source of his mystical poetry. He sang: "The same stream of life that runs through my veins night and day runs through the world and dances in rhythmic measures. It is the same life that shoots in joy through the dust of the earth in numberless blades of grass and breaks into tumultuous waves of leaves and flowers. It is the same life that is rocked in the ocean-cradle of birth and death, in ebb and in flow" (*Gitanjali,* p. 65). Tagore sought God in daily experiences, in the joys and sorrows of everyday life. His poems were his individual responses to life's varied experiences. They were the "unconscious expression of his soul, the outpourings of his devotional heart."[4] Tagore sought to understand himself through his work. The experience of death, in particular the deaths of those near him, was repeatedly explored. We should, therefore, turn to his life and poetry to ascertain his attitude towards and responses to the universal phenomenon of death.

Tagore felt a deep love of nature. The absolute separateness of nature and God was unacceptable to him. It was through nature that he encountered, responded to, and adored the Divine. He saw the same light dwelling both in the world of nature outside and the world of the spirit within. Tagore was eighteen when he had a profound religious experience for the first time:

> One morning I happened to be standing on the verandah. . . . The sun was just rising through the leafy tops of those trees. As I continued to gaze, all of a sudden a covering seemed to fall away from my eyes, and I found the world bathed in a wonderful radiance, with waves of beauty and joy swelling on every side.[5]

I suddenly felt as if some ancient mist had in a moment lifted from my sight, and the morning light on the face of the world revealed an inner radiance of joy. The invisible screen of the commonplace was removed from all things and all men, their ultimate significance was intensified in my mind.[6]

This vision brought home to his mind an awareness of the divine presence behind the phenomenon of nature and of the awesome depths and transcendent meaning of the mundane. The commonplace facts of life "found a great unity of meaning," the fragments lost their isolation, and the world revealed the creative joy of the Supreme: "the joy that makes the earth flow over in riotous excess of the grass, the joy that sets the twin brothers, life and death, dancing over the wide world, the joy that sweeps in with the tempest, shaking and waking all life with laughter, the joy that sits still with tears on the open red lotus of pain, and the joy that throws everything it has upon the dust and knows not a word" (*Gitanjali*, p. 58). After four days the vision faded. But again and again, throughout his life the veil was rent by sudden experiences of heightened consciousness.

Tagore's first encounter with the terrible reality of death took place at the age of twenty-four, when his dearly loved sister-in-law, who had taken the place of his mother,[7] suddenly committed suicide. It was a terrible tragedy and first great sorrow of his life. Till then, he had not realized that there could be "gaps in life's familiar patchwork of smiles and tears." When death created a sudden gaping void, he felt utterly lost. He asked himself whether life and death could ever be reconciled. His ponderings on the meaning and purpose of death led him to a most dramatic "breakthrough" which discloses the greatest turning point in his attitude toward death.

The bottomless chasm of darkness which had thus appeared in my life seemed to exercise a kind of fascination over me and to draw me to its brink day and night. I would stand on its edge and gaze below into darkness, wondering what was left in place of what has been. The human mind cannot understand absolute emptiness and imagines that what is not must be unreal and what is unreal is not. Hence our unceasing search to find something where we see nothing. Just as a plant hemmed in by darkness stretches itself upward to gain access to light, even so when death puts up its black screen of negation and says, it is not there, the mind of man struggles desperately to break through the screen of darkness into the light of affirmation. But when one discovers that the way out of darkness is itself shrouded in darkness, what agony can equal this?

And yet in the midst of suffocating darkness, there would suddenly blow over my heart, now and again, a breeze of gladness taking me by surprise. The painful realization that life was not everlasting itself turned into a source of comfort. That we were not prisoners for ever within the impregnable walls of life's solid actuality—this indeed was welcome tidings to gladden the heart. I had to let go what I had clung to—so long as I viewed this fact as my own loss I was unhappy, but when I learnt to look at it from the point-of-view of life being liberated through death, a great peace fell on my spirit. . . . As this sense of detachment grew within me, Nature's beauty assumed a deeper significance on my tear washed eyes. Her death had given me the necessary distance and detachment to see life and world in their wholeness, in their true perspective, and as I looked at the picture of life painted on the vast canvas of death, it seemed to be truly beautiful.[8]

Tagore had to face later many bereavements—of his wife, father, two daughters, son, elder brother, grandson, etc.; death ceased to be a stranger in the family. However, even upon the death of his wife whom he dearly loved, his son relates that "his inward peace was not disturbed." Passing through the baptism of death, he attained a spiritual poise that gave his sorrows the dignity of tragedy and his joys the strength of understanding. Knowledge of death gave a new depth and richness to his knowledge of life. He felt continuity of experience between life and death. In the light of death, he saw the truth of undying life. "Life in its progress has ever and again to face death's challenge, seeking to halt it and lay it low, but death always is beaten by life; always after annihilating death, life fulfills itself in new and dynamic forms." [9] Tagore did not fear death anymore. When his grandson died, he wrote:

> You seemed from afar
> Titanic in your mysterious majesty and terror.
> With palpitating heart I stood before your presence,
> Your knitted brows boded ill
> And sudden came down the blow
> With a growl and a crash.
> With bowed head I waited
> For the final fury to come.
> It came.
> And I wondered, could this all be the menace?
> With your weapon in suspense,
> You looked mighty big.
> To strike me you came down
> To where I crouched low on the ground.
> You suddenly became small
> And I stood up.
> From thence there was only pain for me
> But no fear.
> Great you are as death itself
> But your victim is greater than death.[10]

The mystery of life never ceased to fascinate Tagore. He loved life passionately and would never turn away from it. The pain he suffered, the cruelty and sordidness he witnessed, instead of causing a revulsion of life made him love his kind all the more. Indeed, his profound understanding of life was the result of deeply experienced sorrow and loneliness. He had sought God in beauty and found him in sorrow. To suffer pain is the right of man; he is born to it and reaches his aim through it. For without pain and death, there can be neither love nor joy.

By the ocean-side of creation
I woke up.
I found that the world
Was not a dream
In letters of blood
I saw my own frame.
I came to know myself
With every hurt, with every pain.
Truth is hard,
I came to love that truth . . .
It never cheats one,
A sorrowful penance in this life
Till the very end.
To receive the hard reward of truth
The debt has to be paid in full
By the way of death.[11]

Tagore looked upon death as the obverse of life and as one with it. "The game of life consists of both life and death, as walking consists of raising the foot and bringing it down." [12] He held that life is ever moving and renewing itself, and death is what helps to renew it. "And thus life, which is an incessant explosion of freedom, finds its metre in a continual falling back in death. Every day is death, every moment even. If not, there would be amorphous desert of deathlessness eternally dumb and still." [13] Life is replenished with death, and death never dies. "Death does not hurt us, but disease does, because disease constantly reminds us of health and yet withholds it from us." [14] In the progress towards perfection, man owing to the weakness of his flesh has to renew his body, and this renewal is what we call death. Tagore in his seventy-seventh year suddenly fell ill and suffered a total lack of consciousness for two days. After his recovery, he described his experience:

This body of mine—
The carrier of the burden past—

Seemed to me like an exhausted cloud
Slipping off from the listless arm
Of the morning.
I felt freed from its clasp
In the heart of an incorporeal light
At the farthest shore of evanescent things.[15]

And in a poem addressed to the Lord of Life (*Jīvan-devatā*), he expresses the wish for the renewal of the old in new forms:

But have my days come to their end at last,
  Lord of my life,
While my arms round thee grow limp,
My kisses losing their truth?
Then break up the meeting of this languid day.
Renew the old in me in fresh forms of delight;
And let the wedding come once again
In a new ceremony of life.[16]

Tagore believed in a developing continuity of life, an evolution both physical and spiritual pointing to higher levels of being yet unreached. He looked upon death as a preparation for fuller life. The soul has to pass through many lives before the goal is reached. "Thou hast made me endless, such is thy pleasure. This frail vessel thou emptiest again and again, and fillest again with fresh life" (*Gitanjali,* p. 1). Death, therefore, is not man's enemy, but rather a friend coming to set him free from intolerable pains, bondage, and unquiet.

Tagore does not, however, look upon the body as a tomb or prison of the soul from which it has to be liberated. For him, man is bound up with nature. The human spirit is bound up with material organism. Contact with body, instead of being a tainting of the purity of the soul, is just the condition necessary for developing its nature.

Regarding future life, Tagore held a twofold view of immortality and rebirth:

So long as man identifies himself with his finite, fleeting personality, he is subject to the law of infinite progress and perpetual approximation. . . . His destiny is not fulfilled. He goes from life to life, and death becomes only an incident in life, a change from one scene to another. But when the individual gives up his selfish nature, and completely surrenders himself to Universal Life, he gains the bliss of heaven and shares life eternal. He is lifted above the travail of births and deaths, and above mere succession in time, to which alone death is relevant.[17]

This idea is best expressed in one of his poems in *Poems Old and New:* "Far as I gaze at the depth of Thy immensity, I find no trace of sorrow or death or separation. Death assumes its aspect of terror and sorrow its pain only when, away from Thee I turn my face to my own dark self."[18]

The infinite is realized by the surrender of the finite. The surrender of the finite self is not however the "negation of self, but the dedication of it." "The flower must bring forth the fruit . . . but when the time of fruition arrives, it sheds its exquisite petals and a cruel economy compels it to give up its sweet perfume. For the flower to develop, the bud has to die, for the fruit the flower, for the seed the fruit, for the plant the seed. Life is a process of eternal births and deaths. Birth is death and death is birth. All progress is sacrifice."[19]

Tagore looked upon the soul of man as something very great; he saw no end to its dignity "which found its culmination in Brahman himself." "The revealment of the infinite," says Tagore, "is to be seen most fully not in the starry heavens but in the soul of man" (*Sādhanā,* p. 41). Any limited view of man would be an incomplete view. Of all manifestations of the Divine, man is incomparable. The human self is unique, because in it God reveals himself in a special manner. In terms of reality we can assert that while nothing is wholly unreal, nothing is as real as man. "God has many strings to his lute, some are made of iron, others of copper; but man is the only golden string in God's lute." [20] If we detach the facts from their setting in the whole, they look awry and unintelligible. "Only when we detach one individual fact of death do we see its blackness and become dismayed. We lose sight of the wholeness of life of which death is a part." [21] The physical event of death enables man to give up the body as a last offering to God; death is not finally dark, for it transmits to him the fount of light which is eternal.

Tagore accepts death in all its fullness and wonder thereby turning sorrow into joy. Not only does he see God in beauty and life, but also in death. "In sorrow after sorrow it is His steps that press upon my heart" (*Gitanjali,* p. 34). Indeed for him, death finds its place and meaning in relation only to God. "The supreme spirit is the concrete dynamic of life at the centre of things, giving rise to the roar of the winds and the surge of the seas. It is the final truth of the cosmic dance of life and death." [22] Thus seen in its setting, death "loses its sting and grave its victory." Death becomes a messenger of and gift from God.

> Death, thy servant, is at my door.
> He has crossed the unknown sea and
> brought thy call to my home.
> The night is dark and my heart is
> fearful—yet I will take up the lamp,
> open my gates and bow to him my
> welcome. It is thy messenger who
> stands at my door.
> I will worship him with folded hands,
> and with tears. I will worship him

placing at his feet the treasure of my
heart.
He will go back with his errand done,
leaving a dark shadow on my morning;
and in my desolate home only my
forlorn self will remain as my last
offering.

(*Gitanjali,* p. 79)

Śrī Aurobindo[23]
Death: A Process of Life

Birth is the first spiritual mystery of the physical universe, death is the second which gives its double point of perplexity to the mystery of birth; for life, which would otherwise be a self evident fact of existence, becomes itself a mystery by virtue of these two which seem to be its beginning and its end, and yet in a thousand ways betray themselves as neither of these things, but rather intermediate stages in an occult processus of life.[24]

Śrī Aurobindo affirms that the ultimate reality, transcendent and indescribable, manifests itself in two terms, a *Being* and a *Becoming.* The being is the fundamental reality; the becoming is an effectual reality. It is dynamic power and result, a creative energy and working out of being, a constantly persistent yet mutable form, process, outcome of its immutable essence (*The Life Divine,* 2, 556). He regards matter and spirit as two ends of one indivisible reality. Matter is not inconscient; it is veiled consciousness or the Spirit involved. The evolution of matter is possible only because there has been an involution of the Spirit into matter. Life is present everywhere even in what appears to be inconscient; consciousness is the very nature of being. "If matter were not living, it could not support life; if some element of life were not present in it, matter could not continue to exist."[25] The Spirit holds all the potentialities of matter, life, and mind in itself and manifests itself in an evolutionary graduation.

Life is the eternal movement of the *conscious force*.[26] It is the cosmic energy that "builds, maintains and destroys forms in the world." It brings forms to existence and again reduces them to nonexistence. Life is all pervading; all existence here is a universal life and takes form of matter. Life manifests itself in diverse forms —plant, animal and man. In matter, it appears like inanimate force; in man, animal, and plant, it is animate. In material elements, life takes the submental and subconscious forms.

Disintegration and renewal are unceasing processes of life. Aurobindo holds that death is not opposed to life. "Disintegration of substance and renewal of substance, maintenance of form and change of form are the constant processes of life; death is merely a rapid disintegration subservient to life's necessity for change and variation of formal experience. Even in the death of the body, there is no cessation of life. Only the material of one form of life is broken up to serve as material for other forms of life (*The Life Divine*, I, 269).

Life is impelled to go on creating eternally. In all its forms—plant, animal, and man—life is characterized by birth, growth, decay, and death. Life depends on matter for its continuation and growth. It helps life by nourishment to remain, to increase, and to express itself. When some bodily function is impaired, life withdraws from it; it is not destroyed. When we say "a man is dead," we mean that the body organism has become completely unusable by life. "Nothing in life that is manifested perishes. It is always renewed. It seems to perish because that is a process of life. Death itself is a process of life."[27]

Man is the epitome of evolutionary process; in him already has been accomplished physical, vital, and mental consciousness. His emergence as a self-aware being is a great fact of evolutionary life. However, man is not conscious of the whole range of his being. He does not know himself fully. He is cut off from the universal consciousness. He does not experience his unity with the omnipresent reality. He finds himself subject to time and death.

Aurobindo regards the individual as a persistent reality, an eternal portion of the eternal spirit. He is not different from the Absolute, but an ingredient poise of the Absolute itself. There is an essential and inherent unity in them. The individual is the medium through which the spirit discloses its being. Behind all the changes of our personality and upholding them, there is a real spirit, a true *Puruṣa*. The spiritual Puruṣa is the supreme spirit dwelling within us and is an essential condition of the discovery of the cosmic self. "The human birth in this world is on its spiritual side a complex of two elements, a spiritual person and a soul of personality; the former is man's eternal being, the latter is his cosmic and mutable being" (*The Life Divine,* I, 709). The individual Puruṣa in working out his cosmic relations with the supreme Spirit assumes a body. This assumption of the body is what we call birth. Only through it is it possible to have a progressive depth of our conscious being toward unity with God and with all in God. Birth is an essential condition of the manifestation of the Puruṣa on the physical plane. "The body is a convenience, the personality is a constant formation, action and experience are instruments" [28] for his development. The psychic being descends into the evolution of empirical self and guides it through its physical, vital, and mental elements.

The soul or the psychic being is the highest representative of the self in our being. It is the permanent being in us which employs mind, life, and body as instruments, but itself remains unaffected by their operation. It is the ever pure flame of divinity in things. Aurobindo points out that it is the psychic being that survives the death of the body and the dissolution of the vital and mental sheaths. So immortality in the sense of durational continuation of existence belongs to the psychic being.

When a man dies, his soul or psychic being after a time goes to the psychic world and takes rest there till the hour comes to take birth again in another body upon earth. . . . Once in its place of rest, the soul enjoys profound peace and delight and is in a kind of luminous sleep. There it assimilates all the experiences of last life, that is to say, imbibes out of them all the substance that goes to increase and strengthen its consciousness, the sap that lends to the growth of the build and stature of the being. A broad planning too is made here, a scheme in outline of the kind of experiences that will need for the particular growth of consciousness envisaged. All this, however, is not the deliberate rational process of the mind; it is something spontaneous, involved, a luminous brooding and incubation as it were, something like the trance of Brahman within which the seed of creation is about to germinate. Also the human soul is not a simple and unilateral being, it is a little cosmos in itself. The soul is also a developing fire that increases and enriches itself through the multiple experiences of an evolutionary progression.[29]

The Puruṣa manifested in each soul-form is really the One. But when the Puruṣa is completely identified with form and movement, then it becomes the ego. It is caused by the separation of man's consciousness from its origin, the Divine. "Each ego feeling itself as it were the centre of the universe creates division not only from the Supreme, but from each other. This creates disharmony and struggle. . . . The formation of the ego brings into existence a self-aware entity, a subjective self, an individual who experiences pain and suffering, duality and death, and all kinds of distortions."[30] Human ego is to be overpassed in order to enable man to achieve progress. It is an inevitable condition through which the evolution has to pass in order to go beyond. Disharmony and death exist so that man may seek a radical cure for them.

Death is not unreal; it is not brought into existence by an anti-divine element. It is the operation of *truth-consciousness* under the conditions of material inconscience; when matter becomes living, it tries to control life; when it succeeds, it returns to its original inconscience—that is death.[31] "Death is imposed on the individual life both by the conditions of its own existence and by its relations to the All-Force which manifests itself in the universe (*The Life Divine, 1,* 293). Aurobindo affirms that all life is a progressive revelation of an immanent divine power and envisages growing displacement of its characteristics of ignorance, incapacity, and death by the emergent verities of knowledge, power, and immortality.

The world of man is a world of ignorance. It is mixed with much falsehood and error which disables him from living a full life. *Avidyā* "ignorance" is the lack of self-knowledge. It comes into play when the individual loses contact with the true self, the Divinity within. Under its influence, one perceives the particular, not the universal. Ignorance, however, is not absolute falsehood; it is, rather, a distortion of truth, a partial knowledge. Indeed the experience of ignorance is itself a sign of awakening; it is operative in human beings only. "It is as if an actor playing a part so completely identifies himself with the character that he totally forgets his true self. That is effective ignorance. So long as he remembers his true self which is all the time behind the actor, he can always go back to it. But if he forgets his true self, he would not even think of going back to it. Then he would be really ignorant. Something of the same nature happens to the human being when he gets enclosed in ego-consciousness." [32]

Life has a meaning deeper than the appearance it bears. To be born, to live, and to drift to death along the pathways of pleasures and pain, hope and grief, is not the object; man has to wake up and recognize that there is a greater power, a larger reality than the puny self. He has to grow out of his limited personality into the greater being of the Divine.

This then is the necessity and justification of Death, not a denial of Life, but as a process of life; death is necessary because, eternal change of form is the sole immortality to which the finite living substance can aspire and eternal change of experience the sole infinity to which the finite mind involved in the living body can attain. This change of form cannot be allowed to remain merely a constant renewal of the same form-type such as constitutes our bodily life between birth and death; for unless the form-type is changed and the experiencing mind is thrown into new forms, new circumstances of time, place and environment, the necessary variation of experience which the very nature of existence in Time and Space demands, cannot be effectuated. And it is only the process of Death by dissolution and by the devouring of life by Life, it is only the absence of freedom, the compulsion, the struggle, the pain, the subjection to something that appears to be Not-Self which makes this necessary and salutary change appear terrible and undesirable to our mortal mentality.

(*The Life Divine*, I, 295-96)

The birth of an individual soul, in human or any other form, is not an isolated phenomenon. It must be continued in other births and must have been preceded by other births. Aurobindo prefers the term "rebirth" to reincarnation because, first, it renders the sense of the sanskrit term *Punarjanma* correctly, and, second, and more important, there is no *definite* psychic entity getting into a new case of flesh through rebirth. "There is a metempsychosis, a reinsouling, a rebirth of a new psychic personality as well as birth of a new body. And behind is the Person, the unchanging entity, the Master who manipulates this complex material, the Artificer of this wonderful artifice." [33] To view one as such and such a personality getting into a new case of flesh is to stumble about in ignorance. Rebirth in this sense is the necessary means for the evolution of the soul into ascending grades of form and consciousness. All birth is a progressive self-finding. It is rebirth that gives to the birth of an incomplete being in a body its "promise of completeness and spiritual significance." Aurobindo sees rebirth as an inevitable logical conclusion if the evolutionary principle is accepted in nature along with the reality of the individual soul.

> If there is an evolution of consciousness in an evolutionary body and a soul inhabiting the body, a real and conscious individual then it is evident that it is the progressive experience of that soul in Nature which takes the form of this evolution of consciousness: rebirth is self-evidently a necessary part, the sole possible machinery of such an evolution. It is as necessary as birth itself; for without it birth should be an initial step without a sequel, the starting of a journey without its farther steps and arrival.
>
> (*The Life Divine*, 2, 718)

Human destiny is to exceed the present life and evolve into higher and divine life; it is neither survival nor rebirth, but the transcendence of life and death. It is the unfoldment of the latent potentiality in man. "If a spiritual unfolding on earth is the hidden truth of our birth into Matter, if it is fundamentally an evolution of consciousness that has been taking place in Nature, then man as he is cannot be the last term of that evolution because he is too imperfect an expression of the spirit." [34] He has to rise out of domination of mind, life, and body into the full consciousness and possession of the spiritual reality within. The nature of perfection visualized by Aurobindo is of an integral character. It is not only the soul that is to gain its freedom, but equally the other members of man's being, his whole instrumental nature as well.

> To transcend, to exceed the consciousness of the body, not to be held in the body or by the body, to hold the body only as an in-

strument is a first condition of divine living. To transcend mind and handle it as instrument, to control it as a surface formation of self is a second condition. To be the self and spirit, not to depend on life, not to be identified with it, to transcend it and control and use it as an expression and instrumentation of the self is a third condition. All this can become complete in him only when he has evolved out of the ignorance into the knowledge and through knowledge into the supreme consciousness and its dynamis and its supreme delight of existence.[35]

Life is not an individual phenomenon; it represents a universal existence and breathing of a mighty Life-Spirit. That which comes out of the divine must inevitably return to the divine. The goal of evolution is continual growth of divine knowledge, strength, love, and purity; it is growth into supermanhood or gnostic being. As man emerged out of animal, so out of man is to emerge superman; and in the process, ignorance, evil, and death are to be transcended. Emanicipated from ignorance and egoism, the superman engages himself in a supreme effort to turn the body into a medium of the spirit's manifestation in matter. He enters into conscious co-operation with divine power which secretly guides the process of evolution. And there comes a time when the soul is consciously immortal, aware of itself both in its eternal immutable essence and eternal mutable moment:

The man who rises above the conception of himself as a life and a body, who does not accept the material and sensational touches of the world at their own value or at the value that the physical man attaches to them, who knows himself and all as souls, learns himself to live in his soul and not in his body and deals with others too as souls and not as physical beings. For by immortality is meant not the survival of death—that is already given to every creature born with a mind—but the transcendence of life and death.[36]

Mahatma Gandhi [37]
Death: Reminder of Duty

Gandhi looks upon birth and death as eternal verities; they are not different states, but different aspects of the same thing. He does not see any reason to deplore death and celebrate birth. While he does not regard death as complete annihilation, he discourages too much curiosity about the nature of postmortem existence. "What would be the plight of a child of five," he asks, "if it desires to know what is going to happen to him after fifty? . . . Where is the need, however, to know what is to happen after death? Is it not sufficient to know that good actions are well rewarded and evil actions bring forth evil fruits? The fruit of best actions is *mokṣa*." [38]

For Gandhi, man is not all body, the body is merely the abode; the body cannot be preserved for any length of time after the soul has left it. Man's real concern, therefore, ought to be for the immortal Ātman, though unfortunately he seems to be concerned only with the body. However, Gandhi does not ask us to disregard the body:

> We must perform the duties arising from the existence of the body. Eating, bathing, going from place to place—all these we do, thinking them to be legitimate activities (*yajña* of the body). . . . There is no sin in taking proper care of one's health, but it is a great sin to forsake one's Dharma for the sake of one's body. We should treat the body as the field in which the Ātman strives and wins liberation, and take every innocent measure to preserve it. . . . It is to the evolution of the soul to which our faculties are to be devoted. All that we have to concern ourselves with is whether it is the Ātman or the body we serve.
>
> (*Works*, *12*, 400; *25*, 481; *32*, 365)

It was the sense of duty that motivated Gandhi's life. He saw that all men are caught in the jaws of death; they have to depart from this world soon. "Then why stray from the path of duty? Why waste time in anger and pleasure seeking?" (*Works*, 39, 70) he asked. In his own life, whenever there was a lapse in the performance of duty due to the weakness of the flesh he did not forgive himself. "For persons who have dedicated themselves to service, there is only one way to mourn death, and that is to dedicate themselves all the more to such service" (*Works*, *14*, 197). This tendency can be discerned in him from his early years. His reaction to the death of his father illustrates the point; he considered it a great misfortune that he was not able to serve his father in his last moments. He was conscience stricken because he was with his wife in bed at that time.

I felt deeply ashamed and miserable. . . . I saw that if animal passion had not blinded me, I shall have been spared the torture of separation from my father during his last moments. I should have been massaging him, and he would have died in my arms. . . . The shame to which I have referred, is this shame of my carnal desire even at the critical hour of my father's death, which demanded wakeful service. It is a blot that I have never been able to efface or forget, and I have always thought that, although my devotion to my parents knew no bounds and I would have given up anything for it, yet it was weighed and found profoundly wanting because my mind was at the same moment in the grip of lust.[39]

In the face of death Gandhi did not surrender to emotion, but turned from sorrow to his strong sense of duty, thereby finding relief in action. A good example of this is found in Gandhi's reaction to his mother's death. His mother died when he was away in England. His brother withheld the news till he returned to India. "The sad news was given to me. . . . My grief was even greater than over my father's death. Most of my cherished hopes were shattered. But I remember that I did not give myself to any wild expression of grief. I could even check the tears, and took to life as though nothing had happened."[40]

Gandhi felt that any metaphysical speculation on death only took one away from duty here on earth. In a letter to the Ashram children, he wrote: "Those who die are to be born again and those who live are destined to die. Why then be glad about life or lament death? Yes, there is one thing to remember. Having known this we should strive to discover our duty and then stick to it until the end" (*Works, 33,* 204). The same attitude pervades the letters contained in the *Complete Works of Gandhi.* As a matter of fact, we do not find a single letter which does not advise the mourner to remember his duty and find solace in it. A good example of this is found in Gandhi's letter to Kemprabha Das Gupta on June 2, 1931: "Dharma and true *śraddhā* consist in increasing work of service in the name of the departed one. . . . So wake up; forget Nikhil's death and try to improve your body for the cause of service" (*Works, 46,* 285). Or again in a letter to his sister: "How can I console you? Pass your time in the performance of duty, looking upon it as the source of happiness and peace" (*Works, 35,* 286).

Gandhi found his answer to the question of death in the Bhagavad Gītā. In it Krisna tells Arjuna to forget his sorrow and perform his duty. "The soul cannot be wounded by weapons; it is up to us to do our duty." The Gītā says that the body is the *Dharmakṣetra,* the battlefield where the eternal duel between right and wrong goes on. The body is capable of being turned into a gateway of *Mokṣa* or seedbed of sin. It is therefore the duty of every seeker to take care of his body and make it an instrument of Dharma.

The fear of death is the greatest obstacle in the performance of our duties. The very idea of death frightens most of us out of our wits and entirely paralyzes our reasoning faculty. But according to Gandhi, the fear of death is unnatural; there is nothing striking about death. Not a moment passes when someone is not born or is not dead in the world. In South Africa, Gandhi was once beaten up by some assailants. As the blows started, he uttered "He Ram" and lost consciousness. Considering him dead, the assailants left him. Recalling this incident later, Gandhi wrote: "On reflection, we fear death needlessly. I believe that I have not known such a fear for a long time. And I have grown more fearless after this incident. If I had not gained consciousness, I would not have felt the suffering that I went through later. We can thus see that there is suffering only as long as there is intimate union with the body. I became aware of suffering only when the soul's union with the body was restored" (*Works, 14,* 510).

Gandhi was more concerned about the way of dying than death itself. He found happiness in living only if God gave "strength to die willingly and gladly while suffering innumerable hardships and tyrannies. . . . There is no salvation in death," he said, "there is salvation in death when dying willingly, when dying gladly" (*Works, 22,* 271). Death can be the utmost assertion of our individuality. It was in this sense, for example, that he thought of the Jews; if they were to die, he believed it was better to assert their individualities in nonviolent resistance than to allow themselves to be taken to the slaughter like cattle.

> For if, at the beginning of their persecution, the Jews of Germany and Austria had resisted with sufficient drama they might not have survived—they did not survive in any case—but they would have made the world less ready to find excuses for Hitler and might have started a well of sympathy, a beginning of resistance among German people. It is just conceivable, moreover, that such tactics

might have obliged the Nazis to let more Jews out of Germany and that lives would have been saved.[41]

The idea of perishing for a cause, for other men, occurs frequently in the writings of Gandhi. He had always held that *Satyāgraha* implies the willingness to accept not only suffering but also death for the sake of a principle. "Just as one must learn the art of killing in the training for violence, so one must learn the art of dying in the training for non-violence." Gandhi sought his peace among disorders; he had shown his willingness to die.

He was only twenty-seven when he was nearly lynched in the streets of Durban; eleven years later he was belaboured in Johannesburg by a rugged compatriot; in 1934 a bomb narrowly missed him while he was on his way to Poona Municipal Hall. Several of his fasts brought him to the verge of collapse; in at least two of them his survival seemed a miracle. As a soldier of non-violence, he had probably run more hazards than many a general had done on a battlefield.[42]

In Gandhi's spiritual and political realms, death was a weapon; he wielded tremendous power in his fasts and swayed a subcontinent by holding his life balanced on a fingertip as it were. And he succeeded because he was so sincerely and obviously intent upon death if he failed to convert the opponent.

Gandhi used to say, half-seriously and half-humorously, that he aspired to live for 125 years. He was, however, so unhappy at the communal riots and large-scale killings during and after partition of the country that he repeated again and again that he did not want to be "a living witness of fratricidal strife." And during his final days in Delhi, where he held his last great fast to bring the Hindu and Moslem communities of the capital together, he succeeded where the police had failed. However, his efforts to protect the minority communities and end the massacres increased the enmity of the fanatical.

On January 30, 1948, at the hour before nightfall, Gandhi, walking to his meeting, was shot by a fellow Hindu and died calling the name of Rama. He died without anger and without fear, in the act of service, with a smile on his face and the name of God on his lips. In his death, the nonviolence for which he stood won a real victory and life gained a deeper meaning.

Sarvepalli Radhakrishnan[43]
Death: Awakening into a New Life

Radhakrishnan surveys the different schools of Indian thought in his monumental two-volume study, *Indian Philosophy*. His own philosophical views are discussed in his well-known works, *An Idealist View of Life, Eastern Religions and Western Thought,* and *The Hindu View of Life*. Although a champion of Advaita of Śaṃkarāchārya, he is not slow in pointing out the limitations of the traditional understanding of the *Advaita*.

Radhakrishnan holds that man is a "compound of self which is immortal, and body which is mortal." [44] Of these two aspects, one makes for finiteness and involvement in nature, and the other makes for transcendence of such involvement; the one sees man as a tissue of evanescent changes, and the other as a spiritual entity, birthless and deathless. One is the empirical self and the other the essential self. In ignorance, the former is mistaken for the real self. The essential self, conditioned by body, sense organs, mind, and intelligence, is the individual self *(jīva)*; it is a knot of intelligence and nonintelligence. It is subject to finitude and limitations.

We cannot attribute substantiality or simplicity to individual ego. It is not an atomic unit, but a very complex structure. It is the systematic unity of conscious experience of a particular centre, which is itself defined or determined at the outset by bodily organism and other conditions. The body, the senses, etc., enter into its experience and introduce a sort of unity and continuity into it. The consciousness linked up with the organism is a purely finite one, which includes bodily states as part of the content of consciousness. As the body is built up gradually, so also is its conscious experience. The finite self is not the ultimate cause of its own consciousness. The ego is the felt unity of the empirical consciousness, which is evolving in time.[45]

The self of man is essentially independent of his physical body. The entire psycho-physical organism slowly reveals itself to human consciousness as an instrument of the self. Body serves as the locus of consciousness of the physical world. It is produced of the five elements of fire, water, earth, air, and ether, the evolutes of *Prakṛti.* Prakṛti is the principle of matter; it has three strands *(guṇas)* which by appearing in different proportions produce the variety of actual existence. The entire world of outer nature including the body, mind, and ego belongs to the category of the changeful. It is conditioned by time and subject to causality. It is affected by the "sixfold waves of change," namely, birth, growth, transformation, decay, destruction and death. At the death of an individual, only the physical body is dissolved into the respective elements out of which it is produced. Death destroys only the physical body.

The term "body," however, includes not only the gross physical body *(sthūla śarīra)*, but also the subtle body *(sūkṣma śarīra)* which constitutes the entire inner world of thoughts and feelings, memory and impressions, and the causal body *(kāraṇa śarīra)* which persists in the condition of deep sleep. In human experience, the three bodies manifest themselves in waking, dream and dreamless sleep respectively. The subtle body which is the core of man's personality survives physical death and is subject to the laws of Karma and reincarnation. The individual self *(jīva)* persists in other forms and conditions of existence to gain experience and knowledge and achieve fulfillment.

> When the physical body is annihilated, there is left behind a seed which brings forth a new organism according to its kind. . . . The soul is independent of the body, and its identity makes possible recollection, etc. Though our bodies may be shattered to dust, still there is something in us which survives; and it is this which determines our future life. The knowledge which we have gained, the character which we have formed will pursue us into other lives. The moral and the pious rise, while the immoral and the impious sink in the scale. The nature of the future life depends on the moral quality of the past life.[46]

Radhakrishnan believes that each individual soul rises higher in the process of evolution, passing through various births and rebirths, always reaping the results of its actions, being governed by the law of Karma. "All acts produce their effects which are recorded both in the organism and the environment. Their physical effects may be short lived, but their moral effects *(saṃskāra)* are worked into the character of the self. Every single thought, word and deed enters into the living chain of causes which makes us what we are." [47] Individuality is due to Karma. Our present was determined by our past and our future will be determined by our present.

The entire world of sense perception, including the ego, fall within the field of time and network of cause and effect relation; it belongs to the category of the relative. It is the sphere of Māyā. It is the sphere of death. There is no "changeless centre or immortal nucleus in these pretenders to selfhood. . . . Illness and death come, if not today then tomorrow, to ourselves and those whom we love, and nothing remains of all we love on earth but dust and ashes. Nothing on earth can offer a sure foothold for the soul of man." [48]

Ignorance *(avidyā)* is the cause of man's egoism and alienation; it is the "innate obscuration of knowledge." It is involved in the very roots of human existence. It is another name for finitude. It is the basis of selfish activity, conflict, and strife as well as the source of man's suffering and anxieties. It cannot be demonstrated by reasoning, since reasoning itself can never stand apart from ignorance. Under its influence, man clings to his individuality and the phenomenon around him and imagines that his very existence is threatened.

> *Firstly,* he thinks and imagines an uncertain future which rouses his hopes and fears. The rest of nature goes on in absolute tranquility. But man becomes aware of the inevitability of death. He worries himself about ways and means by which he can overcome death and gain life eternal. His cry is, who shall save me from the body of this death? Though he is born of the cosmic process he finds himself at enmity with it. Nature, which is his parent, is imagined to be a threat to his existence. An over-mastering fear thwarts his life, distorts his vision, and strangles his impulse. *Secondly,* man's naive at-oneness with the living universe, his essential innocence or sense of fellow-feeling is lost. He does not submit willingly to a rational organization of society. He puts his individual preference above racial welfare. He looks upon himself as something lonely, final and absolute, and every man as his potential enemy. He becomes an acquisitive soul, adopting a defensive attitude against society. *Thirdly,* the knowledge of death and the knowledge of isolation breed inner division. Man falls into fragmentariness. He becomes a divided, riven being, tormented by doubt, fear and suffering. His identity splits, his nucleus collapses, his naivete perishes. He is no more a free soul. He seeks for support outside to escape from freezing fear and isolation. He clings to nature, to his neighbors, to anything. Frightened of life, he huddles together with others.[49]

So long as the self is under the influence of Avidyā, it cannot find fulfillment; at best it is only a question of indefinite progress in time and not of final attainment.

Regarding the nature of life after death, Radhakrishnan holds that it cannot be completely different from the present one. Death cannot profoundly alter the life of the self. "If the self wakes up after dreamless sleep and feels its continuity with the self that went to sleep, death need not mean discontinuity." Death is part of a continually recurring rhythm of nature, only marking a crisis in the history of the individual.

The future life is not one of deathless existence, but "a process marked by periodic mortality of the body." So long as the self is growing, periodic death also is a fact.

> The process of gradual improvement must go on after the death of our present bodies and it is reasonable to assume that this life is followed by others like it, each separate from its predecessor and successor by death and rebirth. . . . Whatever we may think of the compatibility of death with absolute perfection, it is certainly compatible with absolute imperfection. Life after death is continuous with our present existence.
>
> (*Idealist View of Life*, p. 236)

Radhakrishnan dismisses the theory of personal immortality as a product of confused thinking. "Supposing we are allowed the choice, which grade of one's earthly existence is to be perpetuated, the body as it was at the dying moment or in the prime of life or the body at birth. We do not want endless youth or endless age. Whatever it be, if it is endlessly continued, we will be sick unto death" (*Idealist View of Life*, p. 223). He also discards "conditional immortality" as it confuses immortality with survival. He holds that not only saints but sinners also survive. The law of Karma demands survival. Besides, every individual soul is of infinite value, and even the sinner will be ultimately saved. Similarly, the theory of a "soul without a past but with a future" does not commend itself to Radhakrishnan. If the soul has a beginning, it must have an end. "It is difficult to admit that a being which begins to exist at a certain time is immortal in future like a string with only one end" (*Idealist View of Life*, p. 237).

According to Radhakrishnan, the "hypothesis" of rebirth is a reasonable one. The subtle body survives physical death and manufactures new physical bodies for itself; the impelling force is provided by the actions it had done and the knowledge it had gained in previous life. It assumes the body necessary for its efficiency at its next birth by attracting physical elements to itself, and so rebirth is only a renewing of the instrument through which the self works. In this view, the self is not a new entity at each birth, but is a continuing process, a transition, conceived from one situation to another at physical death. "There is such a thing as psychic gravitation by which souls find their level, i.e. their proper environment (*Idealist View of Life*, p. 234).

Rebirth is a movement with a meaning; it is genuine growth into personality and character:

> It recognizes that the values won and character achieved are conserved as mind and purpose which accompany us even through death. The future depends on what we make of this plastic raw material which receives determination by our free choice. Until one attains liberation, one is under the pull of the body and the sense organs, and it is this pull that gravitates the soul to new physical formations to work out its own *karma*.
>
> (*Idealist View of Life*, p. 239)

The mortal man becomes immortal by realizing his infinite, eternal dimension. He is liberated from death.

> At the spiritual level, the individual becomes aware of the substance of spirit, not as an object of intellectual cognition but as an awareness in which the subject becomes its own object, in which the timeless and spaceless is aware of itself as the basis and reality of all experience. . . . The awakened man draws back from his

mind, life and body and all else that is not true being and knows himself to be one with the eternal spirit which is the soul of all phenomenon.

(*Idealist View of Life*, pp. 239-40)

Salvation is different from survival, liberation *(mokṣa)* from rebirth *(saṃsāra)*; it is the reality of life eternal or release from rebirth. It is a supreme status of being in which the individual knows himself to be superior to time, birth, and death. To seek liberation from the wheel of births and deaths is nothing more than awakening to the spiritual level from the merely ethical. It is a new dimension altogether, dealing with things eternal. Regarding the question whether the self loses or retains its individuality in the state of freedom, Radhakrishnan observes:

While the released soul attains at the very moment of release a universality of spirit, it yet retains its individuality as a centre of action as long as the cosmic process continues. . . . The freed soul, so long as the cosmic process continues, participates in it and returns to embodied existence not for its own sake but for the sake of the whole. He has the feelings of kinship with all *(sarvātmabhāva)*. He identifies himself with the universal movement and follows its course.

(*Idealist View of Life*, p. 243)

Conclusion

The phenomenon of death continues to exercise the minds of modern Hindu thinkers deeply. Their solutions, however, revolve around the traditional Hindu doctrines. They reinterpret these doctrines and extend their meaning and sometimes draw new implications from them. They are one in holding that death is not the end of life. Life is one continuous, never-ending process; death is a passing phenomenon which every soul goes through to gain experience for its further evolution. Death comes as a necessary drop scene between two births. It is a drop scene inasmuch as the activities go on behind the curtain. The individual soul travels from life to life assimilating diverse experiences. Birth and death are doors of entry and exit on the stage of this world.

There is death for the physical body which is a compound of five elements. It does not end personality and self-consciousness. Death is separation of the soul from the physical body; it becomes a starting point of a new life with fresh opportunities. It opens the door for higher forms of life; it is a gateway to fuller life.

The individual soul builds various bodies to display its activities and gain experiences from the world. Body is an instrument of all sensual enjoyments. Therefore man is intensely attached to the body. Through ignorance, he identifies himself with the body which is impermanent and nonsentient. The physical body may die and disintegrate, but the impressions of his actions do not die. The individual has to take birth to enjoy the fruit of his actions. So he is caught up in the whirlpool of birth and death. Body is the result of *Karma*, the good and bad actions. Therefore, *Saṃsāra* or phenomenal existence is without beginning and end.

The process of transmigration continues till the individual is purged of all impurities and acquires a true knowledge of the Imperishable. The purpose of transmigration is, therefore, betterment of the individual. The individual soul can never grow without death. Rebirth gives ample opportunities for man's rectification, growth, and gradual evolution.

The root cause of egoism is ignorance. By destroying ignorance through knowledge of the Imperishable, it is possible to annihilate egoism. If one frees himself from likes and dislikes and does not do any actions with a selfish motive, one can free oneself from Karma. He who realizes the eternal soul which is infinite and unchanging frees himself from the jaws of death.

Notes

1. Swami Vivekananda, *Complete Works,* 8 vols. (Calcutta: Advaita Ashrama, 1955-60), vol. 2, pt. 2, p. 226.
2. Rabindranath Tagore was born in Bengal in an extraordinary educated and cultured family. Although he had very little formal schooling, he grew up into an unusually well-educated youth. He read Hindu scriptures and Indian classics along with *Vaishnava* poets and Bengali literature. He also read Western literature and philosophy. He developed a passion for romantic poets. With the publication of his *Prabhat Sangit,* Tagore emerged as a major poet. Tagore's genius overflowed in every literary medium—poetry, drama, short story, and essay; a succession of poetical masterpieces culminated in the Nobel Prize, and the author's worldwide fame. He formed the Visvabharati University at Shantiniketan. He traveled and lectured widely.
3. R. Tagore, *Gitanjali* (London: Macmillan & Co., 1913), p. 87.
4. S. Radhakrishnan, *The Philosophy of Rabindranath Tagore* (Baroda: Good Companions, 1961), p. 4.
5. R. Tagore, *My Reminiscences* (London: Macmillan & Co., 1917), p. 217.
6. R. Tagore, *The Religion of Man* (Boston: Beacon Press, 1961), pp. 93-94.
7. Rabindranath's mother died when he was thirteen years old, too young to feel its impact. As she was laid out on a bedstead, she looked to him as if she was enjoying "a calm and peaceful sleep." Only when the body was carried to the cremation grounds did he feel a storm of grief at the thought that "mother would never return by this door and take her accustomed place in the affairs of her household."
8. Krishna R. Kripalani, *Rabindranath Tagore: A Biography* (London: Oxford, 1962), p. 115.
9. Nihararanjan Ray, *An Artist in Life* (Trivandrum: University of Kerala, 1967), p. 205.
10. See Kripalani, *Rabindranath Tagore,* p. 34.
11. R. Tagore, *The Diary of a Western Voyage* (New York: Asia Publishing House, 1962), p. 1.
12. See Kripalani, *Rabindranath Tagore,* p. 175.
13. R. Tagore, "Religion of an Artist," *Contemporary Indian Philosophy,* ed. Radhakrishnan and Muirhead (London: Allen and Unwin, 1966), p. 37.
14. Tagore, *Religion of Man,* p. 189.
15. Quoted by Kripalani in *Rabindranath Tagore,* p. 384.
16. Ray, *An Artist in Life,* p. 339.
17. S. Radhakrishnan, *The Philosophy of Rabindranath Tagore* (Baroda: Good Companions, 1961), p. 41.
18. See Amiya Chakravarti, *A Tagore Reader* (New York: Macmillan, 1961), p. 347.

19. R. Tagore, *Sādhanā* (New York: Macmillan, 1913), p. 99.
20. An address delivered in 1931 at *Shantiniketan.*
21. Radhakrishnan, *The Philosophy of Rabindranath Tagore,* pp. 56-57.
22. *Ibid.,* p. 177.
23. Aurobindo Ghose was born in 1872 in West Bengal. His father sent him to England for schooling when he was barely seven. He was introduced to Western literature and Bible early in his life. He studied at St. Paul's, London, and King's College, Cambridge. On his return to India in 1893, he joined the Baroda State Service and started an intensive study of ancient Indian literature, philosophy, and religion. He also took an active part in the struggle for national freedom and was arrested in 1908. During his incarceration in the Alipur Jail, he had a profound spiritual experience. He decided to immerse himself in Yoga to be able to broadcast "the eternal message" of India. He started an *ashram* in Pondicherry where he lived the rest of his life. The *ashram* continues to attract philosophers and seekers from all over the world.
24. Sri Aurobindo, *The Life Divine* (Calcutta: Arya Publishing House, 1940), vol. 2, pt. 2, p. 683.
25. A. B. Purani, *Sri Aurobindo's Life Divine* (Pondicherry: Aurobindo Ashram Press, 1966), p. 179.
26. According to Sri Aurobindo, it is the power of Pure Being to create forms; it is at the root of all phenomenal existence.
27. Purani, *Sri Aurobindo's Life Divine,* p. 178.
28. V. Madhusudan Reddy, *Sri Aurobindo's Philosophy of Evolution* (Hyderabad: Osmania University Press, 1966), p. 282.
29. *Ibid.,* pp. 287-88.
30. Purani, *Sri Aurobindo's Life Divine,* p. 45.
31. *Ibid.,* p. 279.
32. *Ibid.,* p. 185.
33. Sri Aurobindo, *The Problem of Rebirth* (Pondicherry: Aurobindo Ashram Press, 1969), p. 26.
34. Madhusudana Reddy, *Sri Aurobindo's Philosophy of Evolution,* p. 274.
35. *Ibid.,* p. 342.
36. Sri Aurobindo, *Essays on the Gita* (Pondicherry: Aurobindo Ashram Press, 1959), p. 58.
37. M. K. Gandhi was born on October 2, 1869, to a pious *Vaishnava* family. He studied the Rāmāyaṇa, Bhāgavata, the *Vaishnava* poets of Gujrat, and popular writings of Jains. In 1888, he went to England for legal studies, which he completed in three years. After he returned to India, he tried unsuccessfully to establish a law practice. Later he went to South Africa and became involved in a struggle against racial discrimination. He followed with great interest the religious and ethical movements of the day. He studied Ruskin, Thoreau, and Tolstoy. He studied the various religions—Jainism, Islam, Christianity, and Buddhism. It was from Hinduism that he

derived the maximum spiritual satisfaction. On his return from South Africa, he assumed the leadership of the movement for national independence. He attempted to establish Hindu-Muslim unity and to improve the conditions of the backward classes in general and the "untouchables" in particular. India became independent in 1947, but the country was partitioned. A fanatic Hindu assassinated Gandhi, who was trying to quench the flames of religious hatred.

38. M. K. Gandhi, *Complete Works of Mahatma Gandhi* (New Delhi: Government of India Publication, 1958), vol. 25, p. 309. Hereafter cited in text as *Works*.
39. M. K. Gandhi, *An Autobiography* (Boston: Beacon Press, 1957), p. 31.
40. *Ibid.*, pp. 87-88.
41. George Woodcock, *Mohandas Gandhi* (New York: The Viking Press, 1971), pp. 116-17.
42. B. R. Nanda, *Mahatma Gandhi* (Boston: Beacon Press, 1958), p. 509.
43. Dr. Radhakrishnan, a philosopher of religion and historian of ideas, was born September 5, 1888. His parents were Orthodox Hindus. He was educated at Lutheran Mission High School (Tirupati) and later at Madras Christian College. He started his career as a teacher of philosophy at the Presidency College and plunged into a thorough study of Indian classics—*Upaniṣads, Bhagavadgita, Brahmasutras,* the basic texts of orthodox schools, Jainism, and Buddhism. He also studied ancient and modern philosophies, European literature, Marxism, and existentialism. He has traveled widely and met leaders of almost every trend of thought. He has arrived at his conclusions on the basis of his innermost experiences.
44. Sarvepalli Radhakrishnan, *The Bhagavadgita* (London: Allen and Unwin, 1953), p. 111.
45. Sarvepalli Radhakrishnan, *Indian Philosophy* (London: Allen and Unwin, 1958), p. 603.
46. *Ibid.*, p. 649.
47. Sarvepalli Radhakrishnan, *An Idealist View of Life* (New York: Barnes and Noble, 1964), p. 218. Cited in text as *Idealist View of Life.*
48. *Indian Philosophy,* volume 2, p. 631.
49. Sarvepalli Radhakrishnan, *Eastern Religions and Western Thought* (London: Oxford University Press, 1964), pp. 43 f.

VI
China
D. T. OVERMYER

Acceptance in Context: Death and Traditional China

Heaven is my father and Earth is my mother, and even such a small creature as I find an intimate place in their midst.
Therefore that which fills the universe I regard as my body and that which directs the universe I consider as my nature.
All people are my brothers and sisters, and all things are my companions.
In life I follow and serve [Heaven and Earth]. In death I will be at peace.

Death does not sever the relationship of the departed with the living; but merely changes it to a different level. Far from being characterized by fear, the attitude of the living toward departed members of the family or clan is one of continuous remembrance and affection.[1]

These passages from the writings of an eleventh-century Neo-Confucian scholar and a twentieth century anthropologist sum up the classical Chinese world view and its implications for death. In this perspective, since man is an integral part of the universe, death is a natural development in a continuum with life. To be sure, traditional Chinese regretted early death, and some sought longevity or immortality, but they ultimately accepted death as a necessary part of the cosmic process, a process which is essentially good.

Though acceptance was the dominant attitude toward death, there were of course many variations and dissenting views. In what follows I shall outline three major patterns in the Chinese understanding of death which were indigenous in origin or function, viz., those of Confucianism, Taoism, and popular religion. Since Buddhism developed in India, its concepts will be discussed only insofar as they shaped popular understanding after the T'ang Dynasty (618–907). Chronologically my emphasis will be on the period between the beginning of the Han and the end of the Sung Dynasties (206 B.C.–A.D. 1279), though it will be necessary to spend some time as well with pre-Han philosophers and the findings of modern ethnologists. My primary concern will be with conceptions of death and afterlife, not death rituals or ancestor worship.

The burial of objects with the dead in prehistoric China was a common practice indicating belief in some sort of afterlife. This practice was continued and amplified in the Shang Dynasty (c. 1500–1050 B.C.), particularly by the ruling elite who accompanied their dead with prodigious wealth, including chariots, horses, elephants, and human beings.[2] From the Shang Dynasty, too, we have written appeals to ancestors to intercede on behalf of their descendents with the high god Shang-ti. From the Chou period (c. 1050–222 B.C.), before the time of the philosophers, we have many texts such as the *Shih Ching* [Book of Poetry] and the *Shu Ching* [Book of History] which describe the ancestral cult and the developing ideas of the soul. For purposes of a brief survey, however, it is perhaps most useful to begin with the perspectives of late Chou philosophy, particularly the two schools which later became dominant, Confucianism and Taoism.

Death and Confucian Thought

The dominant Confucian attitude can be summed up as humanistic and moderately skeptical, though not to the point of denying some form of afterlife. Its tone was set by Confucius (551–479 B.C.) in a dialogue with one of his disciples, Tzu-lu:

Chi-lu [Tzu-lu] asked about serving the spiritual beings. Confucius said, "If we are not yet able to serve man, how can we serve spiritual beings?"

"I venture to ask about death."

Confucius said, "If we do not yet know about life, how can we know about death?" [3]

Though Confucius was not an agnostic, he was much less concerned about propitiation of deities and spirits than most of his contemporaries. For him the center of religious sensibility was T'ien, or Heaven, the ancient Chou Dynasty high god from whom Master K'ung believed he had received a charge to reform the political structures of his day. It follows that ancestral cult in the *Analects* is discussed as an extension of filial piety toward the living, with no emphasis on seeking assistance from spirits of the dead. Veneration of ancestors is an expression of that ritual harmony which should pervade all life.

The psychological and ethical emphasis implicit in Confucius' attitude toward death is stated more explicitly by Hsün Tzu (*fl.* 298–238 B.C.), a Confucian scholar whose stress on the psychological efficacy of ritual came to dominate the *Li Chi* [Book of Rites]. Hsün Tzu writes as follows:

The sacrificial rites originate in the emotions of remembrance and longing for the dead. Everyone is at times visited by sudden feelings of depression and melancholy longing. A loyal minister who has lost his lord or a filial son who has lost a parent, even when he is enjoying himself among congenial company, will be overcome by such feelings. If they come to him and he is greatly moved, but does nothing to give them expression, then his emotions of remembrance and longing will be frustrated and unfulfilled, and he will feel a sense of deficiency in his ritual behavior. Therefore, the former kings established certain forms to be observed on such occasions so that men could fulfill their duty to honor those who deserve honor and show affection for those who command affection. Hence the sacrificial rites originate in the emotions of remembrance and longing, express the highest degree of loyalty, love, and reverence, and embody what is finest in ritual conduct and formal bearing. Only a sage can fully understand them. The sage understands them, the gentleman finds comfort in carrying them out, the officials are careful to maintain them, and the common people accept them as custom. To the gentleman they are a part of the way of man; to the common people they are something pertaining to the spirits.

When conducting a sacrifice, one divines to determine the appropriate day, fasts and purifies oneself, sets out the tables and mats with the offerings, and speaks to the invocator as though the spirit of the dead were really going to partake of the sacrifice. One takes up each of the offerings and presents them as though the spirit were really going to taste them.[4]

Though Hsün Tzu did not concern himself directly with the immortality cult developing in his day (to be discussed below), his perspective laid the foundation for attacks on this cult by other scholars during the Han Dynasty (206 B.C.–A.D. 220). Chief among these were Yang Hsiung (53 B.C.–A.D. 18) and Wang Ch'ung (A.D. 27–c. 100).

In his *Fa Yen* or "Model Sayings," Yang Hsiung is sharply critical of the common acceptance of spirits and immortals:

Someone asks: "What about the many spirits in the time of Chao?" I reply: "As to the existence or non-existence of vague and uncertain supernatural prodigies, the sage does not discuss them."

Someone asks: "Are there immortals such as people talk about?" [I reply]: "Bah! Even of [the culture heroes] Fu Hsi, Shen Nung, Huang-ti, Yao and Shun, I have heard that death and decay came to them all." "Where there is life there must be death, and where there is a beginning there must be an end. Such is the natural course." Yang concludes that efforts to prolong life are useless.[5]

Wang Ch'ung's critique is more lengthy and explicit; he devotes a whole chapter of his *Lun Heng* [Critical Essays] to a discussion of popular ideas of death. His opinions are straightforwardly stated:

People say that the dead become ghosts, are conscious, and can hurt men. Let us examine this by comparing men with other beings:

The dead do not become ghosts, have no consciousness and cannot injure others. How do we know this? We know it from other beings. Man is a being, and other creatures are likewise beings. When a creature dies, it does not become a ghost; for what reason then must man alone become a ghost, when he expires? Man lives by the vital fluid. When he dies, this vital fluid is exhausted. It resides in the arteries. At death the pulse stops, and the vital fluid ceases to work; then the body decays, and turns into earth and clay. By what could it become a ghost? Anterior to man's death, his mental faculties and vital spirit are all in order. When he falls sick, he becomes giddy, and his vital spirit is affected. Death is the climax of sickness. If even during a sickness, which is only a small beginning of death, a man feels confused and giddy, how will it be, when the climax is reached? When the vital spirit is seriously affected, it loses its consciousness, and when it is scattered altogether [*sic*].

Human death is like the extinction of fire. When a fire is extinguished, its light does not shine any more, and when man dies, his intellect does not perceive any more. The nature of both is the same. If people nevertheless pretend that the dead have knowledge, they are mistaken. What is the difference between a sick man about to die and a light about to go out? [6]

Wang goes on to support his position by numerous appeals to physical evidence and to what he considers common sense.[7]

While these ancient Chinese skeptics are most interesting, it would be a mistake to conclude that their views were shared by the majority of educated Confucians, or that their attitude toward death is the same as that of their modern Western counterparts. In practice, most *literati* assumed the continued existence of the soul as a necessary precondition for ancestor worship. In addition, with a few exceptions, even the skeptics were not annihilationists, but assumed that human substance returns to the natural process from which it comes, there to reenter the cosmic cycles of production and dissolution. As Wang Ch'ung writes:

When a man dies, his spirit ascends to Heaven, and his bones return to earth. . . .

Some say that ghost and spirit are names of activity and passivity. The passive principle opposes things and returns, hence its name *kuei* (ghost). The active principle fosters and produces things, and therefore it is called *shen* (spirit), which means "to extend." This is re-iterated without end. When it finishes, it begins again. Man lives by the spiritual fluid (*shen ch'i*). When he dies, he again returns to this spiritual fluid.[8]

Despite the impact of Taoism, Buddhism, and more complex theories of the soul, the orthodox Confucian perspective retained its integrity throughout the Imperial Period. The fully developed combination of humanistic scepticism with psychocosmological theory is stated by the great Neo-Confucian systematizer Chu Hsi:

Let us attend to those things that should be attended to. Those that cannot be attended to, let us set aside. By the time we have attended thoroughly to ordinary daily matters, the principles governing spiritual beings will naturally be understood. The positive and negative spiritual forces are so called with respect to function. . . . The refined material force (*ch'i*) [integrates] to be things. [As it disintegrates], the wandering away of its spirit becomes change. This is the principle of life and death.

Man is born as a result of integration of refined material force. He possesses this material force only in a certain amount, which in time necessarily becomes exhausted. . . . When exhaustion takes place, the heavenly aspect of the soul and the vital force return to Heaven, and the earthly aspect of the soul and body return to earth, and the man dies. Thus, as there is life, there is necessarily death, and as there is a beginning, there must be an end. . . . When a man dies, his material force necessarily disintegrates. However, it does not disintegrate completely at once. Therefore, in religious sacrifices we have the principle of spiritual influence and response. Whether the material force of ancestors of many generations ago is still there or not cannot be known.[9]

Death and Taoist Thought

"Taoism" includes many different traditions, ranging from mystical quietism to eschatological rebellion. Here we can discuss the attitudes toward death of only two of these strands; those of fourth century B.C. philosophy and the immortality cult so prominent during the Han Dynasty. On the surface, at least, these two approaches appear antithetical, for one encourages peaceful acceptance of death, while the other seeks either to overcome it or postpone it as long as possible. While this paradox cannot be completely resolved, it can be made more understandable through analysis of differing historical origins and through realizing that identification with Tao can mean power as well as acceptance.[10]

Perhaps the most lyrical affirmation of death in world literature is found in the writings of Chuang Tzu (lived between 399–295 B.C.), the most important Taoist thinker after the author of the *Tao-te Ching*. Chuang Tzu was a poet who believed that life and death are human distinctions made by those who do not understand the unity of all things in Tao. But let him speak for himself. If there is a distinctive Chinese contribution to man's understanding of death, no one states it better than Chuang Tzu. His ground theme is, "The ten thousand things are one with me." Since this is so, there is "nothing that is not acceptable," not even death. "The sage leans on the sun and moon, tucks the universe under his arm, merges himself with things [and] . . . achieves simplicity in oneness. For him, all the ten thousand things are what they are, and thus they enfold each other." [11]

Chuang Tzu continues:

Life is the companion of death, death is the beginning of life. Who understands their workings? Man's life is a coming together of breath. If it comes together, there is life; if it scatters, there is death. And if life and death are companions to each other, then what is there for us to be anxious about?

The Great Clod (the earth) burdens me with form, labors me with life, eases me in old age and rests me in death. So if I think well of my life, for the same reason I must think well of my death.
You have the audacity to take on human form, and you are delighted. But the human form has ten thousand changes that never come to an end. Your joys then must be uncountable. Therefore, the sage wanders in the realm where things cannot get away from him, and all are preserved. He delights in early death; he delights in old age; he delights in the beginning; he delights in the end.[12]

Chuang Tzu's perspective is continued in the *Lieh Tzu* (c. A.D. 300) and by other thinkers of the third- and fourth-century Neo-Taoist tradition, such as Wang Pi (226–249) and Kuo Hsiang (d. 312).[13] Since their positions are so close to that of Chuang Tzu, it is perhaps more interesting to note that some Chinese carried the Taoist view to a practical conclusion by demanding that they be buried naked, the better to immediately blend with the life force from which they came. Again the theme was set by Chuang Tzu:

When Chuang Tzu was about to die, his disciples expressed a desire to give him a sumptuous burial. Chuang Tzu said, "I will have heaven and earth for my coffin and coffin shell, the sun and moon for my pair of jade discs, the stars and constellations for my pearls and beads, and the ten thousand things for my parting gifts. The furnishings for my funeral are already prepared—what is there to add?" "But we're afraid the crows and kites will eat you, Master," said his disciples. Chuang Tzu said, "Above ground I'll be eaten by crows and kites, below ground I'll be eaten by mole crickets and ants. Wouldn't it be rather bigoted to deprive one group in order to supply the other?" [14]

We do not know if the sage's request was followed by his disciples, but in the Han Dynasty a few such burials were actually carried out, in sharp contradiction to the usual Chinese practice of preserving the body as long as possible in a heavy sealed coffin. For example, in the first century B.C. a certain Yang Wang-sun instructed his sons that, "I desire to be interred quite naked, in order that I might return to the original matter out of which I was created." His sons reluctantly complied.[15] Huang-fu Mi (d. A.D. 282) expressed similar sentiments in his will:

"It is my special desire that I be laid in the pit quite naked, that my body may come into immediate contact with the earth. . . . Thus may my flesh and bones become one with the earth and my soul blended with the primordial life substance (*yüan ch'i*)." [16]

All of this concern to harmonize with natural necessity of course depends on what one considers natural. There were other Taoists convinced that man's natural state was to live one hundred years, or even millennia, and who therefore concentrated all their efforts on overcoming harmful physical habits which wasted life force or impeded its free circulation. For them unity with Tao was not resignation to fate, but a call to action, action to physically restore within the self man's primordial state. Such activity could include special diet, control and circulation of the breath, ritual exercise, taking drugs, and engaging in beneficial forms of sexual intercourse. Here we have time only to note a few of the more important manifestations of this tradition.

In the *Lao Tzu* (4th century B.C.) there are several passages which imply that the perfect man of Tao is impervious to harm, does not waste his energy in anxious movement, and is therefore able to live long. This is a direct result of his identification with the source of cosmic change which itself remains constant.[17] At about the same time that this text was written, other Chinese began experimenting with alchemy and indigenous forms of Yoga in hopes of attaining long life. It is, perhaps, not surprising that these experimentalists turned for textual authority to the more pragmatic emphases of the philosophical school. In any case, by the time of the Han Dynasty, Taoism and the quest for immortality were firmly wedded in the Chinese mind.[18]

In his excellent article, "Life and Immortality in Han China," Yü Ying-shih of Harvard demonstrates that concern for long life *(shou)* is found on early Chou bronzes, while terms for immortality, such as "no death" *(pu-ssu)*, do not appear until the eighth century B.C. He writes, "In general, during the Western Chou period [to 771 B.C.], people prayed only for limited longevity and natural death. But during the Ch'un-ch'iu period (722–481 B.C.), people became more avid and began to pray for escape from old age, as well as 'no death.'" Among terms describing different forms of immortality there are three which imply a kind of transcendence, "transcending the world" *(tu-shih)*, "ascending to the distant place" *(teng-hsia)*, and "becoming an immortal *(ch'eng-hsien)*. Yü maintains that these three terms

> indicate immortality of a different kind, and probably of a different origin as well. This is the immortality of the immortality cult.

. . . To achieve this new immortality was not to live permanently on earth as a man, but rather to leave this world as a *hsien* or immortal. . . .
The new conception of immortality is, therefore, essentially other worldly in nature.[19]

He goes on to state that such *hsien* immortality first appeared in the late fourth century B.C.[20] Where do these immortals go? They proceed to islands of the immortals in the Eastern Sea (Pacific Ocean), to Mount K'un-lun far to the west with its peaches of immortality, or simply to the sky, where they fly freely in space.

Though the tradition of immortals living detached from the world persisted as a continuing goal for Taoist adepts, by the late Han Dynasty much of its flavor of transcendence had been lost through popularization and absorption by the "longevity" tradition. Yü discusses this "Worldly Transformation of the Immortality Cult" in some detail. The most important factor in this process was single-minded pursuit of immortality by Ch'in (221–206 B.C.) and Han emperors, with all the wealth and power of the state at their disposal. Since these emperors wanted to combine immortality with imperial power, they were not interested in transcending the world except, perhaps, as a temporary means of obtaining herbs and charms from immortals. As Ssu-ma Hsiang-ju (179–117 B.C.), a famous Han poet, wrote, "The hsien take their residence in mountains or swamps and look rather emaciated. But this is not what the emperor means by hsien.[21]

Yü goes on to demonstrate the increasing popularity of the immortality idea all through the Han Dynasty including the conviction that with the proper drugs one could escape death and be translated into another realm along with his whole household, including children, domestic animals, and even the house itself. He summarizes by writing,

> The idea of physical immortality struck deep roots in popular thought. . . . People generally believed in various ways of attaining immortality . . . [by] ascension to heaven by performing . . . sacrifices . . . ; by taking immortality drugs . . . ; or by drinking an elixir of gold and gems and, eating the flowers of the purple boletus, which, it was said, would make the body light. . . . There were also people who believed that physical immortality could be achieved by following Lao Tzu's teaching of quietism and dispassionateness, by abstaining from eating cereals, by regulating the breath as well as cultivating nature, or, even more strangely, by metamorphosing the human body into the shape of a bird.
>
> There was also a tradition that people could ascend to heaven in broad daylight simply on the basis of virtuous deeds rewarded by "celestial deities." [22]

Thus, there was a powerful tradition of Chinese thought which looked at death as an obstacle to be overcome on one's way to perfect existence. There is a rich literature on the various methods of attaining such felicity, a discussion of which would take us far afield into complex matters dealing more with techniques of avoiding death than with attitudes toward it. Here let us content ourselves with citing part of Max Kaltenmark's excellent summary of Chinese alchemy and with a brief look at "embryonic breathing."

Kaltenmark writes: "Gold and cinnabar were always the two main ingredients in Chinese alchemy. The first because of its incorruptibility, the second because of its color and chemical properties." In describing the earliest extant alchemical text by Wei Po-yang (second century), he continues:

> The central idea is that natural mutations can be speeded up in the alchemical crucible. In particular, it is possible to obtain purified cinnabar by subjecting it to a series of sublimations. When absorbed by the body, this cinnabar "dissipates the harmful vapors in the body and fumigates the four members of their extremities, whereupon the complexion becomes wonderfully clear, white hairs

turn black, and teeth grow again where they had fallen out; old men grow young again, and from old women one gets young girls. It is possible to change one's appearance in order to escape from worldly peril. Such men deserve the name *chen-jen* [a Pure Man, i.e., a Holy Man who has regained his original pure nature]." It was generally admitted that man's essential life principle was composed of "Primordial Breath" (*yüan-ch'i*), in other words a fragment of chaos, though some authors held that this essence was a mixture of Yin and Yang, the differentiations that occurred within chaos when the universe took form. Sickness and death are caused by an imbalance of Yin and Yang within the body, resulting in the loss of some of this breath. Physicians can increase this breath when it is deficient, but, according to the alchemists, only cinnabar and gold can really restore to the human body the primordial state in which the Yin and Yang were so closely united that they could not be distinguished from each other. This was the meaning they gave to Lao Tzu's injunction "Embrace the Unity." [23]

Such returning to the primordial state brings immortality.

"Embryonic breathing" assumes the whole system of Chinese esoteric physiology, centered on the unhindered circulation of *ch'i* and the perfect balance of its Yin and Yang modes. The Taoists believed that *ch'i* circulates in the embryo in a closed circuit. Since the embryo was a symbol of new life and vitality, recapitulation of its form of circulation could bring renewal. Thus the adept held his breath *(ch'i)* as long as possible, consciously circulating it within his body, combining its elements together in the "Sea of Breath" *(ch'i-hai)* at the base of the abdomen. There, little by little, developed a new "embryo body," a replica of the self, which at death could fly away to a paradise of the immortals.

Henri Maspero sums up the intention behind this process as follows: "The ancient Taoists, for whom immortality was possible only in the survival of the material body, had to work to transform the heavy mortal body into a light immortal body." [24]

This they attempted to achieve through first restraining the causes of mortal decay, and then by creating a new subtle body or embryo within the self, a form of internal rebirth.[25] Such effort amounted to a more detailed technique for attaining the immortality of transcendence popular in the early Han Dynasty. It is instructive to note that in both cases existence in the body was not rejected, but used as a means to transform itself.

Death and Popular Conceptions

It remains to outline the mainstream of Chinese conceptions of death in the medieval period, conceptions not limited to the peasantry but shared to some extent by almost everyone. We will look briefly at fate, conceptions of the soul, and images of afterlife.

Fate. No discussion of our topic would be complete without some reference to the pervasive concept of fate which controlled much of the Chinese attitude toward death and the events of life. In this context fate is but a more abstract formulation of the sense of irrevocable immersion in the cosmic process mentioned often above.

Fate or destiny first appears in the texts as the Heaven-decreed destiny of rulers and states *(t'ien-ming)*. From at least early Chou times it was believed that the king ruled only by Heaven's favor, a favor which would be withdrawn if his administration became corrupt and ineffective. Before long this principle was extended to the people as well. As we read in the *Shu Ching,* "Heaven beholds the people on earth, and weighs their righteousness. After this examination, Heaven gives to each long life or short, according to his merits." [26]

Confucius had a strong sense of personal destiny dependent on Heaven's will and is reported to have said that "Life and death are the decree of Heaven; wealth and honor depend on Heaven," [27]

Mencius (lived between 370–290 B.C.), his most important successor, agreed: "Nothing, but is preordained. We should accept obediently our rightful lot." [28] At this point the Taoists were one with the Confucians, though for them fate was more a mysterious inexorable reality than a guarantee of moral order. Chuang Tzu says it well:

> Life, death, preservation, loss, failure, success, poverty, riches, worthiness, unworthiness, slander, fame, hunger, thirst, cold, heat—these are the alternations of the world, the workings of fate. Day and night they change place before us and wisdom cannot spy out their source.[29]

Though there were a few dissenting voices, such as Mo Tzu (fl. 479–438 B.C.) and Hsün Tzu, the great majority of traditional Chinese believed implicitly in the divine/cosmic direction of life. Even the skeptic Wang Ch'ung devotes a whole chapter of his *Lun Heng* to a discussion of the impersonal operations of destiny, concluding that "length and shortness of life are gifts of Heaven," and "every mortal receives his own destiny; already at the time of his conception, he obtains a lucky or unlucky chance." [30] How all of this operated at the popular level has been well summarized by the anthropologist D. H. Kulp:

> Fate decides all things. Fate determined the time of birth and it will determine the hour of death, the manner of death, and the experiences between birth and death. It is useless to strive against fate. All one can do is to learn the will of fate and conform in the best possible way. One may try to outwit fate but sooner or later one is doomed to defeat. Such are the attitudes that people hold regarding the great events and experiences of life.[31]

This understanding of fate served to further place death in context and give consolation to the bereaved.

Souls. Fully developed Chinese thought maintained that man has two soul elements, each described in terms representing both psychological and cosmic modes. The *hun* or *shen* category is associated with intelligence, light, and the Yang principle. At death the *shen* ascends to heaven, though a portion may also reside in the ancestral tablet. The *p'o* or *kuei* is associated with physical function, darkness, and the Yin principle. After death the *kuei* remains with the body in the grave. In some texts these soul elements are further divided into groups of three *hun* and seven *p'o*. The consensus seemed to be that the souls remain viable after death for only a relatively short time; the *kuei* until the body completely decays, and the *shen* for no more than six or seven generations, while ancestral sacrifices are still offered regularly to its tablet. After that, as Wieger says, "The rite had been performed. The dead had what was due to them. It was for them to know if they existed or not." [32] Except for the Taoist immortality cult, the Chinese had no theory of long-term survival after death until the arrival of Buddhism with its infinite cycles of rebirth.

What became the standard view in medieval times was succinctly stated by Wei Liao-weng, a thirteenth-century scholar:

> Those parts of the universal breaths [Yang and Yin], . . . having attained the highest development, expand [to] form *shen;* but those which revert and retreat, form *kuei.* When implanted in man, they are his *hun,* composed of Yang substance, which forms his *shen;* and his *p'o,* consisting of Yin substance and forming his *kuei.* When these two universal breaths mix [in his body], the *hun* agglomerates and the *p'o* consolidates, and thus they produce his life. But when they leave his body, the *hun* ascends and [again] becomes a *shen,* while the *p'o* descends to become *kuei.*[33]

Of course all these terms simply express different modes of one universal vital essence, *ch'i.* As Chu Hsi writes, "What integrates and disintegrates is material force." [34]

Though we are told here that the "*hun* ascends and becomes a *shen*," in ritual practice grave offerings were often explicitly dedicated to the *shen* as well as the *kuei*, as de Groot demonstrated long ago.[35] From this and linguistic evidence, the famous Dutch scholar concluded that before the theory of dual souls developed there was only one soul, dwelling in the tomb, corresponding to the medieval *kuei*. This *kuei* remained associated with the body only for a time, after which it returned to the earth from which it came. Hence, all the elaborate precautions taken to prevent decay by placing pieces of jade in bodily orifices and by burial in heavy airtight coffins.

However, by the early Chou Dynasty, there also developed the belief that the ancestral spirits of at least the nobility lived on above in association with Heaven. For example, in the *Shih Ching*, which includes material from 1000–600 B.C., we read of one of the deceased founders of the Chou Dynasty:

> King Wen is on high;
> Oh, he shines in Heaven!
> Chou is an old people,
> But its charge is new.
> The land of Chou became illustrious,
> Blessed by God's charge.
> King Wen ascends and descends
> On God's left hand, on his right.[36]

The Chou aristocracy also practiced an elaborate ancestral cult, centering on clan feasts at which the deceased was represented by a temporary impersonator, often a grandson.

There are many other Chou examples of a surviving spirit separate from the body, but perhaps the most dramatic is found in the *Chao Hun* (Summoning the Soul), a third-century B.C.

poem from the southern state of Ch'u. In this poem a shaman named Wu Yang tries to call back the soul of a man who has just died:

> The Lord God said to Wu Yang:
> "There is a man on earth below whom I would help:
> His soul has left him. Make divination for him."
> Wu Yang replied:
> "The Master of Dreams . . .
> The Lord God's bidding is hard to follow."
> [The Lord God said:]
> "You must divine for him. I fear that if you any longer decline, it will be too late."
> Wu Yang therefore went down and summoned the soul, saying:
> "O soul, come back! Why have you left your old abode and sped to the earth's far corners,
> Deserting the place of your delight to meet all those things of evil omen?" [37]

This calling back the soul became a standard element of death ritual during the Han Dynasty.[38]

Eventually the two early concepts of the soul were combined to form the *hun/p'o* theory, as we can see from a passage in the *Tso Chuan* attributed to Tzu Ch'an in 534 B.C.:

> In man's life the first transformations are called the earthly aspect of the soul (*p'o*). After *p'o* has been produced, that which is strong and positive is called the heavenly aspect of the soul (*hun*). If he had an abundance in the use of material things and subtle essentials, his *hun* and *p'o* will become strong. From this are developed essence and understanding until there are spirit and intelligence. When an ordinary man or woman dies a violent death, the *hun* and *p'o* are still able to keep hanging about men and do evil and malicious things.[39]

In about the fourth century B.C. this theory of two souls was integrated with Yin/Yang cosmology with the result indicated above in the passage from Wei Liao-weng.[40]

There are many interesting corollaries of this understanding of soul nature that would take us too far from our topic. Among them are the conviction that every particular aspect of the universe is animated by a *kuei* or *shen,* that souls of the unhappy dead can take the form of animals, and that if the corpse has not decayed, it is possible for its *hun* and *p'o* souls to reunite, thus bringing about resurrection. Details concerning these and many related phenomena can be found in volume four of de Groot's *The Religious System of China.* For our purposes it is sufficient to point out that indigenous Chinese soul theory ends where Taoist mysticism ends, with reintegration into the cosmos. From this perspective it appears as an attempt to explain multiplicity while remaining firmly grounded on the unity which underlies all.

Afterlife. As has been implied above, except for paradises of immortals, the Chinese had no clear vision of an afterlife before Buddhism brought its elaborate systems of heaven and hell. What the *shen* did in Heaven is never explained; and indeed the meaning of the term Heaven itself oscillated between sky, quasi-anthropomorphic deity, and a vaguely indicated celestial court. The most important form of afterlife was that sustained by family ancestral ritual and remembrance. In fact, it could be argued that continuation of the family line was the real locus of effective afterlife. As Taiwanese villagers are told by their priests, "People must marry, since the parents have given us our bodies and we must give the parents another body—a descendant."[41]

In fully developed Taoist mythology there are one hundred and eight paradises, of which P'eng-lai, an island mountain, is one of the most famous. Werner gives a summary description of P'eng-lai as follows:

> It is still the home of the Eight Immortals, and a great host of those who have won the blessing of eternal life. The houses are made of gold and silver. The birds and animals are all white. The pearl and coral trees grow there in great profusion. The flowers and seeds all have a sweet flavour. Those who eat them do not grow old nor die. There they drink of the fountain of life, and live in ease and pleasure. The Isles are surrounded with water which has no buoyancy, so it is impossible to approach them. They are inhabited only by the immortals, who have supernatural powers of transportation.[42]

While such paradises are an important aspect of Chinese religious thought, they remained esoteric to the aspirations of most common people.

The Pure Lands of Maitreya and Amitabha were the first paradises presided over by compassionate deities who provided easy means of salvation accessible to all. Though the orthodox Buddhist Pure Land concept is beyond our purview here, it is important to note that it became a part of folk tradition, in which Amitabha's "Western Heaven" functioned as an alternative to hell for the truly pious, perhaps in part because it was amalgamated with the indigenous paradise of the Mother Queen of the West, Hsi Wang-mu. Gallin summarizes the views of villagers in modern Taiwan:

> The villagers believe that the individual has three spirits. At death one spirit remains in the grave, another remains in the incense pot in the ancestral-worship room of the family home, and the third journeys to the underworld to be judged by the gods of the underworld for its past deeds in life. These gods determine the fate of the spirit, which may be eternal punishment and torture in the underworld, a punishment appropriate to the seriousness of past deeds, or rebirth in another world as anything from an insect to a member of the gentry or an even higher status. However, the

spirits of people who have lived extraordinary pure and good lives are permitted immediate entrance to the "Western Paradise," never again to undergo the uncertainty and misery of earthly life.[43]

Francis Hsü also refers to a "Higher World of the Spirits" and the "Western World of Happiness" in addition to hell, or the "Lower World of the Spirits." The "Western World of Happiness" or the "Western Heaven" is presided over both by the Buddha and the "Golden Mother of the Western Heavenly Lake." The relationship between these two figures is not clear, but it is significant to note that one of Hsi Wang-mu's titles is "Golden Mother of the Jasper Pool."

In any event it was the system of eight or ten hells to which most spirits went to be punished and sorted out for eventual rebirth. This system was the dominant image of afterlife in medieval popular religion, existing side by side with continued worship of ancestors enshrined in their tablets. The multiplicity of souls made it easy for the Chinese to adopt several systems of afterlife at once. Each hell had its chief judge, supported by many other officials, responsible for meting out punishment appropriate to specific crimes. Since with all its sub-hells, Hades had as many as 152 separate departments, it took a long time for souls of the dead to move through the complex process of purgation. All was organized into a bureaucracy paralleling civil administration; at each point there were forms to fill out, sins to list, and fees to pay. The officials of hell were themselves former human beings, assigned only temporarily to their roles, so they, too, could make mistakes and be bribed, just like their counterparts on earth. But despite all obstacles, the soul finally reached the last hell, where it was given a drink to wipe out all memory and then it was sent forth again to be reborn.

There is no need to describe here the structure of Chinese

purgatory. Our question is, What attitude toward death does all this imply? The answer is fear in a context of familiarity. No Chinese wanted to go to hell, but all knew that most did, and once there, one found a replica of the human world. Even the excruciating punishments were deserved and fitted to one's crimes, and they didn't last forever. One knew that relatives on earth would perform rituals at the time of each crucial judgment to propitiate or bribe the officials, and that eventually rebirth would come.

This spirit is well expressed in two communications from souls in hell to living relatives through a medium. Both messages were learned of by Francis Hsü in field research conducted between 1941 and 1943. The first is from a man who died at the age of twenty-seven to his wife:

> It was the natural result of my last life that I died so early; it is a pity that two birds in the same bush have to be separated by one departing before the other; however, decrees have been issued for my reincarnation; it is hoped that my behavior will vindicate me during my next life.

The second is from the spirit of an old woman to her son:

> It is a happy thing that I died a natural death; it is a result of good accumulated in my last life; happily my case has been noticed, and I have asked for immediate reincarnation; already I have the document and am only waiting for my turn to say farewell to the Tenth Judge.[44]

Conclusion

What we have said so far should not be understood to mean that traditional Chinese did not fear death. On the contrary, they spent a tremendous amount of time and effort reassuring themselves that in death one meets the familiar; a reassurance that by our standards implies anxiety. This same anxiety can be discerned in the prevalent fear of ghosts and in the concern to provide for ancestral spirits lest they become angry.

At a more literary level we find some for whom death was the cause of utter despair, a despair which often led to hedonism and drinking bouts. Perhaps the most explicit example is found in the Yang Chu chapter of the *Lieh Tzu* written about A.D. 350:

A hundred years is the term of the longest life, but not one man in a thousand lives so long. Should there be one who lives out his span, infancy and senility take nearly half of it. The nights lost in sleep, the days wasted even when we are awake, take nearly half the rest. Pain and sickness, sorrow and toil, ruin and loss, anxiety and fear, take nearly half of the rest. Of the dozen or so years which remain, if we reckon how long we are at ease and content, without the least care, it does not amount to the space of an hour.

Busily we compete for an hour's empty praise, and scheme for glory which will outlast our deaths; even in our solitude we comply with what we see others do, hear others say, and repent of what our own thoughts approve and reject. In vain we lose the utmost enjoyment of the prime of life, we cannot give ourselves up to the hour. How are we different from prisoners weighted with chains fetters?

It is in life that the myriad things of the world are different; in death they are all the same. In life, there are clever and foolish, noble and vile, these are the differences. In death, there are stench and rot, decay, and extinction; in this we are all the same. Some in ten years, some in a hundred, we all die; saints and sages die, the wicked and foolish die. In life they were Yao and Shun, in death they are rotten bones; in life they were Chieh and Chou, in death they are rotten bones. Rotten bones are all the same, who can tell them apart? Make haste to enjoy your life while you have it; why care what happens when you are dead? [45]

There are similar sentiments in Chinese poetry. First, the fourteenth of the anonymous "Nineteen Han Poems":

I drive my chariot down through the East Gate,
From afar I see the graveyard below the North Wall.
The white aspens are sighing, sighing.
Pines and cypresses line the broad road.
Under the earth are men who died long ago.
Dark, dark are their long nights of rest.
Far, far below the Yellow Springs
For a thousand years they lie in unchanging sleep.
The *yang* and *yin* change in their seasons;
Like morning dew are our destined years.
The term of life has not the strength of metal or stone;
The mourners themselves become mourned.
Neither saint nor sage can escape this evil.
Seeking the food by which to become immortal spirits,
Many have suffered from strange medicines.
Better to relish fine wine
And clothe our bodies in silks and satins.[46]

And again, from T'ao Yüan-ming (d. 427), "Substance, Shadow and Spirit":

Heaven and Earth endure eternally,
Mountains and streams will never change;
The plants know their natural course,
They wither and flourish in frost and dew.
Man should be above them in intelligence,
But he alone is unlike them:
A while ago he was living,
Now he is gone and will never return.
No one ever awakes from the dead;
Friends and relatives will not long remember him.
Looking at the things he used in his life,
Our eyes fill with tears.
I have no mortal magic to overcome death:
Certainly death will overtake me.

I hope you will take my advice.
Whenever you have a chance, never refuse a drink.[47]

The Chinese are capable of as much variety in mood and expression as those in any other culture. Nonetheless, for all the anxiety and occasional despair, the dominant attitude was one of acceptance, from the resignation of the Confucians to the affirmation of Chuang Tzu. At the social level all were part of the "infinite continuum of lineage," [48] within which individual death was subsumed in the life of the clan. And beyond all human change the cosmos continued as before, carrying all within its never-ending cycles of transformation.

Chuang Tzu's wife died. When Hui Tzu went to convey his condolences, he found Chuang Tzu sitting with his legs sprawled out, pounding in a tub and singing. "You lived with her, she brought up your children and grew old," said Hui Tzu. "It should be enough simply not to weep at her death. But pounding on a tub and singing—this is going too far, isn't it?" Chuang Tzu said, "You're wrong. When she first died, do you think I didn't grieve like anyone else? But I looked back to her beginning and the time before she was born. Not only the time before she was born, but the time before she had a body. Not only the time before she had a body, but the time before she had a spirit. In the midst of the jumble of wonder and mystery a change took place and she had a spirit. Another change and she had a body. Another change and she was born. Now there's been another change and she's dead. It's just like the progression of the four seasons, spring, summer, fall and winter.

Now she's going to lie down peacefully in a vast room. If I were to follow after her bawling and sobbing, it would show that I don't understand anything about fate. So I stopped." [49]

Notes

1. Chang Tsai (1020-1077), *Hsi Ming* (Western Inscription), quoted in Wing-tsit Chan, *A Sourcebook in Chinese Philosophy* (Princeton: Princeton University Press, 1963), pp. 497-98; Francis L. K. Hsü, *Under the Ancestors' Shadow* (1948; reprint ed., New York: Doubleday, 1967), p. 243.
2. For Shang burial practices see: Kwang-chih Chang, *Archaeology of Ancient China*, 2nd ed. (New Haven: Yale University Press, 1968), pp. 209-26; Judith M. Treistman, *The Prehistory of China* (New York: Doubleday, 1972), pp. 107-16; and Herlee Glessner Greel, *The Birth of China* (New York: Frederick Ungar Publishing Co., 1937), pp. 197-216.
3. *Analects* 11:11, in Chan, *Sourcebook*, p. 36.
4. Hsün Tzu, "A Discussion of Rites," in Burton Watson, trans., *Hsün Tzu, Basic Writings* (New York: Columbia University Press, 1963), pp. 109-10.
5. Yang Hsiung, *Fa Yen* (Model Sayings), quoted in Fung Yu-Lan, *A History of Chinese Philosophy*, trans. Derk Bodde (Princeton: Princeton University Press, 1953), vol. 2, p. 149.
6. Wang Ch'ung, "On Death," in his *Lun Heng* (Critical Essays), trans. Alfred Forke (1907; reprint ed., New York: Paragon Book Gallery, 1962), vol. 1, 191, 196.
7. Another famous critic of immortality and soul doctrines was Fan Chen (A.D. 450-515) who attacked what he conceived to be Buddhist theories of a transmigrating soul in his *Shen mieh lun* (Essay on the Extenction of the Soul). His basic thesis is: "The soul and the body are identical. Therefore, while the body survives, the soul survives, and when the body perishes the soul is extinguished." On Fan Chen, see Etienne Balazs, "The First Chinese Materialist," in his *Chinese Civilization and Bureaucracy*, ed. Arthur F. Wright, trans. H. M. Wright (New Haven: Yale University Press, 1964), pp. 255-76.
8. Wang Ch'ung. *Lun Heng*, volume 1, 191-92. These meanings for *kuei* and *shen* are based in part on those of different characters with similar pronunciations which mean "to return" and "to extend," respectively.
9. Chu Hsi, *Chu Tzu ch'üan-shu* (Complete Works of Chu Hsi), 1714 ed., in Chan, *Sourcebook*, pp. 644-45.
10. For good discussions of these modes of Taoism within philosophical texts, see Henri Maspero, *Le Taoisme* (Paris: Civilisations Du Sud, 1950); Herlee G. Greel, *What is Taoism?* (Chicago: University of Chicago Press, 1970); and a recent article by Ellen Marie Chen, "Is There a Doctrine of Physical Immortality in the *Tao-te Ching?*," *History of Religions*, 12 (February, 1973): 231-49.
11. Chuang Tzu, "Discussion on Making All Things Equal," in Burton Watson, trans., *The Complete Works of Chuang Tzu* (New York: Columbia University Press, 1968), p. 47.

12. Chuang Tzu, "Knowledge Wandered North," in Watson, trans., *Complete Works,* p. 235 and "The Great and Venerable Teacher," pp. 80-81.
13. On Neo-Taoism, see Fung, *History,* 2, 168-236; Chan, *Sourcebook,* pp. 314-35; Balazs, *Civilization and Bureaucracy,* pp. 226-54; and A. C. Graham, trans., *The Book of Lieh Tzu* (London: John Murray, 1960).
14. Chuang Tzu, "Lieh Yü-k'ou," in Watson, trans., *Complete Works,* p. 361. The articles Chuang Tzu refers to here are standard burial items intended to ward off decay.
15. *Ch'ien Han shu* (History of Former Han Dynasty), chap. 67, in J. J. M. de Groot, *The Religious System of China,* vol. 1 (Leiden: E. J. Brill, 1892), p. 306.
16. *Chin shu* (History of the Chin Dynasty), chap. 51, in de Groot, *Religious System,* 2, 686. Translation modified by the author.
17. On this see, for example, *Lao Tzu,* chaps. 22 and 50; *Chuang Tzu,* pp. 33 and 182 in Watson, trans., *Complete Works;* and *Lieh Tzu,* p. 46 in Graham, trans., *Lieh Tzu.*
18. For two of many discussions of Chinese alchemy and Taoist yoga, respectively, see Ko Hung, *Pao-p'u tzu nei-p'ien,* tr. James R. Ware, *Alchemy, Medicine, Religion in the China of A.D. 320* (Cambridge, Mass.: M.I.T. Press, 1966); and Chang Chung-yüan, "Processes of Self-Realization," in his *Creativity and Taoism* (New York: The Julian Press, Inc., 1963), pp. 123-68.
19. Ying-shih Yü, "Life and Immortality in Han China," *Harvard Journal of Asiatic Studies,* 25 (1964–1965): p. 88.
20. *Ibid.,* pp. 88-91. For a detailed discussion of an immortal in a later period, see Anna Seidel, "A Taoist Immortal of the Ming Dynasty: Chang San-feng," in William Theodore de Bary, ed., *Self and Society in Ming Thought* (New York: Columbia University Press, 1970).
21. Quoted in Ssu-ma Ch'ien, *Shih Chi* (Historical Records), chap. 117, p. 18, cited in Yü, "Immortality," p. 102.
22. Yü, "Immortality," pp. 107, 110, 112.
23. Max Kaltenmark, *Lao Tzu and Taoism,* trans. Roger Greaves (Stanford: Stanford University Press, 1969), pp. 130-31.
24. Maspero, *Le Taoisme,* p. 89.
25. *Ibid.,* pp. 90, 107.
26. *Shu Ching* (Book of History), "Kao-tsung yung-jih" section, in Leo Weiger, *A History of the Religious Beliefs and Philosophical Opinions in China,* trans. Edward Chalmers Werner (1927; reprint ed., New York: Paragon Book Reprint Corp., 1969), p. 22.
27. *Analects* 12:5, in Chan, *Sourcebook,* p. 39.
28. *Mencius,* 7A. 2, trans. W. A. C. H. Dobson, *Mencius* (Toronto: University of Toronto Press, 1963), p. 144.
29. Chuang Tzu, "The Sign of Virtue Complete," in Watson, trans., *Complete Works,* pp. 73-74.
30. Wang Ch'ung, *Lun Heng,* Forke, trans., 1, 137, 139.

31. Daniel H. Kulp II, *Country Life in South China* (New York: Teachers College, Columbia University, 1925), p. 171.
32. Weiger, *History,* p. 124.
33. *Hsing-li ta ch'üan-shu* (Complete Collection of Writings on Natural Principles), chap. 28 (first published in A.D. 1415), in de Groot, *Religious System,* 4, 50.
34. Chu Hsi, *Chu Tzu ch'üan-shu,* in Chan, *Sourcebook,* p. 645. For a good summary discussion of Chinese soul concepts, see D. Howard Smith, "Chinese Concepts of the Soul," *Numen* 5 (1958): 165-79.
35. De Groot, *Religious System,* 4, 5-8.
36. *Shih Ching* (Book of Poetry), poem 241, in Arthur Waley, trans., *The Book of Songs* (New York: Grove Press, 1960), p. 250.
37. "Chao Hun" (Summoning the Soul), in David Hawkes, trans., *Ch'u Tz'u, The Songs of the South* (London: Oxford University Press, 1959), pp. 103-104.
38. For an important Han reference to calling the soul, see *Li Chi* (Record of Rites), in the translation by James Legge, *The Sacred Books of China,* pt. 3 (London: Clarendon Press, 1885), pp. 108, 368-69.
39. *Tso Chuan,* Duke Chao, seventh year, in Chan, *Sourcebook,* p. 12.
40. The classic statement of the dual soul theory can be found in the *Li Chi,* Legge, trans., *Sacred Books of China,* pt. 4, p. 220.
41. Bernard Gallin, *Hsin Hsing, Taiwan: A Chinese Village in Change* (Berkeley: University of California Press, 1966), p. 227.
42. E. T. C. Werner, *A Dictionary of Chinese Mythology* (Shanghai: Kelly and Walsh, 1932), p. 372.
43. Gallin, *Hsin Hsing,* pp. 219-20.
44. Hsu, *Ancestors' Shadow,* p. 174.
45. *Lieh Tzu,* Yang Chu chapter, pp. 139, 140-41 in Graham translation.
46. "Nineteen Han Poems," in Robert Payne, ed., *The White Pony* (New York: John Day, 1947), p. 112.
47. T'ao Yüan-ming, "Substance Shadow and Spirit," in Payne, ed., *White Pony,* p. 134.
48. Hsü, *Ancestors' Shadow,* p. 224.
49. Chuang Tzu, "Perfect Happiness," in Watson, trans., *Complete Works,* pp. 191-92.

VII
Japan
W. R. LaFLEUR

Death and Japanese Thought: The Truth and Beauty of Impermanence

It is difficult to provide a full account of Japanese attitudes with respect to death prior to the introduction of Buddhism from the Asian continent. The reason for this is simple: Buddhism and writing were introduced to Japan at the same time, thus making pre-Buddhist articulations of indigenous views impossible in written form. Buddhism was officially introduced in 538, but undoubtedly present and practiced earlier—especially by Koreans of high status in Japan and by some Japanese themselves. It leaves its impression on the earliest documents in Japan, so we are forced to look elsewhere for information concerning pre-Buddhist views of death.

Archeology has been of some assistance in this matter. From what is referred to as the Jōmon Period (that is, from a period between c. 4000 B.C. to c. 250 B.C.) skeletons have been found with neatly folded limbs. The precise intention of this practice cannot be known, but certain hypotheses can be advanced. "Such a custom may have been based on the belief that a dead person with folded limbs would not haunt the living, or it may have been motivated by an entirely different belief to the effect that those buried in embryonic posture would be assured of rebirth." [1]

A Chinese document written around A.D. 297, the *Wei Chih* or

History of the Wei Dynasty, is one of the earliest written sources referring to the inhabitants of the Japanese archipelago and, fortunately, is one which tells something about Japanese customs regarding death. The *Wei Chih* records the following as having made an impression upon the Chinese observers:

> When a person dies, they prepare a single coffin, without an outer one. They cover the grave with earth to make a mound. When death occurs, mourning is observed for more than ten days, during which period they do not eat meat. The head mourners wail and lament, while friends sing, dance, and drink liquor. When the funeral is over, all members of the family go into the water to cleanse themselves in a bath of purification.[2]

From this we can infer that for the Japanese the social dimension of death was such that those who were in a relationship close to the deceased sought ritual ablution and purification. It would also seem that the dead were in some way an object of fear. Numerous interdictions accompanied the event of death and these were obviously constructed in order to protect the living from either the power of death or from that of the deceased.

In any case, there is other evidence that in early Japan the dead were conceived of as having a continuing relationship with the living. Analysis of Japanese mythology, although complicated by the fact that the myths were not written down until there were already substantial continental influences in the archipelago, suggests that from an early date the Japanese had ideas of multiple dimensions or locations in the universe. Often these were very concretely conceived so that the "other world" or "other worlds" were understood to be mountains or islands beyond the sea. The dead not only went to such places but also were thought to return from time to time. Many pre-Buddhist Shinto rituals are constructed on the theme of welcoming and seeing off various *kami*.[3] And the spirits of the dead—especially in the case of the nobility—were understood to be *kami*. The dead, as *kami*, were thought of as beings with enhanced numinosity and power for good or evil.

What is of special interest in this is not so much the notion that the dead continue to exist and haunt the world of man, since this is a rather common concept and found among many peoples; rather it is the fact that death was interpreted as a *variety of travel*. This not only left open the possibility of "return" to the place of departure, but also occasioned the creation of ritual on the analogy of etiquette appropriate for times of leave-taking and times of welcoming-back. Also, the understanding of death as a variety of travel negates death's finality. This concept has had remarkable tenacity in Japan and even with the introduction of Buddhism was incorporated into the Buddhist structure of belief.

Today it is still believed that during the summer festival of *o-bon*, the dead return to their ancestral homes for the duration of the festival and associate with the living. Precedents for this existed in China, and there is the deep desire to respect one's ancestors in both China and Japan. But research on Japanese folklore has shown the antiquity of the notion of *marebito* or extraordinary visitor, and also the fact that elaborate rites accompany the advent of such a visitor and have done so since ancient times.[4] These concepts were associated so that ritual and etiquette become virtually indistinguishable in such contexts; hospitality becomes a religious rite. What is thought appropriate for the living is all the more proper for the dead who comes as a guest.

Buddhism and Impermanence

The official reception of Buddhism into Japan in 538 was soon accompanied by its official adoption as the religion of state in the year 594. It has at times been argued that between the date of its introduction and the Kamakura era, which began at the end of the twelfth century, Japanese Buddhism was little more than a thin veneer over the indigenous religious patterns and systems of belief. The truth is that both doctrinal and magical forms of Buddhism were present during these many centuries. One of the major attitudes concerning death during this time was that it was something that might be forestalled, outwitted, and escaped by means of semimagical operations and precise knowledge of the "whereabouts" of death and danger. Various documents from the Heian period (794–1192) show that Japanese of the courtly class took elaborate precautions and sometimes put themselves in situations of considerable inconvenience to avoid being in places through which danger or death might pass in its movement.[5] It became a matter of professional expertise to be able to know the direction and route taken by things inimical to certain individuals, and in such a context death became primarily an enemy to be outwitted.

Nevertheless, traditional Buddhist understandings filtered into the mind of the age even while accommodating themselves to older patterns of thought concerning things such as life and death. During this era one term especially came to have importance in the linguistic currency of the day, and through it Buddhist understandings of death penetrated into Japanese thinking and life. This was the term *mujō*, the Japanese way of rendering the Sanskrit *anitya* and the Pali *anicca*.[6] In its Buddhist sense it means "impermanence" or the fact that nothing abides, but it is intended as a positive term.[7] It is no exaggeration to state that *mujō* became not only a fundamental term in the vocabulary of the period, but also that through it was opened to the Japanese a new mode of apprehending death. Even though older modes persisted, the options were multiplied.

Although it is beyond my purpose to review here the history of this term in Japanese thought,[8] it is necessary to point out that texts—both explicitly religious ones and those of a more general literary type—which used this term gave it a status so that in some sense it became the category under which thoughts concerning death appeared. This in itself is significant since it was part of the Buddhist conception at the time that death must rightly be understood as one event in an entire pattern of changes. To some extent the concept of *mujō* or impermanence relativizes death by making every moment a type of "dying." Change becomes all-pervasive. A novel such as the *Genji Monogatari* or Tale of Genji,[9] written around the year 1000, is so thoroughly imbued with a sense of the change and ephemerality of all things that *mujō* makes all experiences, relationships, loves, and plans to be necessarily of short duration. It is as if "endings" are distributed throughout life and only illusion forces us to focus upon death as if it were an extraordinary event, something to be feared.

In traditional Buddhist teaching it was Śākyamuni Buddha whose understanding of *anitya* or impermanence set the pattern for later Buddhists. He was released from his own illusions concerning the world and his own imperishability when, according to the legend, he saw in series an old man, an ill man, a corpse, and a mendicant holy man. Deeply impressed by his face-to-face confrontation with the fact of inevitable change and inevitable death, he left the household life in his father's palace and began his religious quest for Nirvāṇa.[10] This ultimately led not only to his enlightenment, but also to his "Great Death" or his capacity for meeting death with complete composure and equilibrium. In Buddhist teaching this direct confrontation with, and acceptance of the fact of, impermanence becomes the fulcrum upon which the balance is tipped from being caught in illusion to unity with the truth. In addition, it makes possible an eventual "Great Death."

This concept of *mujō* is of primary importance for understanding the impact made by Buddhism upon the Japanese mind and sensibility. Japanese literary historians have discovered that it runs throughout the history of their verse and prose. The evanescence of life and things is the major theme of innumerable literary works. Ivan Morris has rightly called attention to it:

> The Buddhist stress on evanescence has had a major influence on the literature of the Heian period and later. It is characteristic of the Japanese absorption with nature that their *memento mori* should be not a grinning skull nor the crumbling wall of a deserted house but live, poignant images like the scattering of blossoms or the yellowing of autumn leaves, which served to remind them that all beautiful things must soon pass away.[11]

But a significant modification within Buddhism occurs here. Whereas in South Asia and Tibet the importance of Śākyamuni's observation of a corpse became paradigmatic, so that Buddhists there felt at times that meditations within the context of cemeteries and in the midst of mouldering corpses was a *sine qua non* for enlightenment,[12] Buddhists in East Asia and Japan conceived of the *entire world of phenomena* as a place where one could observe and meditate upon impermanence and death. In Japan this became known as *mujō-kan*, a compound phrase in which the element '*kan*' can refer either to the "sense" of impermanence or, when written with a different character also pronounced '*kan*,' the empirical "observation" of impermanence. A link is implied between the observation of ephemerality in the world and the development within one's self of a sensitivity or sensibility.

Observation comes to be joined with appreciation. And in this process there comes into being, not only a concern for truth, but also for beauty. By the empirical observation of the nonabidingness of things in the world, one refines one's sensibility so that the things of the world become, in their quick passing, not only *memento mori,* but also the educators of a person's aesthetic awareness. Thus, it was natural that *mujō* became a dominating theme in the rich literature of the Heian period and in later eras as well. Observation of the ephemeral nature of all things in the world, the "deaths" that quickly overtake them, became not only a way of following the ancient Buddhist paradigm, but also a way of eliciting from those phenomena what was taken to be their characteristic beauty.

Of course, this involves a certain selection. Theoretically all things pass away in time, but it is true that certain things seem to "die" more quickly than others. And to those things which die quickly and with seeming "effortlessness," an unusual beauty was attributed: cherry blossoms, snow that disappears in the morning sunlight, mists, etc. Things come to be beautiful to the extent that they are ephemeral. But it is also significant that in their passing they not only are thought to recapitulate the paradigmatic acts of Śākyamuni, but also in their own way teach men the *ars moriendi.* Observation of such things by man is that which simultaneously impresses on him the truth of Buddhism and the beauty discoverable in the world.[13]

The poems of the twelfth century poet-monk Saigyō illustrate this very well. His verses frequently celebrate the seeming ease and "naturalness" with which things in the natural world accept their passing, but he does so by verbally creating scenes that have in them the stark, monochromatic effect we usually attribute to certain Zen-influenced painters of China and Japan. In the following verse we sense that even as the lush and variegated colors of summer and fall are gradually being exchanged for the sharp and cold monochromes of winter, life is ebbing away with striking beauty:[14]

kirigirisu	With each night of Fall
yozamu ni aki no	Grown colder than the one before,
naru mama ni	The cricket's cry seems
yowaru ka koe no	More feeble—as each night it
tōzakari yuku	Moves farther into distance.

Analysis of this poem shows that in it the poet is suggesting the presence here of multiple and somewhat coordinated "deaths." The time of day is evening or night and, more precisely, a series of nights, each longer and darker than the one before. The season is that in which fall is gradually but definitely yielding to winter. The voice of the solitary insect is heard less distinctly each evening as the cold of winter deepens. Its sound becomes progressively more faint and feeble. But in the last line of the poem the cricket is presented as moving deliberately and purposively—an aspect of the sense of the verb *yuku* here—into the distance, although it appears to be an analogue between a spatial and a metaphysical distance. The cricket dies as it moves. As the cry of the insect becomes more feeble, it seems to move into its own death with comparative ease.

To this extent the insect becomes by implication an instructor of man in the art of dying. There is sadness in death, but also the possibility of eliciting from death a beauty that transforms it into something positive rather than negative. In the following verse Saigyō refers overtly to his own death; the colophon attached to the verse refers to sadness, but also to the "beautiful pathos"—what in Japanese is called *aware*—in the situation.[15] We learn from the colophon that here, too, the insect referred to is a cricket.[16]

sono ori no	When the time comes at last
yomogi gamoto no	My head will lie down forever
makura nimo	Pillowed by sagebrush,
kaku koso mushi no	So this insect's sharp cry is
ne ni wa mutsureme	What will become most close to me.

Saigyō in this verse anticipates his death apart from human society and the presence of human beings on that occasion. Since he was an itinerant monk, this was a not unreasonable anticipation. The headnote tells us that the poem is written when he could hear that a cricket was approaching him; his reaction to this is to realize that such a cricket will probably be close to him both spatially and emotionally at the poet's own passing from life to death. But the cricket's presence is not merely fortuitous; it will be there because its mode of being in the world is one which combines fragility of body with ephemerality of life span. This implies that it draws close to the poet to teach him the lesson of *mujō*.

It is, therefore, the impression that things gain in beauty to the extent that they are ephemeral and transitory that becomes one of the basic components in a characteristic Japanese posture with respect to death. Slightly later than Saigyō and actually living during the Kamakura period, Yoshida Kenkō (1283–1350) expressed in his *Tsurezuregusa* what had come to be a tight nexus between death, beauty, and emotion when he wrote:

If a man were never to fade away like the dews of Adashino, never to vanish like the smoke over Toribeyama, but lingered on forever in the world, how things would lose their power to move us! The most precious thing in life is its uncertainty.[17]

There may be something inherent in Buddhist teaching that forged an early and sustained connection between perception and aesthetics or between the observation of truth beyond the veils of illusion and the creation of beauty.[18] The Japanese particularity does not lie in first forging this unity, but in bringing truth and beauty together under the aegis of the concept of *mujō* so that subsequent eras return to this again and again as a touchstone for their own creativity. Consequently, the treatment of death and transitoriness in the arts and in literature—and there remains much of this right into the present era—is not conceived of as the surface beautification of something essentially ugly, but the elicitation from death of a beauty in it, a beauty which in some sense perhaps makes a type of "transcendence" of death possible. To this extent the arts and literature of Japan at an early date became religious without sacrificing standards and goals requisite for the arts.[19] Within the structure of *mujō-kan* it was expected that attentive perception of the world's phenomena reveals the truth of Buddhism; therefore, the expression of this in art or literature is not the addition of a didactic to an aesthetic purpose, but the harmonization of these two. The arts present exemplars both from nature and from human history to show the *ars moriendi.*

Both Saigyō and Kenkō imply that death brings the individual into unity with a larger totality; the human being is not only like the dew and the blossom, but in death is united with the totality of the cosmic and natural process. And if the death occurs apart from society and its observation of it, that is, if it is "hidden," the unification with nature and the beauty of death are enhanced.

In Buddhist teaching the existence of an individual and continuing ego (*ātman*) is denied; therefore, death becomes the occasion within which one has the opportunity to look for psychological attunement with this ontological principle. Free, unprotesting entry into death reveals freedom from attachment and the absence of illusion and anguish. Thus, any possible note of death as *tragedy* is totally absent here.

Dōgen and a Zen View of Death

Zen was only minimally present in Japan prior to the Kamakura era which began with the transfer of real political power from Heian-kyō (Kyoto) to Kamakura in the east of Japan at the end of the twelfth century. Its existence as a separate form of Buddhism in Japan began when Eisai (1141–1215) and Dōgen (1200–1253) traveled to Sung China and brought to their native land the Ch'an (Zen) traditions of China and established the Rinzai and Sōtō schools of Zen respectively.

Although the Rinzai school's teachings are probably better known in the West than those derived from Dōgen and the Sōtō school, the Sōtō school is the largest school of Zen in Japan. Dōgen was one of the greatest intellectuals of his era and since he wrote an essay on life and death, his thoughts on death deserve attention here. It is not unlikely that the loss of both his parents at an early age not only influenced his decision to enter a monastery at the age of thirteen, but also drove him in a quest for a truly enlightened person, which he claimed to have found in China when he met and studied under Ju-ching, a master of the Ts'ao-tung (Sōtō) school of Ch'an or Zen.[20]

Dōgen's thought is subtle but also rich in psychological insight. In his essay entitled *Shōji* (Birth/Death) he seems to write out of an awareness that often there develops in a person either a great fear of death and consequent attachment to life or a fixation upon death as a positive release from a life which has become loathsome. In *Shōji,* Dōgen seems to teach that an attachment to either life or death is not only disruptive psychologically, but also contrary to

Buddhist teaching. But he entitles his essay "Birth/Death," employing the character for "to be born" and the one for "to die," two characters which when together in a compound are an equivalent in East Asia for the Sanskrit term Saṃsāra. Whereas the tradition which Mahāyāna Buddhists somewhat pejoratively referred to as Hinayāna (Small Vehicle) had seen Saṃsāra as the realm of cyclical births and deaths in contrast to Nirvāṇa, the state of being released from such an ongoing cycle of dying and being born again, Dōgen follows the Mahāyāna (Great Vehicle) tradition by claiming that there is no Nirvāṇa apart from Saṃsāra. Therefore, in *Shōji* he writes:

Only when one comes to understand that birth/death [saṃsāra] is the same as nirvāṇa does [the process] of being born and of dying become something which is not loathed and only then does "nirvāṇa" come to be something which one does not seek after. Then for the first time a [real] release from birth/death comes into being.[21]

For Dōgen it seems that the root of illusion and also of pain lies in the psycho-mental attempt to be other than where one is at any time. To imagine that life/death is an evil from which one wants release and entry into a Nirvāṇic state is precisely that which transforms life/death into something experienced as loathsome; this occurs when man becomes attached to a "Nirvāṇa" which is imagined to be other than the time and the place of his present existence. Paradoxically, one has a real release from Saṃsāra, existence apprehended as evil, precisely when one realizes that existence in the Saṃsāric realm is the only existence man has and is for that reason good. And death for the same reason is good; it is something to which one ought to have no attachment either positively or negatively.

But in his essay *Shōji,* Dōgen also redefines the concept of *mujō* or impermanence by pushing it to new and striking conclusions:

The notion that there is movement from birth to death is a mistaken one. . . . In that time referred to as "being born" there exists nothing other than birth; in that time referred to as "dying" there exists nothing other than death. For this reason at the time of being born one ought to face life only and at the time of dying one ought to face death only. Do not detest one [or the other] and do not desire one [or the other].[22]

Masao Abe in an important essay on Dōgen's thought writes that Dōgen holds to:

complete discontinuity of time, negating a transition from one state to another, immortality of soul, and eternal life after death. Life is absolutely life, death is absolutely death; spring is absolutely spring, summer is absolutely summer; each in itself no more no less—without the slightest possibility of becoming.[23]

This is not to be understood as the rejection of *mujō.* As we shall see below, he insisted on the importance of impermanence. On the contrary, it is the rejection of an interpretation of *mujō* which would see it merely as the equivalent of "process" or would limit it to the notion of "becoming" in contrast to one of "being." For Dōgen, *mujō* is too important a matter to be limited to the idea that all beings are bound to change with the passing of time;[24] it is not "becoming" because the notion of "becoming" negates the fullness of time which Dōgen attributes to each and every moment of time. Abe writes:

The idea of anticipation or waiting for the fullness of time in the future, however dialectic it may be, is not entirely freed from a naturalistic view of time. Only by the realization of the complete discontinuity of time and of the independent moment, i.e. only by negation of temporality, does time become real time. For Dōgen there is no time that is not fullness of time.

And again:

In Dōgen's realization it is not that the fullness of time occurs at a particular time in history but that any moment of history is fullness of time because for him at every moment time fully manifests itself.[25]

It is Dōgen's purpose to move men out of their habit of attachment to, and fixation with, any moment other than the present one, for such attachments deprive the moment of being born of the fullness of time in it and the moment of dying of the fullness of time in it. In his frame of reference, *mujō* is not a "negative" term or one expressive of a deprivation; on the contrary, it suggests a plenum. And this is why he, on the basis of a phrase in the work of the Chinese master Hui-neng, used the combination *mujō-busshō* or "impermanence-Buddha nature."[26]

In Dōgen, psychology and ontology inhere in one another. In the quotation which follows he advises the empirical observation of impermanence. For Dōgen such observation removes what we might call the "repression" of the fact of death, a repression which impairs life. Also, such observation of impermanence in the empirical world is direct perception of, and contact with, the Buddha Nature. He states in his *Shōbōgenzō-Zuimonki* the following concerning *mujō:*

Impermanence is a fact before our eyes. Do not wait for the teachings from others, the words of the scriptures, and for the principles of enlightenment. We are born in the morning and die in the evening; the man we saw yesterday is no longer with us today. These are facts we see with our own eyes and hear with our own ears.[27]

Again we have here the stress upon the empirical observation of *mujō*, but Dōgen is less interested than others in the aesthetic aspect and benefits of *mujō-kan* and more interested in its psychological and religious benefits; the observation of impermanence is the removal both of illusion—the Buddhist notion of *avidyā*—and that which elicits from the present moment the fullness inherent in it.

But it would be irresponsible to neglect to mention that Dōgen seems to have viewed the practice of Zazen or sitting meditation as another and perhaps even more basic means for overcoming attachments to either death or life. For Dōgen, himself a master of words, was of the conviction that ultimately words must yield to practice to arrive at truth. Thus, concerning what he had written about life and death in *Shōji,* he advised as follows: "Do not just mentally grasp this point and do not merely express it with words. Rather, cast yourself—both body and mind—and throw it into the abode of buddhahood." [28]

It seems impossible to escape the conclusion here, since he refers to the joint casting of both body and mind into the abode of buddhahood, that Dōgen is advising the practice of Zen-sitting for those who wish to understand life and death and overcome attachments to one or the other. For it is one of the peculiarities of Dōgen's teaching that he so insisted upon the necessity of Zen meditational sitting that he emphasized both the complete adequacy of "just sitting in Zen fashion" [29]—what he called *shikantaza*—and the oneness of practice and achievement. In his statement that "in Buddhism practice and enlightenment are one and the same,"[30] Dōgen eliminates all notions of Zazen or Zen-sitting as "means" to an end apart from itself—Satori or enlightenment—and expresses something in total harmony with his principle that there is complete fullness in every moment rather than the utilization of one moment to gain the benefits in another one.[31]

In Dōgen's conception of things, one can enter into enlightenment as immediately as one can enter into the activity of Zazen; the two are the same. And this is what he essentially means by his advice that one should "cast oneself—both body and mind—and throw it into the abode of buddhahood" if one wishes to know the truth about life and death. Dōgen insisted upon the importance of Zazen and made no allowances for what we would call "psychosomatic" evasions of practice. He said:

The Zen Master Ta-hui once had a growth on his buttocks. A doctor examined him and found it extremely dangerous. Ta-hui asked: "If it's this serious, am I going to die?"
"There's a good chance that you will," the doctor answered.
"If I'm going to die, I had better practice *zazen* with even greater effort," Ta-hui said. He concentrated on *zazen*, the growth broke open, and that was all there was to the matter. The minds of men of old were like this. When they became sick, they practiced *zazen* all the more vigorously. People nowadays who are perfectly well must not take a relaxed attitude to the practice of *zazen*. I suspect that the occurrence of illness stems from the mind. If you lie to a hiccuping person and put him on the defensive, he gets so involved in explaining himself that his hiccups stop.[32]

But to ignore a potentially fatal illness for the sake of Zazen is in Dōgen's view of things very different from ignoring it because one wants to die. He said:

To have a disease that requires curing and to do nothing about it because you are intent on dying—this is a heretical view. Do not begrudge your life to Buddhism; on the other hand, do not fail to save it if you can. If needed, the use of moxa or medicinal herbs does not become an obstacle to practice. It is wrong, though, to set practice aside and to postpone it until you have cured your disease.[33]

It is in being "intent on dying" that Dōgen recognizes the error and expresses again his insistence upon the full value of the present moment rather than fixation upon what is not present at that moment—either life when one is dying or death when one is living. Insistent upon the orthodoxy of his position as a Buddhist and as a teacher of Zen, he elicits from that position a psychological dimension and attempts to enhance the quality of both life and death.

The "Great Death" of Zen Masters and of Samurai

Although Dōgen personally avoided the forming of political ties between Zen and the newly formed government at Kamakura and in 1247 refused the government's offer of valuable lands for monasteries,[34] in time there was formed a very close bond between Zen and the regency government in Kamakura.[35] As Masaharu Anesaki states it:

Zen was introduced just at the time when the military men were rising to the position of rulers and administrators. There was need of a religion which could fulfill the task of training the ruling classes in mental firmness and resolute action and of satisfying their spiritual aspirations. For this purpose the old religions did not answer.[36]

But even more specifically Zen provided the warriors or samurai of the era with practice in the art of dying.

For a thoughtful warrier, whose life always bordered on death, there was an attraction, even a persuasion, in the belief that truth comes like the flash of a sword as it cuts through the problems of existence. Any line of religious thought that helped a man to understand the nature of being without arduous literary studies was likely to attract the kind of warrior who felt that the greatest moments in life were the moments when death was nearest.[37]

During this era the samurai of Japan went in large numbers to the temples of the Zen schools and also carried meditational practices out in military camp when preparing for battle and possible death.

The calm of the Zen monk's mode of life as well as the equipoise with which great Buddhists—according to what was now becoming a vast collection of stories about the "Great Death" (*daishi*) of saints and masters in China as well as in Japan—met the end of their own lives had an obvious attraction for the warrior.[38] Also the rigor of the Zen monk's daily practice of Zazen was one which the samurai emulated in their own lives, and this had benefits that could be experienced in the course of combat. The regents of the Hōjō period (1205–1334) were strict practitioners of Zen meditation even when they were the military rulers of the land; they even emulated the austerity and frugality of the Zen monks by simplicity in their own style of life.

However, even if the "Great Death" of the Buddhist monk served the samurai as the effective model for his own death in battle, it was the death of the samurai rather than that of the monk that appealed to the popular imagination. It was not the death of an aged monk voluntarily and calmly moving into death,[39] something interpreted as an indication of the spiritual charisma possessed by such a man, but, rather, it was the swift death of a brave and young warrior in battle, an index to his bravery and loyalty to his lord, which became the primary model of a great death during the feudal period in Japanese history. In this context the aesthetics of dying had new importance and the symbol of the cherry blossom, already a symbol of *mujō* in much of Japan's history, was related most especially to the short life and early death of the ideal warrior. The connection here is well summarized by Frits Vos:

> A Japanese adage is: "*Hana wa sakura, hito wa bushi,*" "Among flowers it is the cherry blossom; among men it is the samurai." And what are the characteristics of the cherry blossom? In its form and in its color it is refined and graceful; its fragrance is scarcely detectable; but, above all, it falls off in full bloom—like the rose—without resistence to its own death. These also are the ideals of the samurai: simplicity, modesty, and death in the bloom of life.[40]

The assimilation of the fall of the samurai in battle to the fall of the cherry blossom from the tree is interesting because it imports the aesthetic qualities of the latter into the event of the former while attributing sentience and, therefore, even the capacity for voluntary action, to the blossom. Both the warrior and the blossom enter into their "death" willingly and willfully and the aesthetic nature of the situation attenuates any notion of the presence of violence in the death of the samurai.

The life-style and death-style of the samurai eventually became part of Japanese representation of the ideal type of human existence; it became something stylized as a "way" or mode of religio-ethical realization of goals. It was called *bushidō*, literally, "the way of the warrior." [41] The continued impact of Chinese culture upon Japan during this period stressed the ethical aspects of the samurai's code of behavior. Ideas of loyalty to one's lord and the ideas of fulfilling one's duty, already present in Japan since the early days of Chinese and Confucian influence, were given even greater emphasis when the texts and traditions of Neo-Confucianism had their impact upon seventeenth- and eighteenth-century Japan. Although the Zen principle of the "Great Death" (*daishi*) still is present, it also becomes important that the death of a samurai be one which is not disgraceful to himself, his family, or his feudal lord. Death and its quality come to be related increasingly to ethical and social values even when it continues to be an indicator of aesthetic and charismatic ones as well.

This is classically stated in a seventeenth-century document called *Hagakure*, literally, "Hidden Behind Leaves," a manual in which the samurai is enjoined to face death in the following way:

> I have seen it eye to eye: Bushidō, the way of the warrior, means death. Where there are two ways to choose, let your choice be the one that leads to death. Reason not; set your mind on the way you choose—and push on.
>
> When you fail in your purpose and pay for your failure with death, it is true that your life has been laid down to no purpose; but remember, at least, that your death would bear witness to the quality of your mind. Your death would not be disgraceful.
>
> Every morning make up your mind how to die. Every evening freshen your mind in the thought of death. And let this be done without end. Thus will your mind be prepared. When your mind is set on death, your way through life will always be straight and simple. You will perform your duty; and your shield will be stainless.[42]

The fact that the "Great Death" is here interpreted as something with ethical import and of significance for those with whom the samurai is socially identified is shown by phrases such as "not be disgraceful," "perform your duty," and "your shield will be stainless."

The interaction and mutual exchange between Zen monk and samurai continued for many centuries. Whereas once the monk had been the model for the warrior in the matter of facing death with equanimity, this situation seems to have been reversed to some degree by the sixteenth and seventeenth centuries. We can infer this from the fact the Zen master Suzuki Shōsan (1579–1655), a priest of the Rinzai school who was very concerned about a decline in rigor and a softness that had become a part of Zen, advocated that Zen meditation be done face-to-face with Buddhist images dressed in battle armor, swords, bows, and arrows.[43]

Suzuki Shōsan also suggested that a warrior should write the character for "death" (*shi*) on his chest twenty or thirty times each morning. This insistence upon a mastery of death was carried forward by the Zen Master Hakuin (1685–1768). Hakuin, an immensely popular priest who advocated that the masses practice Zen, wrote the character for "death" in broad brush strokes on a scroll.[44] He also proposed the use of a "death koan," that is, as one of the many paradoxical statements used in Zen—and especially in the Rinzai school—for the dispelling of ordinary logic and for progress in meditation. Hakuin wrote as follows on this:

> If you should have the desire to study Zen under a teacher and see into your own nature, you should first investigate the word *shi* (death). If you want to know how to investigate this word, then at all times while walking, standing, sitting, or reclining, without despising activity, without being caught up in quietude, merely investigate the koan: "After you are dead and cremated, where has the main character gone?" Then in a night or two or at most a few days, you will obtain the decisive and ultimate great joy. Among all the teachings and instructions, the word *death* has the most unpleasant and disgusting connotations. Yet if you once suddenly penetrate this "death" koan, you will find that there is no more felicitous teaching than this instruction that serves as the key to the realm in which birth and death are transcended, where the place in which you stand is the Diamond indestructible, and where you have become a divine immortal, unaging and undying. The word *death* is the vital essential that the warrior must first determine for himself.

Hakuin seems here to be suggesting that the experience of Satori, referred to here as the "decisive and ultimate great joy," is one in which one enters "the realm in which birth and death are transcended" and one in which the person has become "a divine immortal, unaging and undying." Elsewhere concerning this experience he wrote:

Then you will awaken to the Great Matter of true meditation, and all the ordinary consciousnesses and emotions will not operate. It will be as if you had entered into the Diamond Sphere, as if you were seated within a lapis lazuli vase, without discriminating thought at all, suddenly you will be no different from one who has died the Great Death. After you have returned to life, unconsciously the pure and uninvolved true principle of undistracted meditation will appear before you.[45]

It seems that in Hakuin's view of things Satori or the experience of "the great joy" is homologized with that of the Great Death; similarly, the conclusion of the enlightenment experience is spoken of by him as a "return to life."

Although it must be kept in mind that Hakuin in his writings is concerned to communicate Zen teaching to the populace at large rather than to a more "elite" group of students, in the above quotations he implies that the enlightenment experience involves such a quantitative change of consciousness that it is a "death" and one which subsequently transforms the person who has had it into one impervious to death and the fears and anxieties that attend it. This is what he means by saying that one will find that "without any discriminating thought at all, suddenly [he] will be no different from one who has died the Great Death."

It is interesting to note that Hakuin shared Suzuki Shōsan's opinion that the warrior could serve as a model for the monk. Perhaps with a bit of hyperbole included he wrote the following:

In my later years I have come to the conclusion that the advantage in accomplishing true meditation lies distinctly in the favor of the warrior class. . . . Mounted on a sturdy horse, the warrior can ride forth to face an uncountable horde of enemies as though he were riding into a place empty of people. The valiant, undaunted expression on his face reflects his practice of the peerless, true, uninterrupted meditation sitting. Meditating in this way, the warrior can accomplish in one month what it takes the monk a year to do; in three days he can open up for himself benefits that would take the monk a hundred days.[46]

The *Hagakure* of approximately the same era celebrated the samurai and his mode of death in terms of ethical value demonstrated in such a death. Hakuin sees the valiant expression on the warrior's face as an index to the depth and penetration of his Zen meditation. Both celebrate the samurai's mode of life and his mode of death and complement one another in the value system of the time.

Suicide, Mishima and a Conclusion

But the "Great Death" did not always occur in battle. It was sometimes demonstrated in an act of suicide. A long-standing Japanese tradition has refused to view suicide in negative terms and has quite frequently seen in it qualities of nobility, strength, and determination of will—especially when it is done in the traditional manner by cutting the abdomen with a sword. This is termed *seppuku,* although the less elegant word *harakiri* is better known in the West. The positive valorization of *seppuku* increased during the past few centuries although its roots go much deeper in history. It is the theme of innumerable popular entertainments and dramas and an important component in much fiction. The story of "Forty-Seven Ronin"[47] who committed *seppuku* as a group to avenge their common lord in 1703 was one which inspired much public enthusiasm and became a classic known to school children from an early age. It and other tales of suicide based on loyalty became models for patriotic behavior during the 1930s and early 1940s.

However, the motives for *seppuku* were multiple. Frits Vos writes:

> There existed two forms of this suicide, namely, *seppuku* as punishment and voluntary *seppuku*. *Seppuku* as a punishment was granted during the Edo Period (1600–1867) to samurai who had committed serious crimes; in this way they were spared the shame of being put to death by an executioner. Voluntary *seppuku* could be committed for various reasons: in order to follow one's lord into death (*junshi* or *oibara*), in order to escape the fact that one had fallen alive into his enemy's hands, in order to protest against an unjust decision or against unfair treatment by authorities, or when one had been deficient in carrying out his duties, etc.

But aside from these motives for carrying out this painful and dramatic form of suicide there existed another level of meaning in the act, one well summarized by Vos:

> A person's cutting open of his own abdomen in *seppuku* was a declaration—out of an old Japanese belief—that the abdomen was the locus of the vital center. Through an opening of the abdomen one would demonstrate in a symbolic way that this center was undefiled. The most important place of the abdomen was the so-called *tanden* ("the field of vermillion"), a place located approximately one thumb's distance below the navel, a place which filled an important role in the respiration techniques in Taoism and in Zen.[48]

The choice of the abdomen is not arbitrary; it is conceived of as the physiological and spiritual center of a person's existence.

And this conception, having certain roots in Taoist mystical physiology,[49] was something which Buddhist masters in general and Zen masters especially had long held inasmuch as the base of breathing-control seemed to lie there in what was called the *hara*.[50] It was the place of personal control par excellence and, therefore, the Zen-trained samurai, precisely in that act which demanded perfect control in what was often a lengthy act of suicide, chose the *hara* as the place for the insertion of his sword.

In the historical development of the freely-entered-into death sketched above, the creation of this value structure for *seppuku* brings the element of voluntariness to its furthest point. In the act of ritual suicide by *seppuku* a "revelation" is intended. The act is meant to demonstrate to society that, in spite of offense committed or in spite of having fallen into an enemy's hands, there exists within the person an inner strength and all the imperviousness to death that a samurai traditionally possessed.

Although this attribution of high value to ritual suicide has received much criticism by Japanese in the period following the end of the Pacific War, the novelist Yukio Mishima sought to reinstate the earlier ethos. After having written extensively about it and having a film in which he himself as the main actor portrayed the *seppuku* of a famous Japanese general,[51] he committed suicide by *seppuku* on November 25, 1970, in a highly dramatic way. Intimations of this event are present in his book *Sun and Steel* and deserve attention here.

Mishima, who was impressed both with the ritual suicide tradition in Japan and with ideas of the ancient Greeks, lamented what he regarded as contemporary Japan's loss of its traditions and failure to retain the ideal of death as something with aesthetic possibilities. He wrote: "Modern man is almost devoid of the desire of the ancient Greeks to live 'beautifully' and to die 'beautifully.' "

Having committed himself much earlier to what he called "a union of art and life, of style and the ethos of action," he trained his body with intense physical training, but this was apparently eventually related to his desire to die as a samurai would have died, in the so-called bloom of life. But of most interest here is the phrasing he chose to distinguish what he called the "heroic" from the "decadent" death.

> What difference there might be resolves itself into the presence or absence of the idea of honor, which regards death as "something to be seen," and the presence or absence of the formal aesthetic of death that goes with it—in other words, the tragic nature of the approach of death and the beauty of the body going to its doom.[52]

What is of particular interest in this statement is its mention of a "formal aesthetic of death" and its expression of a desire to regard death as "something to be seen." Mishima would seem to be self-consciously relating his own principles to the tradition in Japan.

However, the statement deserves analysis in order to assess whether the "tradition" concerning death in Japan is a unified whole or whether it has had elements of change and discontinuity within it. Most obvious is the presence of the phrases "the tragic nature of the approach of death" and "the beauty of the body going to its doom." Here it appears that Mishima has clearly borrowed concepts from the classical antiquity of the West and assumed that they are compatible with those of the classical period in Japan. But we have noticed above that the entire thrust of Buddhism in earlier Japan was to negate any notion of death as a tragedy.[53]

Furthermore, Mishima's *seppuku* in 1970 was clearly the playing out of a scenario written earlier in writings such as *Yūkoku* (*The Rite of Love and Death*) and *Sun and Steel.* It was intended to be a public protest against modern Japan's loss of the samurai ideal, and to this extent it was Mishima's assertion of his individual self and conviction against the totality of his immediate society. There was present in this sequence a "fixation" with death and the conception of suicide as a histrionic performance. It is far removed from Dōgen's principle of nonattachment either to life or death. It is also hardly consonant with the Buddhist understanding of death as an event which, since there exists no permanent ego, provides a person with an unparalleled opportunity to accept this fact with equanimity and beauty, especially if the death occurs in private and is unobserved. Ironically, on many points Mishima is "Western" and "modern" precisely on the occasion which he intends as a catalyst for the reinstatement of ancient and Japanese understandings of life and death.

But it would be unreasonable to assume that Mishima has personally and suddenly subverted the "tradition" for that would imply that the tradition was a unified and totally coherent unfolding in history. As a matter of fact, the tradition of the "Great Death" in Japan has, like all traditions, involved continuities and discontinuities. It had within itself twists and changes at various points. Sometimes the curvature was such that earlier principles seemed to have been stood on their heads.

An attempt has been made in these pages to sketch briefly this pattern of thinking about death in Japan. Changes in the tradition have been noted because they seem clearly to be present. The early idea—one informed by Buddhism—that death is the prime moment for release from the illusion of having a separate and ongoing ego or soul and the moment for a total unification with truth and also with the cosmic natural processes was quite different from the notion nourished by Neo-Confucianism that death is the occasion for the demonstration of an individual's loyalty, integrity, and honor. The Buddhists see death as part of a *cosmic* process;

Neo-Confucianism focuses on its *social* meaning. Moreover, in spite of the fact that the samurai learned from the Zen monk how to face death with equanimity, the fixation upon death was something at variance with Dōgen's advocacy of seeing "impermanence as a fact before the eyes" so that one might be released from positive and negative attachments to life or to death.

Undoubtedly, social and political factors have been influential in the varying conceptions of death throughout the different eras of Japanese history. Continuation or reinstatement of the "tradition" is at times the aegis under which change of that tradition is carried out, perhaps quite unintentionally. However, impermanence or *mujō* does seem to have been a basic concept which, even when differently applied in different times and places, mediated the meaning and potential aesthetic value of death to the people of Japan.

Notes

1. Joseph M. Kitagawa, "Prehistoric Background of Japanese Religion," *History of Religions* 2 (1963): 320. For a detailed account of archeological research on prehistoric Japan, see J. E. Kidder, Jr., *Japan Before Buddhism* (London: Thames and Hudson, 1959).
2. William Theodore de Bary et al., eds., *Sources of Japanese Tradition* (New York: Columbia University Press, 1958), volume 1, pp. 4-5. See also Charles Haguenauer, "Du Caractère de la Représentation de la Mort dans le Japon Antique," *T'oung Pao,* Second Series, 33 (1937): 158-183.
3. Joseph M. Kitagawa, *Religion in Japanese History* (New York and London: Columbia University Press, 1966), p. 14. Note also that no precise Western equivalent exists for the word *kami;* it refers to sacrality in general and to objects of worship both human and natural.
4. See Alexander Slawik, "Zur Etymologie des japanischen Terminus marebito

'Sakraler Besucher,'" in *Wiener Völker-kundliche Mitteilungen,* 2 (1954): 44-58.

5. See Bernard Frank, "Kata-imi et Kata-tagae. Étude sur les Interdits de direction a l'époque Heian," in *Bulletin de la maison France-Japonaise,* n.s. 5 (1958): 1-246.
6. *Japanese-English Buddhist Dictionary* (Tokyo, 1965), p. 202.
7. "In den Sutras des *Agama* und des *Nikaya* findet man den engen Zusammenhang zwischen den Termini *mujō* und *metsu* (*nirodha,* Vernichten). Der Begriff *metsu* is nicht negativ, sondern im Gegenteil sehr positiv." "Der Gedanke vom *mujō* oder *metsu* führt dahin, dass man das leidvolle Leben vernichtet und ruhig, leidlos und befreit von Schwanken, Angst und Furcht lebt." Mitsuyoshi Saigusa, "Einige Bemerkungen zum Buddhismus in Japan," in Lydia Brüll and Ulrich Kemper, eds., *Asien Tradition und Fortschritt,* Festschrift für Horst Hammitzsch (Wiesbaden: Otto Harrassowitz, 1971), p. 505.
8. Works in Japanese of special value on this topic are Karaki Junzō, *Mujō* (Tokyo, 1965) and Nishida Shōkō, *Mujō-kan no Keifu* (Tokyo, 1969).
9. Lady Murasaki, *Tale of Genji,* trans. Arthur Waley (New York: Random House, 1960).
10. See Richard Robinson, *The Buddhist Religion* (Belmont, Cal.: Dickenson Publishing Co., 1970), pp. 14 ff. and Roy C. Amore, "Death and the Nāstika Systems" in this volume.
11. Ivan Morris, *The World of the Shining Prince: Court Life in Ancient Japan* (New York: Alfred A. Knopf, 1964), p. 110.
12. *Ibid.*
13. For the development of nature's soteriological role in Japanese Buddhism, see William R. LaFleur, "Saigyō and the Buddhist Value of Nature," pts. 1 and 2, *History of Religions* 13:2 (1973) and 13:3 (1974).
14. *Sankashū* no. 2051 in Itō Yoshio's edition, *Nihon Koten Zensho* (Tokyo: Asahi Shimbunsha, 1946), vol. 78. The translation is mine.
15. Concerning this term "*aware*" Robert H. Brower and Earl Miner write that it means "touching, pathetic, beautiful, moving the sensibilities, evoking the proper emotional response. Applied to those aspects of life and nature or their embodiment in art which stir the sympathies of the sensitive person of cultivation and breeding, impressing him with a deep awareness of the ephemeral beauty of a world in which only change is constant." *Japanese Court Poetry* (Stanford, Cal.: Stanford University Press, 1961), p. 503.
16. *Sankashū* no. 846 in Itō Yoshio edition. Translation mine.
17. Donald Keene, trans., *Essays in Idleness: The Tsurezuregusa of Kenkō* (New York and London: Columbia University Press, 1967), p. 7.
18. See, for instance, Herbert V. Guenther, *Buddhist Philosophy in Theory and Practice* (Baltimore: Penguin Books, 1971), especially pp. 43 and 101.
19. A number of terms used as aesthetic criteria in the arts were directly or indirectly informed by the concept of impermanence; for an overview of

these see Sen'ichi Hisamatsu, *The Vocabulary of Japanese Esthetics* (Tokyo: Center for East Asian Cultural Studies, 1963).

20. For an account of Dōgen see Heinrich Dumoulin, S. J., trans. Paul Peachey, *A History of Zen Buddhism* (Boston: Beacon Press, 1963), pp. 151-74. In addition to what is cited below, some excerpts from his writings appear in William Theodore de Bary, et al., eds., *Sources of Japanese Tradition,* vol. 1, pp. 240-50. Abe Masao has been rendering great service by translating parts of the *Shōbōgenzō* by Dōgen in recent issues of *The Eastern Buddhist,* new series. See also Klaus Robert Heinemann, "Shushō-ittō und Genjō-kōan—Welterkenntnis und-verwirklichung bei Dōgen," in Brüll and Kemper, eds. *Asien Tradition,* pp. 184-92.
21. *Shōbōgenzo,* edited by Nakamura Sōichi (Tokyo, 1972), vol. 4, p. 397. Translation is mine.
22. *Ibid.*
23. Abe Masao, "Dōgen on Buddha Nature," *The Eastern Buddhist,* n.s., 4 (1971): 68.
24. Karaki Junzō, in fact, writes of the "metaphysics of mujō" (*mujō no keijijgaku*) in Dōgen. See his *Mujō,* pp. 283 ff.
25. Abe Masao, *Dōgen,* p. 68.
26. *Ibid.*, p. 56.
27. Reihō Masunaga, trans., *A Primer of Sōtō Zen: A Translation of Dōgen's Shōbōgenzō Zuimonki* (Honolulu: East-West Center Press, 1971), p. 39. This work, a more or less popular compendium of Dōgen's thought, is based on talks given by Dōgen and was recorded by his disciple Ejō (1198–1253).
28. *Shōbōgenzō,* ed. by Nakamura Sōichi, vol. 4, p. 389. My translation.
29. See de Bary et al., *Sources of Japanese Tradition,* pp. 247-48.
30. Dumoulin, *History of Zen Buddhism,* p. 166.
31. This is, no doubt, also another example of Dōgen's application of the Mahāyāna principle of equating Nirvāṇa with Saṃsāra to another pair of binary terms.
32. Masunaga, trans., *Primer of Sōtō Zen,* p. 91.
33. *Ibid.*, p. 105.
34. George Sansom, *A History of Japan to 1334.* (Stanford, Cal.: Stanford University Press, 1958), pp. 429-30.
35. Joseph M. Kitagawa, *Religion in Japanese History,* pp. 129-30.
36. Masaharu Anesaki, *History of Japanese Religion* (1928; reprint ed., Rutland, Vt.: Charles E. Tuttle Co., 1963), p. 210.
37. Sansom, *History of Japan,* p. 429.
38. See Kaiten Nukariya, *The Religion of the Samurai: A Study of Zen Philosophy and Discipline in China and Japan* (London: Luzac & Co., 1913), p. 35 ff. See also Daisetz T. Suzuki, *Zen and Japanese Culture* (Princeton, N. J.: Princeton University Press, 1959), a major part of which is concerned with Zen and the samurai and with the development of "military arts" in Japan.

39. In the Zen tradition the reaching of a great age was often interpreted as an indication of great spiritual attainment; there may have been Taoist influence in this.
40. Frits Vos and Erik Zürcher, *Spel zonder snaren: einige beschouwingen over Zen* (Deventer: N. Kluwer, 1965). My translation.
41. See de Bary, et al., *Sources of Japanese Tradition,* pp. 384-433 and especially 389-91; F. Vos, "Knighthood—Translation of the Chapter Shidō from Saitō Setsudō's Shidō Yōron," *Orientalia Neerlandica* (Leiden, 1948), pp. 468-83; and Robert N. Bellah, *Tokugawa Religion: The Values of Pre-Industrial Japan* (Glencoe, Ill.: The Free Press, 1957).
42. Z. Tamotsu Iwadō, trans., " 'Hagakure Bushidō' or The Book of the Warrior," *Cultural Nippon* 7 (Nov., 1939): 33-55 and 7 (Dec., 1939): 57-78. The publication of this work and others on Bushidō during the 1930s is an indication of the importance placed upon the Bushidō tradition in the ideology of the time. (I have "modernized" the English slightly.)
43. Hajime Nakamura, *Ways of Thinking of Eastern Peoples* (Honolulu: East-West Center Press, 1964), pp. 492 and 502.
44. For a reproduction of this calligraphy see R. D. M. Shaw and Wilhelm Schiffer, trans. Hakuin, "*Yasen Kanna,* 'A Chat on a Boat in the Evening.' " *Monumenta Nipponica,* 13:1 and 2 (1957): 101-27.
45. Philip B. Yampolsky, trans. *The Zen Master Hakuin: Selected Writings* (New York and London: Columbia University Press, 1971), pp. 219, 94-95.
46. *Ibid.,* p. 68. On page 17 Yampolsky states that he is of the opinion Hakuin here made "a statement to which he himself could scarcely have given much credence." The last sentence is certainly hyperbolic, but the intention of the whole is quite clear.
47. Anesaki, *History,* pp. 280-82.
48. Vos and Zürcher, *Spel zonder snaren,* pp. 134-35. Translation mine.
49. See *Ibid.*
50. See, for example, K. G. von Dürckheim-Montmartin, *Hara, The Vital Center* (London: Allen and Unwin, 1962).
51. The Japanese *Yūkoku* has been entitled both as *Patriotism* and as *The Rite of Love and Death* in its English translations; it can be found in Yukio Mishima, *Death in Midsummer and Other Stories* (New York: New Directions Book, 1966). The theme of ritual suicide is also important in the recently translated novel *Runaway Horses* (New York: Knopf, 1973) by Mishima.
52. Yukio Mishima, *Sun and Steel,* trans. John Bester (New York: Grove Press, 1970), pp. 54, 47.
53. See *Ibid.*